Just Managing?

What it Means for the Families of Austerity Britain

Mark O'Brien and Paul Kyprianou

Contents

Preface

The era of 'austerity' that followed the UK banking collapse of 2008 has seen a savage and sustained assault on the security and well-being of the working poor. Historically unprecedented cuts to government spending across a swathe of essential services, combined with radical changes to the benefits system, have hit very hard at the least well-off in society.

Throughout this period, ministers have peddled platitudes about having to make 'hard choices' in order to 'balance the budget' and 'reduce the debt'. These ministers' 'hard choices', of course, did not involve that between 'eating or heating'; and the budgets that had to be balanced were not those of families surviving on low incomes. In fact, as weekly budgets have spiralled out of control, those families have been forced into levels of debt that are impossible to manage.

The electorate was told that government austerity policies would at least be 'fair', with the wealthiest sacrificing the most in percentage terms, and the poorest the least. Actually, the poor have sacrificed everything whilst the richest in society have enjoyed entrenchments of their privilege and wealth.

Whilst these political language games have gone on in the rarefied world of Westminster, it has been the grind of life on low and deteriorating incomes that has been the reality for millions of families. However, media commentaries and the establishment political cacophony have drowned out the voices of the very people the debate is about.

In this book, thirty working families who have suffered the brunt of austerity talk about their experience of struggling to hold down jobs, maintain decent homes, stay healthy and achieve a degree of happiness for themselves and their children.

Here, these 'just managing' families of austerity Britain now have their turn to speak.

PART I

BACK TO THE FUTURE?

1. Understanding Poverty: Then and Now

Different world; same problems

On the eve of the outbreak of World War I, a ground-breaking study of working poverty in Lambeth was conducted by researchers connected with the Fabian Women's Group. Published as *Round About a Pound a Week* (1913),[1] the report closely followed the lives and weekly expenditure of families who, though not the most poor, with the man of the household in work, nonetheless struggled to survive on a weekly budget of something close to 20 shillings. The report retains its interest for us today, not just for its historical importance as an example of research that influenced social policy in its era, but one that provides us with a picture of working-class life that still resonates today.

A crucial theme running through that report was a debunking of many of the presumptions and strictures that emanated from middle class moralists and establishment reformers. In their view, the working class were 'unthrifty' in their expenditure and 'improvident' in their procreation. They asked: why could the men not cut down on their drink? Why did these families not rent cheaper basements to afford an extra room and reduce overcrowding? Why could they not buy coal and food in bulk to get better rates? Why did they have so many children?

1 Pember Reeves, M. (1984 [1913]), *Round About a Pound a Week*. Virago, https://archive.org/details/roundaboutpoundw00reevrich

 https://doi.org/10.11647/OBP.0112.01

In fact, the men did not drink; rather they were mainly sober working men who gave the major portion if not all of their wages to their wives, who managed the household budget. Basement rooms tended to be gloomy and damp which meant more having to be spent on coal and gas. Moreover, better if possible to have one room that was well ventilated and sunny though more expensive, than two cheaper rooms that were below ground level with stagnant air and the risk of bronchial diseases that came with it. Coal could not be bought in bulk if there was nowhere to store it. The reason for the monotonous daily food shop was that many of the men were paid daily. It was also the case that these families' houses and rooms did not afford pantries for storing food, and with vermin a constant problem it was impossible to keep food for any length of time without it attracting mice and rats. These families were large because of a combination of early marriage to be able to leave the parental home and the need to establish a household, the effective unavailability of contraception and the uncertain survival of any single child.

There was also the matter of porridge. Some ladies of the Fabian Women's Committee, firmly of the view that porridge would make a fine breakfast for a working man, set about proselytising its virtues to the working-class women they attracted to meetings on the subject. Bags of porridge were left at their houses; the reformers returning the following week, enthusiastic to see the results of 'their work'. To their great consternation the bags were found untouched. Porridge was slow to make and the pan could not be left to boil whilst other tasks were attended to. Porridge left too long would burn and ruin one of the two pans, or even the only pan in the house. Finally, porridge without milk and sugar was revolting to the children and men alike. One women described her children's' reaction: "they 'eaved at it".[2] Another gave her husband's response: "Ef you gives me that stinkin' mess, I'll throw it at yer".[3]

The condescension of the moral crusaders of the day notwithstanding, it was simply not the case that the difficulties of these working families' lives were self-created, the result of poor household management or lack of intelligence. Rather they were the result of brute circumstance and

---

2 *Ibid.*, p. 57.

3 *Ibid.*

the material limitations they had to negotiate daily. As Maud Pember Reeves, commenting upon the question of diet, put it in the report:

> *That the diet of the poorer London children is insufficient, unscientific, and utterly unsatisfactory is horribly true. But that the real cause of this state of things is the ignorance and indifference of their mothers is untrue. What person or body of people, however educated and expert, could maintain a working man in physical efficiency and rear healthy children on the amount of money which is all these same mothers have to deal with? It would be an impossible problem if set to trained and expert people. How much more an impossible problem when set to the saddened, weakened, overburdened wives of London labourers?*[4]

Of course, it is true that much has changed even for the poorest in society. Housing conditions are better, and the extremes of overcrowding that were common in the early part of the twentieth century are gone. Levels of infant mortality have improved radically from the dreadful levels of more than a century ago. Nutrition is better. Sanitation is better. Access to healthcare is better. Education and provision for children is better. There are welfare state benefits. Indeed, many of these social improvements are attributable in part to the efforts of the socialists and reformers who worked on the 1913 Lambeth study and others like it.

However, a horrible truth emerges from a comparison with the circumstances and social experience of the working poor then and today: in fact, there is much that remains the same. As we show here, the sense of balancing always 'at the edge', the constant high levels of worry and stress, the strains on family life, the struggle for decency despite the exhaustions of the weekly grind all attest to a working-class experience that is recognisable from a previous age. It is not that these things are simple continuations of what went before. They are shaped and affected by modern pressures and influences: these problems of life belong to their own time and place. However, if these different generations could meet they would have much in common to compare: the experience of debt; economic insecurity; ill health; arbitrary treatment by employers; the extensions of hours of work to impossible extremes; very long journeys for work; the struggle to make time for their children; and so on. The pernicious effects of poverty are all too evident as stubborn and shameful features of our otherwise prosperous society.

4 *Ibid.*, p. 145.

It is an old observation, though no less true for that, that 'poverty' is a relative term, measured by the prevailing norms and expectations of the society in which it exists. Its impact then, its psychological meaning, its consequences for feelings about life and behaviour and even its physical effects upon health and what today we call 'well-being', cannot be wholly captured by absolute measures. These are important of course. Longevity, morbidity rates and the incidences of infant death within the first year are all related to poverty levels. Beyond matters of basic survival however, it is often the comparison with others that matters most today, particularly in the affluent countries. The work of Richard Wilkinson and Kate Pickett (2009), for example, reported in their best-selling book *The Spirit Level*[5] established with statistical authority that it is the inequalities within a society that properly explain its social outcomes, and not the simple levels of overall wealth.

In the UK, as in much of the industrialised world, a 'great reversal' of wealth occurred between the mid-1970s and the end of the 1990s. The trend today continues, driven by ever more inequitable tax regimes and downward pressures on pay, taking the levels of inequality to ever greater extremes. This shift has, with occasional pauses, accelerated over the decades up to the present times. Between 1979 and 2010, the wealthiest ten percent of British society saw their share of the national pie increase from 21 percent to 31 percent. More egregious still has been the concentration of wealth at the richest pinnacle of the social pyramid. In 1978 the wealthiest one percent of British society between them commanded six percent of the national share. By 2010 this had reached nearly fourteen percent.[6] Just four years later, the wealth of the 1,000 richest people in the UK had risen by 55 percent. This meant that their combined wealth stood at £519 billion, a figure that could have provided every British family with an extra £6,000 in their income.[7] In 2017, pre-tax income for the most affluent ten percent was 24 times higher than that of the least affluent ten percent. The richest fifth of

5 Wilkinson, R. and Pickett, K. (2009), *The Spirit Level: Why More Equal Societies Almost Always Do Better*. Allen Lane.

6 Lansley, S. and Mack, J. (2013), 'A More Unequal Country?', *Poverty and Social Exclusion Newsletter*. 16 April, http://www.poverty.ac.uk/editorial/more-unequal-country

7 Dorling, D. (2015), *Injustice. Why Social Inequality Still Persists*. Policy Press, p. 388.

the UK population had more than 40 percent of total national wealth, compared to the poorest fifth who had just eight percent.[8]

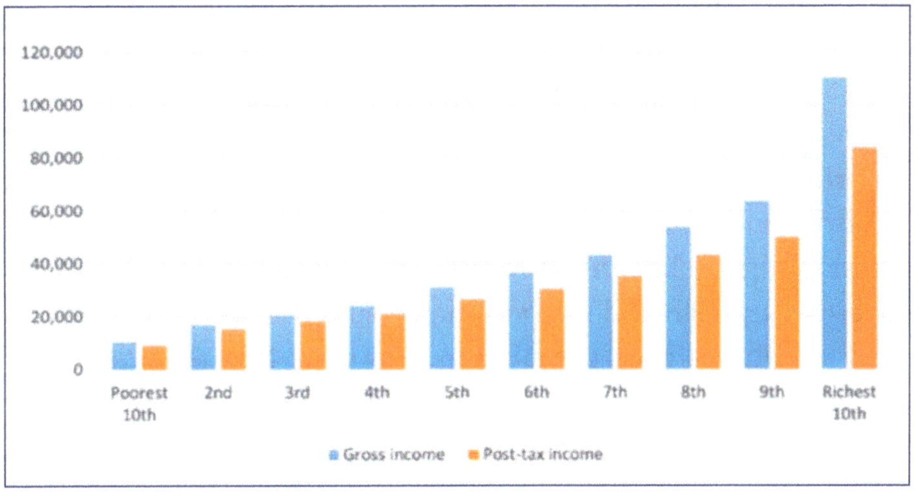

Income distribution in the UK.
Office for National Statistics.[9]

A self-justifying political and media narrative has accompanied this radical alteration of wealth distribution in favour of the already rich. Danny Dorling in his *Injustice*: *Why Social Inequality Still Persists* (2015)[10], with a nod to Beveridge's 'five giants' that had to be slain by the post-War Labour government, lists five myths that have constituted this ideological veneer. These he identifies as: 'elitism is efficient'; 'exclusion is necessary'; 'prejudice is natural'; 'greed is good'; and 'despair is inevitable'. These myths, however, have proliferated not only in the offices of ministerial speech writers and tabloid editors. They have seeped into the processes and methodologies of government policy making, so that the conceptualisations that underpin them become a material reality in the lives of the poor—and (of course, very differently) of the rich. Another aspect to this narrative has been the media construction (once again) of the poor as indolent, feckless and prone to petty criminality; a phenomenon that Owen Jones (2016) has described as the 'demonization

8 Equality Trust (2017), 'The Scale of Economic Inequality in the UK', https://www.equalitytrust.org.uk/scale-economic-inequality-uk

9 Office for National Statistics (2017), https://www.ons.gov.uk/peoplepopulationandcommunity/personalandhouseholdfinances/incomeandwealth/datasets/theeffectsoftaxesandbenefitsonhouseholdincomefinancialyearending2014

10 Dorling, D. (2015).

of the working class'.[11] This media game, however, is connected to real legislative processes. One example of this has been the re-framing of poverty in UK government policy as being no longer a result of low income levels, but rather of behaviour and even 'lifestyle choices'. Within the 'Troubled Families' programme, for example, launched in 2011, the factors of income and living standards were downgraded in importance to give way to such things as parenting skills, parental health, drug and alcohol dependency and family stability.[12]

Considering the life effects for the worst off in society, the growing gap between the rich and the poor has resulted in deteriorations on all life and well-being measures: physical health; frequencies of mental illness; life expectancy; malnutrition; etc. *The Spirit Level* showed this to be a global phenomenon. Along with these types of measure, the authors also considered personal and social outcomes such as educational performance, teenage birth rates, violence within communities, incarceration rates and social mobility across the industrialised nations. On each of these indicators and others, negative outcomes correlated closely with inequality within those nations. The study showed that:

> [...] *among the rich developed countries and among the fifty states of the United States,* [...] *most of the important health and social problems of the rich world are more common in more unequal societies. In both settings the relationships are too strong to be dismissed as chance findings. The importance of these relationships can scarcely be overestimated. First, the differences between more and less equal societies are large—problems are anything from three times to ten times as common in the more unequal societies. Second, these differences are not differences between high- and low-risk groups within populations which might apply to only a small proportion of the population, or just to the poor. Rather, they are differences between the prevalence of different problems which apply to whole populations.*[13]

The question of pay

The social consequences of the inequality we see today are terrible not just for their impact upon individuals and families, but for the quality

11 Jones, O. (2016), *Chavs. The Demonization of the Working Class*. Verso.

12 Lansley, S. and Mack, J. (2015), *Breadline Britain. The Rise of Mass Poverty*. Oneworld, p. 65.

13 Wilkinson, R. and Pickett, K., p. 173.

of social relationships at a larger scale. Regardless of the effects upon the 'social fabric', these trends have been driven deliberately and relentlessly by government policy over a period of more than four decades. Crucial to the descent into ever deeper levels of poverty for the worst off, along with the erosion of the welfare services and protective state benefits, has been the downward pressure on relative wage levels for the working poor. A counter-argument to this assessment is that government legislation has been in place to address the problem of poverty pay for two decades. And yet the reality of worsening income inequality continues. There is something here to be explained.

The National Minimum Wage Act (1998) established for the first time a basic level of pay for all workers regardless of industrial sector. It had been preceded by historical legislation that had provided wage regulation for specific occupations. As far back as 1891 there had been the Fair Wages Resolution Act. This was followed in 1909 by the Trade Boards Act which set basic localised wage levels for the most exploitative industries. In 1912, miners had struck for the minimum wage; the result later that year was the Coal Mines (Minimum Wage) Act. In the years immediately following the Second World War the Wage Council system that had emerged from the Trade Boards further improved wage regulation. By the early 1950s the wages of 3.5 million workers were protected by its provisions. This redistributive policy regime, combined with the wage militancy of the 1960s, drove the favourable shift of the relative working-class portion of national wealth that had occurred by the mid-1970s. It is this period that provides the most meaningful baseline by which to assess the effectiveness of more recent minimum wage policy.

Throughout the 1980s, Wage Councils were eroded in effectiveness and in number. In 1993 the John Major Conservative Government abolished the last of the Wage Councils, thus giving employers a much freer hand in setting remuneration levels. Over this period, as we have seen, the redistributive tide was reversed, as the wealth gap grew wider by the year. Since 1998, the minimum wage, though increased annually, has come nowhere near narrowing the wealth gap to the extent that was seen in the post-war years. Even by the more modest standards of the recent era of government social policy, it has fallen far short of the levels needed to prevent worsening inequality and increasing neediness amongst those on the lowest incomes.

The National Minimum Wage was hailed as a great achievement of the 1997–2010 Labour Government. Overseen by the Low Pay Commission it has held its position against average earnings across the UK. What it has not done however, has been to retain its value against inflation, and this is what matters to working families. Whether measured against the Retail Prices Index (RPI: that includes housing costs) or against the Consumer Prices Index (CPI: which does not) the reality is that its relative value, considered as a 'real consumer wage', has deteriorated for most of the years of its existence.[14] So, in the four years up to October 2013 the real consumption value of the National Minimum Wage had *fallen* by 45 pence an hour. The Resolution Foundation has calculated that it is worth £1,010 less a year than in 2008.[15] Considering the problem in the longer term, minimum wage policy in the UK has failed to protect the low paid against a continuous downward slide in the value of their income since it came into effect in April 1999. Indeed, even a very low paid worker in 1970 was likely to be earning more in real terms, than a worker on the National Minimum Wage in the years following its introduction.[16]

In his 2014 budget the then Chancellor of the Exchequer George Osborne raised the adult National Minimum Wage to £7.20 an hour. This was heralded as a new National Living Wage (NLW), even though it was in fact lower than the UK Living Wage and the London Living Wage established for that year by the Living Wage Foundation as £7.85 and £9.15 respectively. It also left behind over two million workers who were under the age of 25 and therefore ineligible for the new rate. By April 2017, the full adult rate had been increased to £7.50 an hour, the age 21–24 rate to £7.05 per hour and the age 18–20 rate to £5.60 per hour. These figures, however, were amongst the lowest minimum wage levels

---

14 Low Pay Commission (2014), *The Future Path of the National Minimum Wage*, https://www.gov.uk/government/publications/the-future-path-of-the-national-minimum-wage-2014, p. 16.

15 D'Arcy, C. and Kelly, G. (2015), *Analysing the National Living Wage Impact and Implications for Britain's Low Pay Challenge*. Resolution Foundation, http://www.resolutionfoundation.org/app/uploads/2015/07/RF-National-Living-Wage-briefing.pdf

16 Toynbee, P. (2003), *Hard Work. Life in Low Pay Britain*. Bloomsbury, p. 178.

in Europe. Moreover, they remained set far below the Living Wage that would ensure a decent standard of living for all working households. At 2017 prices, the all-UK Living Wage hourly rate would need to have been £8.45 for this to be guaranteed.

Of greater significance is the fact that since 2010, with the election of the Conservative-Liberal Democrat Coalition Government and the 2015 Conservative Government that succeeded it, the failure of the National Minimum Wage to narrow the wealth gap in the UK has been compounded by the largest programme of abolition and reduction of state benefits ever seen in the UK. Changes to the benefits system have impacted enormously on the low paid. The measures introduced by the 2012 Welfare Reform Act, for example, replaced a range of important benefits and tax credits such as Working Families Tax Credit and Child Tax Credit. Shortly after it was announced, Save the Children estimated that a single parent with two children on an income at or near to the National Minimum Wage would be around £2,500 a year worse off as a result of being moved onto Universal Credit, pushing the families of up to 250,000 children into poverty.[17] With each successive adjustment to the Universal Credit since 2013 its real-terms value has fallen.

Moreover, the Universal Credit is calculated annually whereas income for the low paid can vary from month to month, leading to the problem of overpayments and consequent clawbacks (a major reason for resort to pay-day loans). This poses problems particularly for those who are self-employed and whose income, whilst low, also varies monthly. Daly and Kelly (2015) describe the sensitivity of what they term the 'money rhythm' for the poor as they carefully balance their income against expenses and loan repayments from one month to the next. Shifts in the benefits regime will also disrupt these carefully calculated balances established over time for many of those in such straitened circumstances.[18] New types of conditionality for in-work eligibility, trialled in Liverpool in 2016, will also punish those deemed to be taking insufficient steps towards obtaining work. Further harmful

---

17 Save the Children (2012), *Ending Child Poverty: Ensuring Universal Credit Supports Working Mums. How Will Universal Credit Affect Poor Families?*, http://www.savethechildren.org.uk/resources/online-library/ending-child-poverty-ensuring-universal-credit-supports-working-mums

18 Daly, M. and Kelly, G. (2015), *Families and Poverty: Every Day Life on a Low Income.* Policy Press, p. 50.

effects result from the pressure that the Universal Credit, with its new battery of sanctions, creates upon people to move into the 'poverty-trap' of part-time work.[19]

On top of these changes have come successive waves of welfare reform, each of which has introduced further caps, cuts and freezes to benefits. The introduction of the Personal Independence Payment to replace the Disability Living Allowance (DLA) for instance, was designed to save the Treasury £2.2 billion. The Welfare Reform and Work Act (2016) introduced £12 billion of cuts to welfare spending. It also repealed much of the Child Poverty Act (2010) that had set targets for eradicating child poverty. By April 2017, these further changes to the welfare system were being implemented. They included: a freeze in working age benefits and housing allowances for all four successive fiscal years; the setting of the Local Housing Allowance (the term used for Housing Benefit given to tenants in the privately rented sector) at a rate based upon the cheapest 30 percent of properties, rather than the cheapest 50 percent used previously; major reductions in the amount that can be earned before Universal Credit is tapered away entirely; a freezing of the level for Child Benefit; a lowering of the cap on total benefit levels for households; a reduction in the earnings entitlement for tax credits from £5,000 to £2,500; the ending of the family element in both Universal Credit and tax credits; a reduction of the Universal Credit Work Allowance to £397 per month for those not receiving housing costs, £192 per month for those receiving housing costs and removed entirely for non-disabled people without children; and the end of Child Tax Credit after the second child.

Specifically, the loss of the child element of Universal Credit for families with more than two children would affect 256,000 children of 'households in poverty', 266,000 children of households 'at risk of poverty' and 609,000 children of households that were 'just about managing' by 2020. Low income families with a third or additional child would have to make up a difference of £1,737 a year between their needs and their benefit entitlements. As a result of this single policy, 266,000 children were set to join the 2.3 million already living in households in

19 O'Hara, M. (2014), *Austerity Bites: A Journey into the Sharp End of Cuts in the UK*. Policy Press, p. 67.

relative poverty: a 10 percent increase over the parliamentary term.[20] So, whilst the British Prime Minister Theresa May shuttled back and forth between Westminster and Brussels negotiating Britain's exit from the European Union, notwithstanding her stated intention to 'reach out' to struggling families, her government was implementing reforms that would once more impact savagely upon the poorest in society.

Minimum wage policy, then, should not be seen in simplistic terms as an automatic 'good' for those on low pay. It must be balanced against other aspects of state regulation of a low-pay economy. Everything also depends of course, upon the level at which it is set. When set high, representing a meaningful uplift for the poorest, it is of course a gain for working people. However, when set low, and raised at rates lower than consumer prices increases, whilst employers push up the prices of their products and services, it is no longer an instrument of redistributive social policy for most workers. This is an old complaint and was raised at the end of the eighteenth century against the Speenhamland System that set agricultural wages on terms favourable to landowners rather than farm-labourers. So today, the socio-economic meaning of the National Minimum Wage cannot be read in econometric tables, but must be considered in terms of the lived experience of working people.

The forgotten matter of fairness

Whilst the gap between rich and poor has widened since the 1970s, the processes driving it have accelerated over recent years. This has been the result of many factors. A major cause however, has been a wholesale assault upon welfare spending since 2010. In the 2010 Comprehensive Spending Review the Coalition Government announced budgetary reductions of £81 billion by 2014–2015, with £11 billion coming through welfare cuts and £3.3 billion as public-sector pay freezes.

At the local level, the Communities and Local Government settlement was set at a 33 percent reduction of then current spending, with a 42 percent reduction in administration costs, whilst resource 'savings' of 28 percent were set for the Local Government settlement. Capital

20 Ghelani, D. and Tonutti, G. (2017), *The Impact of the Two-child Limit to Tax Credits.* Policy in Practice. April, p. 3.

funding for all departmental support to councils was set to fall by 45 percent over the spending review period. Overall, Central Government funding to councils was reduced by 26 percent. In 2013, the government introduced a further 10 percent reduction in funding for councils. In 2015, £33 billion of cuts in public spending were announced by the new Conservative Government over the five years of its administration.

In 2010, much was made of a new element in the calculations that underpinned that year's budget. This was the Distributional Impact Assessment (DIA) that accompanied it. The Coalition Government made an explicit commitment under the DIA that although the budgetary reductions in public spending over the five-year term of the spending review would be 'painful for all', they would at least be fair. By 'fair', the DIA was clear that this meant any overall reductions in income would be proportionate to existing income levels: in other words those at the top of the income gradient would lose proportionately more than those at the lower end of the income gradient.

In its five-year estimated projections, the DIA predicted a continuous downward distribution of income loss from decile 10 (the ten percent highest income group) to decile 2 (the second lowest ten percent income group) in the proportionate equivalised[21] income loss resulting from budgetary reform.[22] For decile 1 (the lowest ten percent income group) a reassuring note accompanied the chart explaining that the disproportionately high rate of income loss for this group was apparent only, since turnover within it would be high as people left the benefits system and became employed. The DIA made an even more straightforward commitment on the question of 'benefits-in-kind' covering group benefits arising from government spending on health, social housing, travel subsidies, schools and school-based services, free school meals, Local Authority spending etc. Here the impact upon household consumption would be distributed fairly by quintile group with the poorest households losing the least in percentage terms.

---

21 'Equivalisation' adjusts income estimates from purely monetary units into more realistic effective income assessments.

22 HMS Treasury (2014), *Impact on Households: Distributional Analysis to Accompany Budget 2014*, http://socialwelfare.bl.uk/subject-areas/government-issues/social-policy/[Treasury]/impact14.aspx

With the end of the Coalition Government's five-year spending, an assessment of the claims of its impact assessments against the reality of what transpired became possible. It was clear that the actual outcomes of the Coalition Government's cuts in welfare spending and budgetary reform were not proportionate according to income group; with the wealthiest losing the most and the poorest the least in percentage terms. In fact, quite the opposite had occurred: the actual impact gradient was the exact *reverse* of what had been promised. In July 2014, the National Institute of Economic and Social Research[23] simultaneously calling for greater transparency and more standardised impact assessment, reported that certain groups had been disproportionately affected by cuts to spending. These included: the disabled (especially disabled children and those also in low-income groups); women (particularity in relation to cuts in benefits and tax credits relating to children); and Black and Asian households (especially in relation to reductions in education spending and housing allocations). With respect to income and household consumption groups, the report graphically demonstrated the wholly regressive nature of government fiscal policies on a range of measures. It revealed that from decile 1 to decile 8 the pattern of detriment represented a 'mirror-image' of the distribution predictions that had been presented by the Coalition Government.

The most significant cause of this trend was reductions in tax credits and benefits whilst changes for 'indirect tax' (on consumption goods) was also a factor. The overall pattern was that those in the lower income groups lost out more than those in the middle and upper groups up to decile 9. A more comprehensive analytical model, the Landman Economics model,[24] confirmed the contrast between what the public was promised and what transpired. In November 2014, the report produced by the Centre for Analysis of Social Exclusion and the London School of Economics confirmed these findings.

23 Reed, H. and Portes, J. (2014), *Cumulative Impact Assessment. A Research Report by Landman Economics and the National Institute of Economic and Social Research (NIESR) for the Equality and Human Rights Commission.* Equality and Human Rights Commission. Research report 94, https://www.equalityhumanrights.com/sites/default/files/research-report-94-cumulative-impact-assessment.pdf

24 The Landman Economics model uses a wider and more up-to-date set of measures that those used by the HM Treasury, including for instance the effects of localisation of Council Tax Benefit.

> [...] *some groups were clear losers on average—including lone parent families, large families, children, and middle-aged people (at the age when many are parents), while others were gainers, including two-earner couples, and those in their 50s and early 60s.*
>
> *Across the income distribution as a whole, the changes were regressive. On this comparison, the bottom half lost (with the poorest groups losing most as a proportion of their incomes) and the top half gained* [...].[25]

In its income distribution forecast for the period 2016–2017 to 2020–2021, factoring in welfare reform with slight growth in the UK economy for 2014–2015 and using data from the Government's own Office for Budgetary Responsibility, the Resolution Foundation predicted further reductions in living standards for all income groups within the bottom half of the working population. This was based upon: a three-year freeze in the levels of working age benefits; greater than previously forecast price rises; reductions in work allowances following the introduction of Universal Credit; and the loss of benefits for families with more than two children. By region, three quarters of the twenty hardest-hit areas have more than the national average share of households with three or more dependent children and twelve have an Asian population greater than ten percent of the total. A March 2016 report into the unequal effects of welfare reform concluded that the "more deprived the Local Authority the greater the financial loss".[26] The conclusion was that Theresa May's government was set to be "the worst on record for income growth in the bottom half of the working age income distribution"; and would preside over the "biggest rise in inequality since the 1980s, reaching record highs after housing costs by 2020–2021".[27]

25 De Agostini, P. Hills, J. and Sutherland, H. (2014), 'Poor Lose, and Rich Gain from Direct Tax and Benefit Changes Since May 2010—Without Cutting the Deficit', LSE / CASE, November, p. 5.

26 Beatty, C. and Fothergill, S. (2016), *The Uneven Impact of Welfare Reform. The Financial Losses to Places and People*, Centre for Regional and Social Economic Research and Sheffield Hallam University, p. 3, https://www4.shu.ac.uk/research/cresr/sites/shu.ac.uk/files/welfare-reform-2016_1.pdf

27 Corlett, A. and Clarke, S. (2017), *Living Standards 2017. The Past, Present and Possible Future of UK Incomes*. Resolution Foundation Report, p. 10, http://www.resolutionfoundation.org/publications/living-standards-2017-the-past-present-and-possible-future-of-uk-incomes/

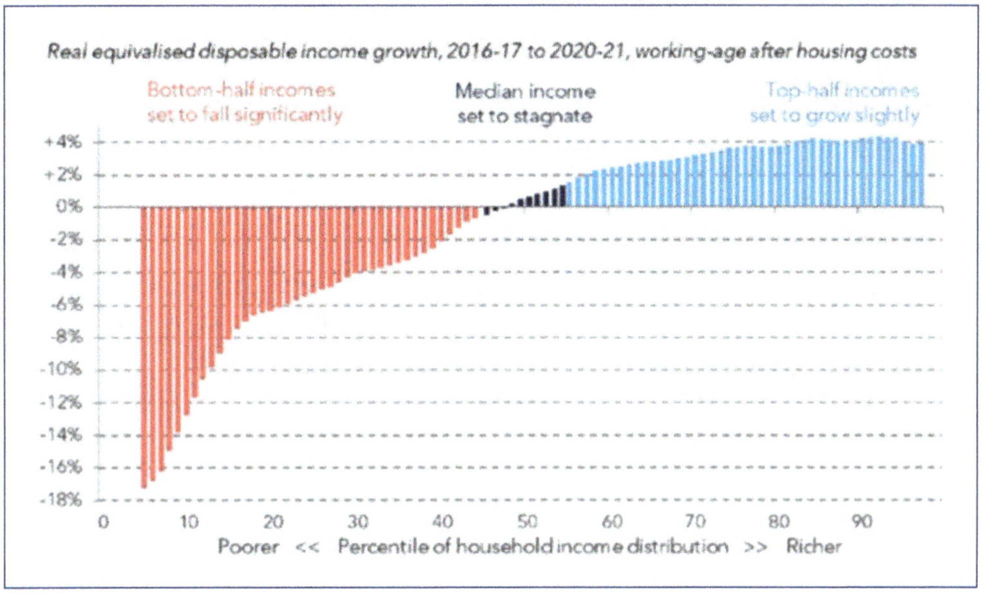

Projected disposable incomes 2016–2017 to 2020–2021.
Resolution Foundation 2017.[28]

The spending cuts then had not fallen 'fairly' across the spectrum of income groups in the UK; they had fallen unfairly. Indeed, the distance between what the Coalition Government had promised the British electorate in 2010 and the real effects after five years made the outcome more than unfair; it made it an injustice and a deceit.

The political refrain of successive governments of the last thirty years has been the intention of breaking a perceived 'culture of dependency' on benefits and moving people into work. At the 2015 Conservative Party conference the then British Prime Minister David Cameron declared in his keynote speech that the vision behind the May budget of that year was one of moving from a 'high tax, low wage' economy, to a 'low tax, high wage' economy. The picture that is emerging, however, is quite different. Rather, we see the creation by policy of an employment market rigged increasingly on terms that are advantageous only towards employers. With relative wages held down and fewer types of state support available, and those set at decreasingly adequate levels, a culture of '*low wage* dependency' has become established for the least well-off in society. In this situation, workers, despite 'staying off benefits' and remaining in employment as they are urged, become trapped in jobs

28 Corlett, A. and Clarke, S. (2017), p. 10.

that do not pay enough for them properly to support themselves and their families. They become vulnerable also to unscrupulous employer practices designed to maximise worker output, with no guarantee of proportionate reward. The result is large numbers of workers who take home less than the National Minimum Wage, are forced to accept 'zero-hour contracts', work in unsafe and unhealthy conditions and work every hour they are able, including the most family-*un*friendly, to make ends meet. The 'low tax, *low* wage' agenda then, is ultimately an 'exploitation charter'.

2. The *Getting By?* Study

The life experiences reported here were given to community researchers as part of the 2014–2015 *Getting By?* study that was supported by the Liverpool City Council Action Group on Poverty. The stories of the families who took part in the project, however, will have been representative of those of many others across the UK. Indeed, it is the wider significance of these families' stories beyond their local setting that makes them important. That said, some local context will deepen our appreciation of the impact of government policy upon thousands of Liverpool working families in recent years.

Since the 1980s a 'structural gap' has existed between Liverpool and the rest of the UK on several socio-economic measures, with the City falling below national averages for employment rates and health indicators. However, throughout the early 2000s there was evidence of improvement in the lives of Liverpool residents.[1] Driven in part by an expanding public sector element in the economic composition of the Liverpool City Region, economic growth continued over the ten years between 1999 and 2009.[2] This meant that 50,000 jobs were created over that period. There was an improvement in educational attainment rates which began to compare well to national averages at National Vocational Qualification (NVQ) Level 2 and NVQ Level 3. Partly attributable to the public health and education initiatives of the City's Primary Care Trust,

1 The Mersey Partnership (2012), *Economic Review 2012*, p. 44, http://www.knowsley.gov.uk/pdf/LC10_MerseyPartnershipEconomicReview2012.pdf

2 Liverpool City Council (2012), *The Liverpool Economic Briefing*, p. 5, http://liverpool.gov.uk/media/9996/liverpool-economic-briefing-february-2012.pdf

 https://doi.org/10.11647/OBP.0112.02

population health measures had also seen improvements over this period. Improvements in the statistics for cardio-vascular disease were evident for example. Obesity measures had also improved, especially amongst children at Year 6. However, by the early years of the 2010–2015 Coalition Government these economic, social and health improvements were beginning to falter.[3]

As a city region for which the public sector in the form of government services and administration comprised around 40 percent of economic composition, Liverpool was especially vulnerable to swingeing cuts to departmental and non-departmental public body budget settlements. Furthermore, many private sector companies in sub-sectors such as business services, retail, sports and leisure, relied in part at least upon public-sector spending within Liverpool and across its economic area. These sub-sectors were now jeopardised by the scale of the reductions in government spending initiated by the 2010 budget. The scrapping of the Liverpool Primary Care Trust in March 2013 also meant the loss of the overarching public health strategy it had provided.

Liverpool already had a high proportion of English 'most deprived small areas', a relatively high proportion of benefits claimants, a high incidence of children living in homes affected by poverty and a high frequency of Incapacity Benefit claimants. This meant that many thousands of Liverpool residents were especially vulnerable to the effects of benefit cuts, the raising of entitlement thresholds and the new benefit caps introduced by the Welfare Reform Act that became law in March 2012. On top of this, major cuts to various types of area support from Central Government, cuts to Local Authority services, the loss of Crisis Loans and Community Care Grants resulting from the abolition of the Discretionary Social Fund and the decimation of funding to Community and Voluntary Sector organisations for free services and neighbourhood-level projects were to add significantly to the problems being faced by Liverpool's working-class communities. This onslaught resulted in a planned four-year £90 million of cuts annually to services

3 O'Brien, M. (2012), *'Fairness and the City'. Public-sector Cuts, Welfare Reform and Risks to the Population of Liverpool and its Wider Region: An Independent Submission to the Liverpool Fairness Commission.* Centre for Lifelong Learning, https://www.liv.ac.uk/media/livacuk/cll/reports/fairness_and_the_city.pdf, pp. 27–39.

across the board. Altogether, the Central Government budget allocation to the City had fallen by £420 million since 2010.

So, on top of Liverpool's unenviable position as one of the most deprived cities in England came reductions in Central Government funding of 58 percent in real terms.[4] By 2021 projected budgets show a reduction of 68 percent. Moreover, the services that have been affected are those that low-income families disproportionately rely upon. This pattern, of areas of high deprivation being hit by the largest cuts, has been evident in many parts of the UK. Specifically, Liverpool has suffered the fifth largest financial reduction in the UK with losses projected to 2020–2021 rising to £157 million each year.[5]

Whilst each of the specific losses were consequential for communities, families and individuals it was the interacting effects of these multiple changes, combined with reductions and removals of services and benefits, that was to create a dangerous downward spiral for those who were already struggling to make ends meet. This was the background against which the interviews for the project were conducted.

A major impetus for the research came from the Hope Conference organised by the office of the Mayor of Liverpool in the summer of 2013. The conference brought together agencies and organisations working on the 'front line' of helping those in need, including the Citizens' Advice Bureau (CAB),[6] credit unions and foodbanks. The intention was to identify priorities and actions to help address the serious challenges Liverpool faced because of the combination of the economic downturn, changes to welfare and the loss of funding for crucial services. Among the messages coming out of the conference was the need to highlight the impact of working poverty, and to get 'beyond the statistics' to tell the stories of the families affected by it. The Action Group on Poverty responded to this by supporting the proposal to replicate the *Round*

---

4 Jaleel, G. (2014), 'Liverpool is the Hardest Hit Major UK City in Government's Latest Round of Funding Cuts', *Liverpool Echo*, 19 January, http://www.liverpoolecho.co.uk/news/liverpool-news/liverpool-one-worst-hit-country-8313557

5 Liverpool City Council (2017), *Welfare Reform Cumulative Impact Analysis 2016. Interim Report February 2017*, p. 4, https://www.lcvs.org.uk/events/report-launch-liverpool-welfare-reform-cumulative-impact-assessment/

6 Citizens' Advice is a government funded service providing free and impartial information and advice about benefits, entitlements at work, debt management, health issues, immigration matters, family law, etc.

About a Pound a Week study. This was initiated and delivered by a Liverpool-based research company, 'Praxis CIC'.[7]

This book joins other studies that have focused upon geographical localities to provide an insight into how life is changing for the poorest communities across the UK. In her coincidentally titled *Getting By: Estates, Class and Culture in Austerity Britain*, Lisa McKenzie (2015)[8] drew upon her close relationship with the St Ann's estate in Nottingham to share an insider's view of the hardships being created by austerity. In *Families and Poverty: Every Day Life on a Low Income*, Mary Daly and Grace Kelly (2015)[9] drew upon research they had conducted with families in Belfast, to explore the impact of poverty upon aspects of family life. In *Tyneside Neighbourhoods: Deprivation, Social Life and Social Behaviour in One British City* Daniel Nettle (2015),[10] using a combination of demographic and ethnographic data in a comparative study explored the negative impacts of socio-economic deprivation upon levels of neighbourhood trust and pro-sociality. In *Whose Benefit? Everyday Realities of Welfare Reform*, Ruth Patrick (2017)[11] explored the impact of benefit reform on the lives of working class people in Leeds. The family testimonies reported here then, are not only relevant to North West of England. Rather they are a local expression of a far more widespread social reality.

The *Getting By?* (2015) study[12] captured the experience over a year of thirty Liverpool families in which one or both parents were in low paid employment. Using weekly spending diaries to track their income and spending and in regular in-depth interviews, they revealed the challenges faced in their daily lives as they struggled to cope in their day-to-day lives. Just about managing on incomes below

---

7 For information about Praxic CIC: http://praxiscic.co.uk/

8 McKenzie, L. (2015), *Getting By: Estates Class and Culture in Austerity Britain*. Policy Press.

9 Daly, M. and Kelly, G. (2015), *Families and Poverty: Every Day Life on a Low-income*. Policy Press.

10 Nettle, D. (2015), *Tyneside Neighbourhoods: Deprivation, Social Life and Social behaviour in One British City*. Open Book Publishers, http://www.openbookpublishers.com/product/398; https://doi.org/10.11647/OBP.0084

11 Patrick, R. (2017), *Whose Benefit? Everyday Realities of Welfare Reform*. Policy Press.

12 Praxis CiC (2015), http://gettingby.org.uk/

the Minimum Income Standard[13] they are experiencing 'austerity Britain' at the sharp end.

The families had not been selected because their situation was extreme: in fact, rather the opposite. These people were in the 'mainstream' of the employment market and of society. They were working in schools, hospitals, hotels, shops and offices. Some were on the national minimum pay level, and others just above it. A few were in better paid employment; but nonetheless, because of specific circumstances, were struggling financially. In some households both parents were in paid employment. For many of the families, part-time employment was all that was available; or was the only option given child-care responsibilities. To reflect the fact that many adults are in some form of training and employment a student nurse in her last year of training, who was also having to do agency work, was included. In addition, three families where a parent was 'self-employed' were included, reflecting the increasing trend towards this type of work practice.

The families then conformed to the type of the 'near poor' who live just above the official poverty line and who, whilst remaining in employment, move in and out of technical definitions of poverty and live close to the edge of intractable financial and social problems.[14] They are the 'just-about-managing' households of austerity Britain. They were drawn from different neighbourhoods in Liverpool. Most were white British; one was from the Liverpool Chinese community; one was a Liverpool-born Black British family; one family was Somali; and one family was from Poland. All the families had at least one child under eighteen years of age. Nearly half were single parent families (although this did not tell the whole story as some had partners they did not live with for financial reasons). Several of the families were living in privately rented property; others were in social housing; and two owned their own home and were paying mortgages.

---

13 The rate deemed by the public in 2014 to be the minimum necessary to achieve an acceptable standard of living. See: Davies, A., Hirsch, D. and Padely, M. (2014), *A Minimum Income Standard for the UK in 2014*. Joseph Rowntree Foundation, https://www.jrf.org.uk/report/minimum-income-standard-uk-2014

14 Shildrick, T., MacDonald, R., Webster, C. and Garthwaite, K. (2011), *Poverty and Insecurity. Life in Low-pay, No-pay Britain*. Policy Press, p. 177.

PART II

THE BIG ISSUES

3. Money Matters

Every penny counts

The decade before the banking collapse of 2008 saw a downward trend in the numbers of families in which nobody worked. A combination of factors had created a favourable environment for people moving into work, either for the first time or after a period of absence from the job market. These included: economic growth in some sectors; the introduction of Working Tax Credit as a direct benefit to those in low paid work; appropriate educational and accreditation opportunities at local colleges and training centres; new types of jobs in public services such as classroom assistants, health support workers etc.; and the introduction of Child Tax Credit that heavily subsidised child-care, as well as free, part-time nursery provision for three- to four-year-olds.[1] Since the crisis of 2008 however, against the backdrop of government budget cuts, these have either been pared down to a fraction of what they had provided as forms of support for low-income families or have been eliminated altogether.

Between the financial years 2009–2010 and 2012–2013 average pre-tax household earnings in the UK fell by 9.4 percent with prices outstripping wage increases.[2] Over these years a 'wage squeeze' worsened income

1 Power, A., Willmot, H. and Davidson, R. (2011), *Family Futures. Childhood and Poverty in Urban Neighbourhoods*. Policy Press, p. 195.

2 Belfield, C., Cribb, J., Hood, A. and Joyce R. (2014), *Living Standards, Poverty and Inequality in the UK*. Institute of Fiscal Studies/Joseph Rowntree Foundation/ Economic and Social Research Council, p. 2, https://www.ifs.org.uk/ publications/7274

 https://doi.org/10.11647/OBP.0112.03

levels with average rates of pay falling by between one and two percent each year.[3] The worst affected were those in insecure employment, moving in and out of work at regular intervals. These workers were most likely to see annual, real-terms cuts in their pay packets.

Whereas low interest rates provided some buffering to many home-owners, no such protection was available to those living in the privately rented sector. Indeed, tenanted households on average saw the proportion of their income going on their housing costs rise by two percent between 2007–2008 and 2012–2013. Since 2013, there have also been marked increases in the numbers of people living in poverty in both the social housing and the privately rented sectors: of 400,000 and 350,000 respectively.[4] Of course for those home-owners who were no longer able to afford their mortgages following a reduction in household income for any reason, the result was often repossession. Over this period, the proportion of people living in a mortgaged home declined by five percent.[5]

The problem of absolute poverty (defined as 60 percent of the 2010/11 median income) is also still with us today with 12.9 million (20.3 percent of the population) living in these circumstances in 2014–2015 (considering disposable income after housing costs). 27.5 percent of all children (3.7 million) live in conditions of absolute poverty.[6] By 2015, 9.6 million people, fifteen percent of the population, were living in what has been termed 'deep poverty'.[7]

More specifically with respect to wages, at the end of the Coalition Government period, the UK had one of the worst records of all industrialised countries for low paid employment, coming second only to the US. A fifth of workers were paid less than the Living Wage; this figure having risen from 3.4 million in 2009 to 4.8 million by 2014. By April 2015, 21 percent of employees (5.7 million) were low paid.

---

3 Corlett, A. and Gardiner, L. (2015), *Low Pay Britain 2015*. Resolution Foundation, p. 14, http://www.resolutionfoundation.org/publications/low-pay-britain-2015/

4 Aldridge, H., Kenway, P. and Born, T. (2015), '*What Happened to Poverty Under the Coalition*'. New Policy Institute, p. 7.

5 Belfield, C., *et al.*, p. 2.

6 Belfield, C., Cribb, J., Hood, A. and Joyce R. (2016), *Living Standards, Poverty and Inequality in the UK*. Institute of Fiscal Studies/Joseph Rowntree Foundation/ Economic and Social Research Council, p. 58, https://www.ifs.org.uk/publications/8371

7 Belfield, C., *et al.*, p. 5.

Six percent (1.5 million) were on the National Minimum Wage; this proportion having increased year-on-year since 2000.[8] In its 2016 report, the Resolution Foundation estimated that based on current trends the proportion of workers on low pay will increase to fifteen percent by 2020.[9]

On top of pay being held down across all sectors, as we have seen the real value of the National Minimum Wage has fallen by five percent since 2010. Moreover, low paid employment is not distributed proportionately across society. Women and young people, for example are far more likely to be in low paid work than men and older workers (except for the very oldest). Women make up 61 percent of all low paid employees; and 25 percent of female employees are low paid compared to sixteen percent of male employees.[10] Rising rates of younger workers are low paid; 80 percent of workers in the 21–25 years age group for instance, are low paid.[11] Low pay is also linked to educational attainment: 35 percent of those with basic attainment levels are low paid compared to just three percent of those with tertiary qualifications. Moreover, nearly three-quarters of people in low paid jobs in the UK in 2002 were still in low paid work in 2012.[12] Rather than being a 'first step' on a route to more secure and better paid employment, these types of employment represent a low pay poverty trap from which those workers affected find it very difficult to escape.

The worst sectors for breaches of minimum wage legislation and low pay generally are: hospitality; retail; restaurant and bar work; hairdressing; child-care; social-care; hotel cleaning; and various types of home-working. In these sectors, even were the National Minimum Wage to be set at a higher level, perhaps at the level of the Living Wage, there would remain the problem of enforcement. Over a quarter of a million workers are not paid the legal minimum after two decades of legislation. Despite this the number of government inspections that were completed has fallen by a half in recent years.[13]

---

8 Stephen Clarke, S. and Conor, D. (2016), *Low Pay Britain 2016*. Resolution Foundation, p. 5, http://www.resolutionfoundation.org/publications/low-pay-britain-2016/

9 *Ibid.*, p. 9.

10 *Ibid.*, p. 19.

11 *Ibid.*, p. 38

12 Buckle, A. (2014), p. 13.

13 *Ibid.*, p. 16.

However, reduced levels of income and the insecurity affecting those in low paid jobs are not simply the product of low wages—rather they are caused by a combination of factors. Such jobs are more likely to be based upon zero-hour contracts for example, which have tripled in number since 2010, affecting nearly 1.4 million workers.[14] Cuts to tax credits and other benefits have also reduced family incomes. There is also the problem of families in the lowest income quintile depending upon wages that are too low to have benefited from the increase in personal tax allowance. The combined effects then of several factors such as low pay, reductions in benefits and credits etc. need to be our focus if we are to understand the growing poverty in the UK under the Coalition and Conservative governments since 2010—and poverty trends in developed countries more generally. Considering welfare reforms, the introduction of the Social Sector Size Criteria (also known as the 'under occupation charge' and the 'bedroom tax') the maximum benefit cap and reductions in Council Tax relief in 2013, reduced overall household incomes for the families affected.

In March 2013, the Coalition Government's Welfare Reform Act came into legislative force. As we have seen, the effects of the welfare reductions introduced by the new Act impacted upon poverty measures almost immediately. Over the next two years the proportion of working age adults living in poverty increased to 22 percent. By April 2015, fourteen percent of pensioners were living in poverty following the first downward annual trends in six years. Over the same period the proportion of children residing in poor households rose to 29 percent; an increase of two percent.[15]

The introduction of the National Living Wage at £7.20 from April 2016 was predicted to benefit 1.9 million workers immediately and six million by 2020; meaning a two percent fall in the proportion of employees on low pay over these years. However, scrutiny of what these figures represented revealed a less optimistic scenario. The Resolution Foundation predicted that over time the National Living Wage was likely to result in a 'bunching' of the pay distribution with large numbers of workers pushed close to, but not over the low pay threshold. This would mean increasing proportions of workers stuck at

14 *Ibid.*, p. 8.
15 Aldridge, H. *et al.* (2015), p. 7.

a level at, or only slightly above, their minimum legal entitlement and for significant periods of time.

> *The NLW is also likely to lead to a significant bunching of the pay distribution. The share of employees paid only their age-specific legal minimum was around 1 in 50 in the years following the introduction of the minimum wage in 1999. In 2014, around 1 in 20 were on the wage floor. With the introduction and growth of the NLW, by 2020 more than 1 in 7 are expected to be paid at or only just above the legal minimum.*[16]

This analysis also found that in 2015 nearly one-quarter of employees (23 per cent, or 6.3 million individuals) were receiving pay below the Living Wage, representing a new high for this measure.[17] Moreover, assessments of the impact of the raised National Living Wage do not include the economic experience of self-employed workers who tend to be lower paid than those with full-time employed status; indeed, more than half (51 percent of self-employed workers) were low-paid in 2013–2014. With 4.5 million workers in this category in the UK, this represents a significant gap for our understanding of what is happening for many on low incomes.[18]

Comprehensively considering the impact of the introduction of the National Living Wage, it will not result in a new era of upward social mobility for the worst off in society. Rather it will result in the 'locking-in' of the low pay threshold for many millions of workers, as employers set their remuneration rates at the lowest levels required. Of course, the National Living Wage does mean that pay levels will improve for the lowest paid workers, and especially those in 'extreme low pay'. However, any assessment of its overall impact on the lives of working families will be overly optimistic unless other income elements are factored in.

In reality, the increase in minimum wage levels will nowhere near make up for the £12 billion worth of cuts to welfare benefits announced for instance by the government in 2015. The greater share of the advantage arising from the National Living Wage will go to households that are already towards the top-end by income of those affected, while

16 Clarke, S. and d'Arcy, C. (2016).

17 *Ibid.*

18 *Ibid.*

welfare reductions will disproportionately affect those households with the lowest total incomes. The result of government wages policy and changes to benefits *combined* will be that many or even most households will be worse off than before.

What we have seen since 2010, has not been a state-driven attempt to help 'the most vulnerable' out of poverty. Rather it has been a concerted move to lock the poorest in society into a new 'low wage dependency'. In this economic model, the 'ways up' from low pay by skills acquisition, career development and so on, are blocked as a large proportion of workers remain stuck at or close to the low pay threshold. Equally, the 'ways out' are also blocked as benefits for working and non-working members of low-income households are removed. The result is a situation in which the room for manoeuvre for workers is constrained to the extreme, and in which employers have no reason to improve the conditions, security or pay levels above the minimum required for their employees. Far from social mobility then, it is a scenario of structural, labour-market *immobility* for these workers and their families.

Family voices

Feeling 'the squeeze'

Even before the 2008 financial crisis, wages were failing to keep pace with price rises. Today, millions of people in the country cannot reach an acceptable minimum standard of living because their wages are too low. Even when wages are subsidised by tax credits, many families still fall short on this measure. In Liverpool alone, 32,600 families in work qualified for Working Tax Credit at the time of the study. Low pay is a fundamental problem; but it isn't the only issue. There are also poor employment practices and working conditions that make work and family life difficult to balance.

Brenda explained how the combination of these and many other pressures affected her. She was having to manage a student debt of £30,000 and had just gone back to work after having her third child. She was working in the hotel and leisure sector. On a weekly basis, her expenditure exceeded her combined income from wages, Child Tax Credit, Child Benefit and Housing Benefit by £98.91, and as a result she was also struggling to pay back a debt of £2,280. Her relationship with her long-time partner had become difficult since having the baby, and she was worried about how she was going to cope with shift work. She was relying on help from her mother.

> *I'm like, I don't have enough time; and if I do have the time, it's either to sleep, to be able to just sit and do nothing or clean up* [...] *but even though things have changed, I'm still only just getting by now. It's kind of like I'm putting all this time in, but I'm not with the kids—and for what? I'm getting by; but you'll see in the diary, my wages went up by only 12p an hour. So I went from £6.19 to £6.31; its minimum wage.*
>
> Brenda

Gill and her partner Pete had two young children, one of whom had health problems. When they were interviewed, Gill was also pregnant. Pete had previously worked for the same large international company for many years before being made redundant. He was unemployed for about eighteen months during which time he was receiving Job Seeker's Allowance and applying for fifty to sixty jobs a week to make sure his benefit wasn't stopped. He then got a job in a well-known fast food outlet.

> *He was working for* [...]. *He was going out and working all hours there and he wasn't seeing us. And that was a trial; a six week trial. At the end of six weeks they just said 'No, you've not got the job'.*
>
> Gill

Following this experience, Pete obtained work in the service sector. He was being paid £6.31[19] an hour on a zero-hour contract. This required him to phone-in every day except Sunday, to see if he was needed. In practice he found he was working every day.

> *He goes in at 8am every morning, and he's there all day. Last week he did 47 hours. The week before that was 50 hours. I think the zero-hour contracts are for holiday cover, aren't they? So they don't have to pay you holiday pay or sick pay.*
>
> Gill

In an average week, the family was spending £95.40 more than their combined income from earnings, Child Tax Credit and Child Benefit.

19 £6.31 was the hourly rate for the National Minimum Wage at this time, prior to subsequent increases.

They could only manage this by drawing upon Pete's redundancy money and the funds Gill's father left after he had died the previous year.

Jenny was a lone parent with one young child. Since she'd left school when she was sixteen, she had always worked and saw that as being very important. Nonetheless, she was struggling financially.

> *Rent, gas and 'leccy bills are just outrageous; water bills, everything. You can't go a week without having a bill. There is always a bill there; and it needs to be paid, no matter what. By the time you get to the end of the month, and you think 'Oh, there is a week free'. Then something else happens; and there never is, there never is.*
>
> Jenny

Jenny had been employed in her catering job for about nine months. She was working two shifts: one of ten hours; and the other of six hours. She was being paid £6.19 an hour.[20] If it had been a slow day she would have to wait for her pay, hoping she would get it at the end of the next shift. She would sometimes have to wait until her employer had the money. Jenny wasn't given payslips and although the work itself wasn't difficult, her work situation was stressful.

> *My boss, the bosses that work there, they are just unreal; and she is constantly threatening me with my job, accusing me of everything. But there is nothing I can do; and everyone is like 'Just walk out; go on the dole'. But I can't do that. I know that my job keeps me and* [her son]. *So I couldn't just walk out of work. I have to stay there and take it. It is stressful; especially with the work situation. You feel like you are working for nothing. You are working and working; and you are coming home, and you have still got nothing. It does really get you down.*
>
> Jenny

Both Phil and his partner Dot were being paid the National Minimum Wage. Dot had two jobs, working as a care worker and as a cleaner, while Phil worked full-time in the hotel and leisure sector. They were living in social housing near to the city centre and had one child. Even with their combined income, including tax credits, they were finding it hard to make ends meet. Phil compared their situation to what he remembered of how things had been a few years previously.

---

20 Jenny was still being paid at the old rate.

> *Oh no, much worse. I'd say over the last two years we've noticed. The likes of tax credits* [...] *we used to get like £100-odd off them in 2010, and it's only £50-odd now. The wages haven't gone up; they're only rising with the minimum wage. And we were on minimum wage then. So basically, the money hasn't 'gone up', it's only gone up with the minimum wage; but the tax credits and things like that are going down. And it's not what we had in 2010. We could afford to say 'Yeah, we can pay that bill'. But now we've got to 'rob Peter to pay Paul'. We struggle, basically, we really struggle; juggling bills. So what generally happens now is a lot of companies are always pressuring us to pay more and more, like electricity and gas. But our financial situation doesn't allow us to do that. So we just pay what we can pay.*
>
> Phil

Gaynor was a lone parent with one child. She had three jobs, including working in a well-known supermarket. She was struggling to pay off rent arrears on her privately rented property, as well as a pay-day loan. On average, she was left with just £8.39 a week, once her weekly expenditure was taken away from her combined earnings, tax credits and benefits.

> *Yeah, the living wage is £7.50, but we're only on £6.50 minimum wage and this is what's happened. I'm getting penalised because I have to do extra hours to get the money in, because I've got more going out than I've got coming in. And I'm getting hit in other places because I've done a few extra hours. My rent and my Council Tax benefits, that all went down when my wages went up. Now I'm even thinking 'Is it even worthwhile working?' I've worked nearly all my life apart from for five years where I brought my daughter up. I've worked since I was sixteen and sometimes I feel like, well, 'what is the point?'*
>
> Gaynor

The wage freeze

Carol and Ric had two children. Carol had been forced to give up her job due to chronic ill-health and the family was now relying solely on Ric's pay as a residential care worker. He was being paid just above £7 an hour and had not had a pay increase for many years. Despite the long hours he worked, the family was in permanent debt, owing nearly £4,000. Although Ric's hourly rate had stayed the same, changes in how it was calculated meant that he was now earning less.

Money-wise, as well, there's been no raise at all since, I can't remember when. In fact they cut hours. I wouldn't say they fiddle the hours, but Ric works from 12–10pm. It used to be 'twelve-to-twelve' and he was paid for twelve hours; then he'd finish his shift and then he'd get the 'sleep-in' rate; but they've changed that. They've taken the two hours off, and now he only gets paid from 'twelve-to-ten'; and the two extra hours go onto the 'sleep-in', and there's no increase there. So for every shift he's two hours pay down. And even things like staff expenses in work, they're £3 a day and, if the lad [their son] *wants to go to town, that's it gone, isn't it? It's more than gone. There are no expenses for anything like the food and drink, and he's out from 12 noon till 8am the next morning. He'll take his packed lunch with him that he'll have when he comes in at 10 at night and that's it. And they're basic things. There are numerous other things, like the staff bedroom and conditions and that sort of thing really. But you're tied in, what can you do about them at the end of the day? And you're back to that same old thing, you're lucky to have a job; 'like it or lump it' really. You've got no choice about it.*

Carol

Ruth had four children and her partner Mark had been looking for work for a long period. She was working in a clerical job and was being paid £7.80 an hour, or just about the Living Wage. Financially, things were very difficult and the family was struggling with debts of nearly £6,000. Ruth also had not had a pay rise in recent years.

When I started working, the wages were quite good. But I haven't had a wage increase in five years. It's been tough. Don't get me wrong, we got a bonus at Christmas; £200. So that was good. It makes you feel a bit more appreciated. But I would like a bit more pay. I would love a bit more pay. Obviously, when you see someone else getting a three percent rise or a 1.5 percent rise, you're a bit jealous of them like; because we are just left on the same wage.

Ruth

Liz was a lone parent with one child, living in a privately rented property. She was working as a receptionist, but found that her finances were a constant struggle. On a weekly basis, her outgoings exceeded her combined earnings, Working Tax Credit and benefits by £27.08. As a result, she often relied on help from family members. Again, Liz had not had a pay rise that kept up with rising costs for many years.

Nothing, until last year. I think we got something like [an extra] *20p an hour; so I didn't see nothing for it. Five years ago, when we used to have different*

> *bosses, we used to get a raise each year; even if it was like 20p or something. We'd get it every year, but now we don't. That's all we've had in the five years, 20p.*
>
> Liz

Janet was also relying on financial help from her family to cope. She was a lone parent and had two children. She was working full-time as a teaching assistant. Her outgoings were by far exceeding her combined income from wages, tax credits and Child Benefit. Over an average week, she had £134.04 more going out than she had coming in. She had debts of over £3,000.

> *I can't remember the last time my wages went up. They've stayed the same for years now. It's got worse really. I love my job; but everything's gone up apart from my salary. It's not just me; all the other girls and staff in the school are doing three times more than what they use to do. We were only talking about it the other day; how much it's changed. I come home with just over £1,000 a month after tax and everything, and I do overtime. Like today, I've been in since 7:10am. I'm paid for today; it's breakfast club, so we get paid overtime. But by the time you get taxed, it's nothing. And it's only going to get taken out of my Working Family Tax Credit; so you do it out of the goodness of your heart don't you?*
>
> Janet

Cuts in public sector funding had made things hard for the voluntary sector organisation Luke worked at. As a result, he'd had no increase in his pay for six years. He was also getting no additional payment for being on 'stand-by', and having to deal with emergencies. His partner had recently had their second child and was on maternity leave from her job in a supermarket. They had a mortgage which accounted for nearly a third of their outgoings. They were only just about managing financially, with an average weekly surplus of £25.61.

> *In the last one or two years, the budget cutting for the Local Authority and the Government means we haven't got any opportunity to get more funding like there used to be. So we have to think about alternatives. We can generate income but at the moment everyone's salary has been frozen; no increases at all. We provide a critical service to the elderly, so sometimes we've got to deal with emergencies. So, we've got some unexpected working hours during the weekends and evenings. It's classed as 'emergencies'; but it's quite often… and we don't get paid; but we can claim back the time.*
>
> Luke

Working for free

It is remarkable that people already in low paid employment should work with an expectation, or even a requirement, that they do extra unpaid work. However, this was a common experience amongst the families.

Liz was working part-time, which enabled her to take her child to and from school. Whilst this suited her, she found that she was also expected to work unpaid hours by coming in earlier and finishing later than she was contractually obliged to.

> *So, it's only ever like half-an-hour at most; although I suppose during the week that's 2.5 hours, isn't it? I've never thought of that really. But no, I don't get paid for it. It's expected. No flexi-time. I suppose if I wanted to I could note it down and probably push for it to get my time back; but I never have. You just go along with it.*
>
> Liz

Gavin and Phoebe had four children. Gavin was working full-time in manufacturing. Phoebe had previously had a good job but she'd had to give it up for health reasons. The family had debts of nearly £4,000 and each week their expenditure exceeded their income by £104.31. Their financial difficulties weren't helped by the fact that part of Gavin's employment was unpaid.

> *He's salaried, so he's got to work at least ten percent of his hours more a week. He doesn't get paid extra for that, it's just part of his contract.*
>
> Phoebe

Where breaks cannot be taken for any reason, this also means that in effect an unpaid element exists within the working day. This was true of Brenda's workplace experience. Because of the nature of her work she often found that breaks couldn't be taken when they were due. She then got an unsympathetic response from her manager when she raised the issue.

> *I didn't have a break today; but if you were to mention anything it would be 'Well that's your fault' because you chose not to have your break.*
>
> Brenda

As a shop worker on the minimum wage, Karolina was also expected to work unpaid beyond her finishing time.

> *I'm paid minimum wage, plus sometimes I've got to stay. Say I finish work at five thirty on Saturdays; I'm never really out of the place at five-thirty, because we need to cash up the tills. Whoever is cashing up the till can't do it on their own because they need a witness to sign off the money that's there. So I'm spending hours, not getting paid; and I don't think it's right. But then when you come in late to work, you get asked 'Why are you late?'*
>
> Karolina

Once a job had been found, travel to and from work presented its own difficulties. Cath and Nick were spending nearly £2,500 a year putting petrol in their car which Nick needed to get to work. They had three children, one of whom had serious health issues. They were living in social housing. As well as having to travel a long distance outside of Liverpool, Nick was also expected to be available on a 'stand-by' basis.

> *For the people on stand-by, they don't get paid for that time on stand-by. They have to be available at any time; and that's if you want to get paid. And also his time; he's got to leave a lot earlier. So even if he doesn't start till half-six, he's got to leave at half-past four, two hours before so he doesn't get stuck in the rush hour traffic.*
>
> Cath

Escaping low-pay?

Joy was a lone-parent with one child. She was living in privately rented property and had been employed as part-time as a receptionist for twelve years. She was paying back debts of over £2,000. Joy saw no real prospect of improving her situation.

> *There's nothing within my workplace that would affect my pay rate. They can just pay minimum wage, unless there's a manager's role; but we only have like one manager. There's nothing really to increase the pay. I've just picked up a day in work to increase my monthly pay.*
>
> Joy

Apart from increases linked to the National Minimum Wage, Liz didn't think her financial situation or her job prospects would improve.

I've been in the same job for ten years this year. I don't get nothing major; just like when the minimum wage goes up. I don't even know what it is to be honest; but whenever we get a rise, it's not really noticeable, especially because I'm part-time. We get graded on what we do but to be honest with you, they try and keep you at the basic rate if they can anyway. So it doesn't matter what you do. I'm that used to it now, that I'm just like I never think I'll get increases and anything I do get is a bonus. I've never put in for a promotion and because of the hours that I work there probably aren't any opportunities.

Liz

Brenda was in debt after having gone to university as a mature student to improve her employment prospects. She now felt she would have to do further training to escape being on the minimum wage.

I'm not sure [...] *what my plan was for the future. It was to kind of look for a salaried, paid job, rather than shift* [work] *at minimum wage. I'm in £30,000 of debt from uni; so I don't want to be getting minimum wage all my life. I was looking to maybe do a bit more training. Yeah, kind of just look elsewhere for something that pays a salary.*

Brenda

However, Brenda was already having to find a £1,000 a year to keep her training up to date, and couldn't afford to do further training on top of this.

Another one for me is the position that I'm in. For me to improve my training, we have to do continuing development courses every year; it's self-funded isn't it? So, that's another thing for me to keep going. It's like £1,000 a course; it's like £1,400 for that course; and then it's a six-week course.

Brenda

Karolina and her partner Micha were from Poland and had been in Britain for eight years. Karolina was working part-time in a shop. Micha was doing full-time manual work, taking as much overtime as possible to manage financially. Both were on the minimum wage. They had one young child and were expecting their second. Micha had used the last of their savings at the time to pay for training. He was hoping that this would enable him to get a better position at his work; but it hadn't worked out as planned. Karolina didn't feel he had any prospects with his employer.

> *Micha just said that* [he needed] *that 'card' to be able to* [improve his job]. *He had to pay for it, because when he was jobless he got it himself. Because he asked the people in the job-centre if they would arrange that for him and every time they said, 'Oh, we need to find out' or 'We haven't got that course at the moment'. So he spent the last of our money on that. He paid about £300 for it; and he got that done because he was hoping to get a* [better paid] *job. But then he couldn't get the job.*
>
> Karolina

Colette was working full-time as a teaching assistant, on a temporary contract. She had two children and was living in privately rented property. On a weekly basis, her financial outgoings exceeded her combined wages, Child Tax Credit and Child Benefit by £8.46. She had debts of over £1,300. Colette saw training as a way of improving her prospects. However, that meant doing training on top of work, and at the same time as looking after her family. She was finding the situation overwhelming.

> *At the moment I am trained at NVQ Level 2. I've got an opportunity to become a Level 3. But I struggle with that because it is done out of work hours. Also I've got the child-care to worry about; plus the exhaustion. I am absolutely shattered when I come home at the moment. I don't think I could go to university and study; and as you can see, trying to get some peace and quiet! I could only do it when* [the children] *have gone to bed.*
>
> Colette

Being self-employed Emma could only see one way of earning more money.

> *I'm self-employed. The only way I could improve what I'm doing would be to take more hours on. But I'd have to take a huge amount of hours on, because I think the* [threshold] *for the Working Tax Credit—I don't know if it's 30 hours. But then it's picking* [her son] *up; and it's like holidays over the summer. If I work 30 hours, it's getting somebody to mind him for 30 hours; and I couldn't afford to pay for him to go to school clubs or that type of thing. The other thing would be to maybe bring work home with me, like ironing, which I could do at home, in the evenings; and then obviously* [her son] *is with me anyway. So that could be a bit of a boost.*
>
> Emma

Self-employment; the way out?

Self-employment, a 'way out' of poverty much trumpeted by successive governments in Britain since the 1980s, offered no solutions to the family members who had tried it.

Steve was categorised as 'self-employed' even though he had been working full-time for the same company for a number of years. He and Sian had three children. Sian described Steve's work situation. Steve was earning the Living Wage, but that still left the family spending on average £10.72 more each week than they had from their combined wages, tax credits and benefits. They had debts of over £1,200 and frequently needed help financially from family members.

> *He's classed as self-employed; he's been with the firm for seven years. He's on just under £8. They* [the workforce] *asked for a pay rise last year and they* [the employer] *said, 'No'; but he gets his petrol paid. There's a works van they all get in to go to work. But his wages, they're not enough for what he does.*
>
> Sian

Emma had four children. One was working and another was in full-time education. She was working as a self-employed cleaner, earning £6.20 an hour. On a weekly basis her outgoings were exceeding her combined wages, Child Tax Credit and Child Benefit by £59.60 a week. She was paying back debts of £1,584. Emma explained that she would much rather have been working for an employer, than have the insecurity of not knowing whether she would have work from one week to the next.

> *I just find it a struggle to go out to work and then at the end of the week there's nothing left. It's just disheartening; it gets me down. I worry about my credit cards, but saying that though, I still use them. I've got to; there's no other way I can work round it. I think a lot of people are in a very similar situation. I'd like not to be self-employed and work for a company* [so that I] *didn't have to do all the book-work and knew from one week to the next that my job was safe; knew what money was coming in. Being self-employed I can't be off, because I don't get paid. If anyone cancels a job at the last minute, I don't get paid. It's not reliable. I would much prefer to be working for someone; 40 hours a week with a wage and enough money to do stuff.*
>
> Emma

Help from the state?

Changes to tax credits were having a major impact on Ruth's income and were a part of the reason why the family was now over £5,500 in debt.

> *When the government came in last time, the new government, the Coalition, I lost a hundred and twenty* [pounds] *a week in Working Tax Credits. So I only get Child Tax Credits now and my wage. Previously I had had Working Tax Credits, so it was like a massive amount of money to lose. So it's completely different now to then.*
>
> Ruth

This situation had been compounded by the loss of Housing Benefit after her daughter had left school.

> *I just don't think things are made very easy for people for the transition. They stop everything; and I just think, 'If you know that transition is going to happen, why can't it be made that little bit more simple for people? Especially when they* [the landlord] *are sending letters out saying the next step is eviction!*
>
> Ruth

Eileen had seen her tax credits go down by £60 a month. Her finances had also been affected by one of her children turning eighteen.

> *I've got a lot less money coming in now because* [her son] *has turned eighteen. I used to get help towards his rent. I used to get Child Benefit and I used to get a few quid for Family Tax Credit. That's all stopped; even though he's doing nothing. That all stopped; all of a sudden. There's a lot less money coming in. So we're feeling it.*
>
> Eileen

A change in the rules for Working Tax Credit had affected Don and Terri.

> *You could work whatever, like twenty hours a week, and you'd get Working Tax Credits. They stopped my Working Tax Credit without telling me because my partner didn't work enough hours.*
>
> Terri

Amy was told she had been overpaid tax credits and couldn't understand why.

> *From last August, I've lost tax credits for my son because he was at school leaving age. My tax credits had stopped for him, and my family allowance had stopped for him as well. The Child Benefit had stopped for him. But I've had a letter from 'the tax credits' recently saying that there's been an overpayment, although all the changes of circumstances were notified to them. So my tax credits have now reduced as well; and they're taking back money for an overpayment. I will query it when I phone them, because I really don't understand where the overpayments come from. It was a couple of thousand pounds.*
>
> Amy

A forced reduction in her working hours by her employer meant a double loss of income for Gaynor.

> *Mine are like down to thirteen hours a week anyway; that's what my contract is. I lose my working tax* [credit] *below sixteen hours and then I'll be down to £66 a week. Well hopefully, more work will come up because thirteen hours a week just isn't good enough. It took me eighteen months to get the job that I've got now. I don't want to wait another eighteen months for another job. I've had this job for a year and she still hasn't offered me extra hours.*
>
> Gaynor

At the same time as Brenda's wages rose by 10p an hour, she lost her Council Tax Benefit[21] which meant that her Council Tax went up from £20 to £80 a month (including arrears payments) so that she was no better-off. She had been offered more hours, but the effect on her Working Tax Credit would have meant that her overall income wouldn't actually rise.

> *I'd even do more hours, but it doesn't financially benefit me if I did. I'd lose so much in tax credits; so it's not worth it.*
>
> Brenda

Some of the families had experienced considerable difficulties arising from confusion over the payment of Council Tax and Housing Benefit. For some, this has resulted in payments being stopped or reduced, causing a great deal of anxiety and stress.

21 In April 2013, the Council Tax Benefit was replaced by Council Tax Support, under which low income households are obliged to pay Council Tax regardless of their income level.

Brenda had assumed that she didn't need to tell the Local Authority how the increase in the minimum wage had affected her pay. This had led her into serious difficulties over the payment of Council Tax.

> *It's minimum wage and that just happened automatically over the period of a year. Then all of a sudden I got a letter to say 'Have your wages changed?' I was like, 'I didn't think I needed to let anyone know'. It was just a small increase. I said, 'I've only been in proper employment for a few years now'. So I got a letter from work to say the wages had increased, and then all of a sudden I got a letter from the Council saying 'You've been overpaid by', I think it was '£1,400, and we want it back'. It turns out that the overpayment is for the rent, and they want £11.50 a week; and then my Council Tax is £30 a week. So I'm paying out £41.50 a week. That's over £160 a month; for what? For Council Tax, and for my wages going up 10p! I don't get it.*
>
> Brenda

As well as difficulties over tax credits, Amy was having problems with her Housing Benefit through no fault of her own. She had received a letter from her local tax office stating that a previous tenant was living with her. In fact, the other tenant hadn't lived there for fourteen years. Eventually the mistake was acknowledged, but not before she was threatened with eviction and had suffered considerable worry and anxiety.

> *Then I got another letter, saying that they'd stop the payments because they had reason to believe, not only was he living in the property, but that he was earning £499 a week. So I said 'If you find him and he's earning £499, then tell him he can squeeze into the house any time'. But that stopped my Housing Benefit payments; and then that caused rent arrears on my account. I'm in the middle of trying to sort it out now, because they want me to go to court for eviction for my house, even though the letters and everything had gone in.*
>
> Amy

When her daughter went on an apprenticeship scheme, Zoe saw her Housing Benefit unexpectedly cut.

> *My Housing Benefit has dropped to £56 a week. I just thought with my daughter it would be classed as education, training. She gets £90 a week and I didn't think it would affect me that much.*
>
> Sue

She experienced serious stress as a result of mistakes that were made in the way her Housing Benefit was calculated.

> *I think 'Housing Benefit' were a bit naughty though, because they got me so stressed; and, in the end, I hadn't done anything wrong. It was just that I thought I was going to go to court. And all the letters they sent me, showed that I had given them the changes; but it was their fault. So all that worry and all that 'Anything you have to say will be taken down'. I was thinking I was going to lose my place.*
>
> Sue

Liz had also had problems with her Housing Benefit, arising from confusion about what she should have been paying.

> *I get Housing Benefit that changes all the time, because one minute they say I'm entitled to stuff; then they say I'm not entitled to it. Then they say I am again; and then they say I'm in debt to them, and they're taking money off me. Every year, without fail, it happens; every single year. Then half way through the year I'll get another letter off them changing their mind again. My Council Tax, I get the sole home occupancy discount; but my Council Tax is still £77 a month or something like that.*
>
> Liz

There had been uncertainty as to whether Sian and Steve should have been getting Housing Benefit.

> *We don't get any Housing Benefit* [discount] *at all. I recently phoned them up because what they had us down for was a lot more than he actually earned. What they had was sixteen and a half* [thousand pounds]*; and he's only on thirteen and a half.*
>
> Steve

Joy was prepared to go to court over what she felt was the unfair way in which her Housing Benefit and Council Tax arrears were being dealt with.

> *My Housing Benefit was overpaid, and now they have cut it down to £100. I appealed against it, and the Council Tax as well, but I still owe them the money. And whereas I was paying £50 a month Council Tax, they now want £300 a month up until April, and then I will go back onto the £100 per month. I'm not entitled to any help now and I've got to pay everything out of my wages. I thought they had made a mistake, and that's why I appealed; but they have come back for £300. I shouldn't have been getting any Council Tax benefit; but they*

said they are still entitled to claim it back off you. I think I was paying £50 a month instead of £75, over a couple of years. They said 'You can either pay it, or not and wait until they take you to court'. I asked if I could come to some other arrangement and they said 'No, just wait until they take you to court'. Since I got that letter I have made one payment of £100. So I'm not paying, and am going to wait until the court try to sort something out. It was their mistake. Out of my wages, I wouldn't be able to pay the rent and Council Tax and all the other bills with it.

Joy

The Disability Living Allowance had made a significant difference to both Cath's and Amber's families. Cath said that the extra financial support it provided was crucial.

Now, having a child with special needs, we get that extra money. If he didn't have his condition then we wouldn't get that extra money. We would struggle even more because we wouldn't have that extra you get with the DLA. I think it's called a 'premium' with the Child Tax Credits. So you get a little top up; but it's got to be a certain rate though. Not everyone qualifies, so you have to be on a certain rate of the DLA, and then you qualify for a little bit extra. Now that's not a luxury, and I've said many times I would prefer my son not to have anything; to have a normal life.

Cath

Amber had to fight to get Disability Living Allowance for her son.

[Things are] *a lot easier now because I have been awarded DLA. I wasn't awarded DLA two years ago. I can't get him on transport because of the way he is. That was a massive struggle. We lived so far away from the school at that time; so I was getting a taxi every single morning with him at about £7 a taxi. So we are looking at £14 a day. It was outrageous.*

Amber

Both Ric and Carol's children had chronic health problems and they were hoping they would qualify for disability support. However, Carol had not had a good experience of applying for the benefit.

I'm just thinking about applying for DLA for the kids actually. I've applied for myself but they just turned me straight down. I've got this, my leg dislocates; so I spend quite a lot of time on crutches and a leg brace. It certainly is a lot of steps [in the application process] *for a leg brace; but I'm kind of stuck, if you know what I mean.*

Carol

Fiona had two children. She was living with members of her extended family, and not with her partner. She was trying to establish her own business, but until she could draw an income from the business her main source of income was Working Tax Credit, amounting to £840 a month. She was paying back debts of nearly £3,500. She was concerned about the changes to the benefits system and how they would affect her. Particularly, she was worried that she wouldn't be entitled to the new Universal Credit and so would have abandon her business.

> *What is slightly concerning is what will happen if the Universal Credit scheme comes through, because of the limits on how long you can run a business without making a profit. And that's a little bit terrifying, especially because no one seems to know how it will work; what the restrictions will be. I kind of keep watching that with hints of terror.*
>
> Fiona

Amy too had concerns about how Universal Credit would work. She was also very aware of the negative stereotyping of welfare claimants.

> *There's a lot of talk about people being on benefits; people saying 'Go out and get a job'. And then there's other people at the other end of the spectrum, the rich, and when they give statistics about benefits they automatically assume it's people out of work; but for the majority of the time, it's not. It's people who are working on a low-income or part-time wages; and that's where a lot of the benefits bill comes from. But too often it's categorised as the 'too lazy to get off their bums and get a job' lot. We are just forgotten about. I'm OK in that I've got a contract for thirty-seven hours; but there are lots of people with zero-hours. How do you budget with a contract like that? Forty hours one week and ten the next? People need proper contracts and fair pay as well. Pay has to reflect living costs.*
>
> Amy

Karen and Steve had four children; the youngest was just a baby. Karen had been made redundant from her job at the start of the year. They were now relying on Steve's public sector administration job that gave him about £1,000 a month after tax. Karen didn't know what the changes would mean for her.

> *I'm still going to struggle; a massive struggle. You hope something nice is going to happen to you. I don't think there is going to be any help out there for us. There are going to be a lot of changes in benefits like the Universal Credits. Things are changing. I've started with my credit union and I'm trying to put a little bit away. What's going to change? There should be more help.*
>
> Karen

The thresholds that regulate the tax and benefit system were at least partly responsible for the difficulties and mistakes the families had experienced with routine payments.

> *If my partner worked more hours, I would lose my Housing Benefit. So we are in a catch. He works twenty hours; then I get my Housing Benefit. But if he was to go up* [in hours] *I would get working tax* [credit] *but lose my Housing Benefit. So I wouldn't gain.*
>
> Emma

Emma was trying to calculate whether she should try to increase her weekly working hours from sixteen to 24. This would have meant asking her mother to pick up the children from school which she felt would be too much for her. The fact that her son was now working plus the fact that she had recently increased her hours up to sixteen, meant that she now had to pay Council Tax and had also lost free school meals for one of her other children.

> *And the other big thing was when, before I started working the sixteen hours, I didn't have to pay any Council Tax. Now I have to pay £112 a month. Because Sam works as well, it works out that his wages and my wages are on the cut-off. So I don't get any* [discount]. *He works four days; but it's shift work, so it's classed as full-time.*
>
> Emma

Gaynor was also finding that if she increased her hours she would lose her Housing Benefit.

> *I'm only doing sixteen hours for thirty-nine weeks a year; so that entitles me to full Housing Benefit* [discount]. *So as soon as I do any extra hours or the extra weeks, I won't get that; and that's when it's going to hit me.*
>
> Gaynor

She knew that her benefit payments would be affected when her eldest child became eighteen. However she didn't yet know by how much, and whether it explained the reduction she had already received.

> *I seem to be about £70 down a week. I'm not sure why that is. Not sure if it's because of the change; but I'm sure it will level itself out, won't it? But it's £70 a week less than what it was. That's a lot!*
>
> Gaynor

Uncertainty about entitlements was a common experience for the families. Gill admitted that she and Pete didn't understand the system.

> *I've said to Pete 'We'll have to look into it', because you get your Child Tax Credits and we're entitled to Working Tax Credits. But when you don't know the system… I get Child Tax Credits now, but he's entitled to Working Tax Credits. We've just applied for that. Someone told us you had to work a minimum number of hours to get something. I was thinking that maybe we should look at going to the CAB or something.*
>
> Gill

Phil and Dot discovered that they had been overpaid for their Working Tax Credit, but didn't understand how it had been calculated.

> *We've got a tax credit debt for an overpayment that was a couple of thousand that they've paid us; and we have to pay it back. They really haven't explained it. They just lumped the figures together and, honestly, you look at it and you phone them up to contest them, and they said 'No, it's an overpayment'. We've got to pay it back. We are getting tax credits, but we have to pay that back by direct debit; £20 a week. How it is with my partner, she's scared in case they send bailiffs or someone from the* [Local] *Authority round to the house.*
>
> Phil

The level of complexity and the errors and inefficiencies in operating the benefit system, coupled with the need for advice on matters such as personal debt and housing, makes the Citizens' Advice Bureau and other advice services more needed than ever. Carol's debt problems and uncertainty about her entitlements illustrated this.

> *I get Child Tax Credit but we don't get 'working families'* [Tax Credit]. *I'm not sure if you both have to be working for that or not? It's been checked numerous times. I've had lots of help from the CAB. I've been to debt counselling and all that. Actually, I am currently, I'm just coming to the end of a—it's not a bankruptcy order it's the* […]*—I can't remember what it's called. But basically, it only lasts a year; it wiped out all my debts and I started again with a new bank account. So, I can't borrow or anything. Basically, it amounted to £10,000 that I just couldn't pay off. Over the years I'd made an arrangement through the CAB. I was paying them off at like £25 a month.*
>
> Carol

Without the advice they had received from their local Citizens' Advice Bureau, Terri and Don wouldn't have known what to do when the bailiff arrived at their door.

> *I came home one day and there was a letter posted through the door and a man in a van. So I looked at the letter and I said to my partner 'That's a bailiff's letter'. I had only just paid them the £50. So I rang them and said 'What's he sitting outside for?' The man said 'Would you like to come out and speak to me'. So I said 'Yeah, I would'. So I went out and said, 'It's lowered'* [the repayment amount]. *He said, 'No they want you to pay £50 to me as well and I said, 'I can't do that'. So, I flew round to* [name at CAB] *and I said 'He is demanding I pay him as well'. She said 'Hang on' and she rang the enforcement officer for Liverpool City Council and they said 'No, £50 and that's it'.*
>
> Terri

Terri then got advice about her other debts.

> *Well* [name at CAB] *told me to put in for 'support tariff', and 'the water' too. So I did, and I get a letter saying they'd given it to me: which cleared it and put me £15 in arrears. I don't have to pay them now till 7th April.*
>
> Terri

Support and advice services such as Liverpool Citizens Support Scheme and the local Citizens' Advice Bureau play a vital role in assisting people who are in crisis and helping them navigate the complexities of the welfare system. At a time when pressures on these services are increasing, the funding they rely upon is diminishing.

Politicians and the media have made sure that the issue of welfare benefits have never strayed far from the news headlines. Continued media focus on 'benefit scroungers' has created a stigma for those receiving benefits. An old and crude stereotype also perpetuated by the media is that of the lone parent having children to access state support. Both Colette and Liz were lone parents who were only marginally better-off working. Despite the hardships of low paid work and the slightness of the resulting financial advantage, contrary to this stereotype they believed strongly in the importance of working.

> *Funnily enough I was discussing this with my Mum the other day. Because my contract is up for renewal, we worked out the worst case scenario if I lost my job*

> *and could not get another one and had to go back on benefits. I would have to move from here because I wouldn't be able to afford the rent. We worked out I am £10 better-off for working thirty-five hours a week. But I said 'It is about your own self-respect and for what I am showing them'* [the children].
>
> Colette

Liz compared her finances with a friend who was also a lone parent, but not in work.

> *We sat down and worked out that I was £5 better-off than she was a week. I feel like I am working, mainly for my own sanity, and I want to instil it into* [her son] *as well, because I don't want him to think that you can just sit at home and get paid for doing nothing, you know. My Dad never did that; my dad's always worked. My Mum looked after us and brought us up and looked after the home and stuff. But my Dad did work. So in mine and* [her son's] *family, I've got to be both parents to him. So I think I need to be his role model, and I need to work to show him that he's got to work as well when he's older.*
>
> Liz

Even with the importance they attach to working, the families had strong views about low paid employment. Amy and Amber highlighted the failure of the National Minimum Wage to keep pace with inflation.

> *To be honest with you, I think it's 'pie in the sky' isn't it, £6.50? The way things are increasing. Everything is increasing: your rent; your Council Tax; your food; your fuel. Everything is going up; and the rate of pay isn't going up to meet that. To me it doesn't make sense; and when you think that you've got these bigwigs that are on hundreds of thousands of pounds a year, who sit there and get somebody else to do their work for them.*
>
> Amy

> *Like, when you think* [about] *the minimum wage, ten years ago when I was working in a* [well-known fast-food outlet], *it was probably about £5.80 something. So that has only increased by 80p in ten years as opposed to the increases; you know, like, you can't even get a packet of 10p crisps any more. Everything has increased: everything; Council Tax; gas; electric. It is all increasing by a massive percentage and yet the national wage isn't. I think that's wrong. I think as well, there are a lot of jobs now that are minimum wage that ten years ago wouldn't have been.*
>
> Amber

Sue felt that working makes a person feel part of society. She wanted become a nurse so that she could make a difference in the world. She was in the last year of her nurse training and was having to do agency work to cope financially. The agency paid the National Minimum Wage. She estimated that the bursary[22] she was getting as a student nurse paid her about £3 an hour for her weekly thirty hours on the ward. She was paying back a debt of nearly £4,000 and had an average of just £8.57 a week left after necessary expenditure. She had a daughter who was living away from home, and a teenage son on an apprenticeship. She made the point that families on the minimum wage rely on tax credits that in effect subsidise employers.

> *I think we talked about this another time, and I was saying I kind of find that I benefit loads from the Tax Credit system and it's a fantastic short term measure. But I think as a long-term measure, it does allow businesses that could afford to pay people more, not to pay people more. I don't at all see how big, massive corporations can justify declaring massive profits, but relying on the Government to pay their workers extra money if they've got children to care for.*
>
> Sue

Fiona had reservations about how the National Minimum Wage worked in practice.

> *I understand why we have the minimum wage and now we've got it, it absolutely should be a living wage. But again I have that thing of perhaps, even with good intentions, governments mess things up an awful lot of the time. By having a minimum wage you're actually setting a lower bar* [for the employers], *which if they can get away with paying it, they will. So it's good news for people on the minimum wage that there's a rise; but it isn't that much is it? 19p an hour? And it's not going to make a substantial difference for many people. I like the tax threshold increase more.*
>
> Fiona

Increasing wages to improve the incentive to work was suggested by Colette.

> *I think as well, with regards to benefits and stuff, I am £10 better-off working full-time and I want to work. There are plenty of people who would say* [why work] *for the sake of £10? They need to give you more incentive to work and make it more worth your while. Yeah, in that sense wages should go up. You wouldn't want to be on benefits if you knew you would be earning a lot more working.*
>
> Colette

22 The 2015 Spending Review scrapped bursaries for nursing students, effective from August 2017.

Conclusion

Based upon the experience of these families we can see that there is a cruel contrast between government rhetoric regarding 'fairness' and lifting pay levels, and the reality for those struggling on low pay and their families. An uplift in the National Minimum Wage, still far below the Living Wage, does not by itself eliminate the problems of life for those who must survive on the lowest rates of pay. For that to happen the full complexity of the factors that shape the experience of life on low pay would need to be addressed. So, any potential improvements to living standards for such families arising from an increase in the National Minimum Wage to £7.50, are cancelled out for millions of families by weak enforcement, age caps, cuts to in-work benefits, the introduction of charges for a growing range of essential services, increases in school-related costs, insecure contracts and so on. It is the entirety of these financial pressures and more that create the problem of working poverty. This is what needs to be lifted in order to address the unfairness of wealth distribution that has characterised British society for forty years.

The paradox then, of policies that purport to 'end poverty pay' or to 'lift the poorest out of poverty' from successive governments, and the reality of rising poverty rates and the UK's stubborn position near the bottom of the poverty league tables of the industrialised countries is not so hard to understand. For example, whilst the National Minimum Wage rose to £7.50 in 2017, so also did the numbers of workers on zero-hour contracts and with 'self-employed' status even whilst working for the same company over several years. Moreover, the 'bunching' of many workers at or slightly above the National Minimum Wage means that it is a double edged-sword, representing both a floor beneath which wage levels should not fall, and a ceiling above which it is difficult to rise. Given the constraints within which minimum wage policy operates then, it should come as no surprise that relative poverty has continued to worsen, and as the gap between the 'haves' and the 'have-nots' has widened with each successive cycle of employment policy.

This situation also gives the lie to the claims by successive governments over the last thirty years that their employment and welfare policies have aimed to eliminate 'benefit-dependency'. The hollowness of that rhetoric lies in the fact that the real effect has been to create a new type of dependency; the dependency upon low paid work with no escape through significant improvement in wage levels, short-term use of benefits, upskilling or retraining. Whilst the benefits are being reduced and removed, the dependency upon work that is poorly paid and insecure remains. The only real beneficiaries in this situation are the state as it regressively relinquishes its responsibilities towards low paid workers, and employers who continue to pay their workers at or marginally above the minimum required of them.

4. Working Life

The 'dignity of work'

Wages and other sources of family income are of course matters of survival. However, things that affect the experience of work are also important. Where work is satisfying, purposeful and rewarding the effect on the health, well-being and happiness of the person can be positive; even profoundly so. Where it is none of these things it can impact negatively upon the person in all of these respects and more. For the lowest paid and the unskilled, work has seldom ever been anything other than necessary; 'the job' being a means of providing a livelihood and supporting dependents; 'the workplace' rarely a site of personal satisfaction or outlet. However, whilst avoiding a romantic view of working life, it is reasonable to expect minimum standards that should exist regardless of occupation or social status. Work should at least be safe; it should not be compromising to a person's health; there ought to be dignity in work; there should be some predictability of hours and duties; a balance should prevail between contractual obligations and family life; there should be some form of employee representation; and so on.

However, it is just these aspects of working life in which we see a year-on-year erosion of standards and employer obligations, and deteriorations in the quality of working life for the low paid in the UK. Work it seems in many sectors has become more stressful over recent years. Many workers find that they need to add to their basic hours to bring in an adequate family income. Work for the lowest

 https://doi.org/10.11647/OBP.0112.04

paid is increasingly casualised,[1] with contractual permanence far more difficult to achieve than in the relatively recent past. Low paid work is increasingly associated with poor health. The trends for workplaces in the least well-paid sectors are of more arbitrary treatment of employees, higher incidences of bullying and, for a growing number, below minimum standards for basic entitlements and protections.

The problem of stress in the workplace has come under scrutiny in recent years. The Health and Safety Executive identify six common causes of stress at work: difficulties in managing the demands of the job; inability to control work pressures; poor working relationships; workplace change; problems of role definition; and inadequate support.

Those in low paid jobs are also at greater risk of accidents and injuries in the workplace. Often these are trivialised or ignored by the employer so that the individuals affected feel unable to take time off to recover for fear of losing their employment.[2] A further cause of illness can be the culture of the workplace more generally in relation to management attitudes to stress when it is reported. Gender also plays a role, women being more likely to experience stress in the workplace than men. The combination of these factors creates 'vicious cycles' in which stress becomes increasingly severe for the individual, affecting them at many psychological and physical levels of health, wellbeing and occupational function.[3]

A 2015 Trade Union Congress (TUC) study explained that the mental symptoms of stress included disrupted sleep patterns, listlessness and, at the extreme, suicide. The physical consequences it identified included loss of appetite, nausea, heart damage and stroke. Highlighting the extent of the problem it revealed that work-related stress, accounting for 39 percent of all work-related illness, causes 11.3 million lost work-days in the UK. It reported also that between 2013 and 2014 around

1 'Casualisation' refers to the shift from permanent contracts to a pattern of non-standard, fixed-term and zero-hour contracts or uncontacted working.

2 Shildrick, T., MacDonald, R., Webster, C. and Garthwaite, K. (2011), *Poverty and Insecurity. Life in Low-pay, No-pay Britain*. Policy Press, p. 149.

3 Blaug, R. Kenyon, A. and Lekhi, R. (2007), *Stress at Work: A Report Prepared for The Work Foundation's Principal Partners*. The Work Foundation, http://westminsterresearch.wmin.ac.uk/11456/

244,000 new cases of work-related stress, depression or anxiety were diagnosed; equating to one diagnosis every two minutes.[4]

These figures do not tell the whole story, however. Problems of work-related illness are exacerbated by the insecurity which characterises working life for increasing numbers of people. Since 2008, the proportion of workers on standard permanent contracts in the UK workforce has been falling, following a decade in which it had remained relatively constant. In those sectors which have seen rising employment numbers, new jobs have tended to be those with part-time, temporary and self-employed status.

In 2014, 69 percent of organisations (and 78 percent of large employers) were using fixed-term contracts, whilst 36 percent (and 40 percent of large employers) employed workers on casual contracts.[5] According to the Office for National Statistics Labour Force Survey, the numbers of workers in temporary and casual employment has increased year-on-year since 2008. In 2014, 1.7 million workers reported being in temporary work; a rise of 300,000 over six years. Over the same years the number of workers on zero-hour contracts had risen to 1.4 million,[6] effectively doubling within that period.[7] Its March 2017 report revealed more than a threefold increase in the number of employees on zero-hour contracts over the preceding five years.[8] This meant that approaching three percent of the active workforce were on a zero-hour contract, with a far higher percentage of those on low pay. Women and younger workers were also more likely to be in this category. Another type of casualisation that has become far more familiar in the UK, is that of self-employed status for workers within an organisation who would otherwise have been employed with all of the entitlements associated with standard contracts. So, between the years 2010 and 2013, of the

4 TUC (2015), 'Someone Experiences Work-related Stress Every Two Minutes'. Press release, 16 October, https://www.tuc.org.uk/workplace-issues/someone-experiences-work-related-stress-every-two-minutes-says-tuc

5 HRZONE, Acas, CIPD (2015), 'Workplace Trends of 2015. What They Mean for You', 14 January, p. 19, http://www.acas.org.uk/media/pdf/t/e/Workplace-trends-of-20151.pdf

6 *Ibid.*, p. 22.

7 *Ibid.*, p. 16.

8 Office for National Statistics (2017), https://www.ons.gov.uk/employmentandlabourmarket/peopleinwork/employmentandemployeetypes/bulletins/uklabourmarket/mar2017

casual or 'atypical jobs' that accounted for 40 percent of new jobs in the UK, around half were zero-hour contracts; by the following year however, the great majority of new jobs were 'self-employed' positions.[9] By December 2016, the number of self-employed workers had risen to 4.8 million; 15.1 percent of the workforce.

For most employers using the whole range of forms of casual employment the rationale, predictably, is that of filling temporary needs according to market fluctuations and changes in demand.[10] These types of job are characterised by: lack of recognition awards; lack of cover for sickness, maternity and retirement; an absence of training opportunities; exclusion from internal communications; and a lack of clear line management arrangements.[11]

With the introduction of fees for employment tribunals, even the basic statutory workplace rights that exist are less likely than in the past to be enforced. Since the introduction of fees for employment tribunals for instance, applications to court have fallen by 79 percent.[12] One aspect of this erosion of worker entitlements is that whilst the employer is within their rights to allocate hours solely based upon their needs (the definition of 'zero-hours' status), the employee cannot do so without risking their position entirely.

Neither is the impact of casual employment status restricted to the workplace. Home-ownership for instance is often unattainable for those who are in atypical work. Effectively blocked from buying a property by the refusal of banks to offer them mortgages, they and their families will very likely be renting their homes in the private sector. Restricted in their choice of home location, often they will be forced to live at a considerable distance from their workplace that makes expensive travel journeys to and from work necessary. It is unsurprising then that the insecurities and life-pressures for workers in these kinds of jobs lead directly to anxiety, stress and 'depressed mental states'.[13]

---

9 Brinkley, I. (2014), *Zero-hour Contracts: Response to the BIS Consultation*, The Work Foundation, March, p. 4, http://mbsportal.bl.uk/taster/subjareas/hrmemplyrelat/twf/164300zerohour14.pdf

10 HRZONE, Acas, CIPD (2015), p. 19.

11 *Ibid.*, p. 21.

12 *Ibid.*, p. 23.

13 *Ibid.*, p. 24.

Problems of insecurity and the erosion of basic protections affect many other aspects of working life. One such aspect is that of the right and ability to take time off work. In a 2015 report the TUC estimated that each year 1.7 million people, or 6.4 percent of the workforce, are unable to take up their holiday entitlement.[14] This was even though at the time of the interviews paid holidays were a statutory entitlement under the 1998 EU Working Time Directive. Added to this are circumstances in which workers do not feel secure enough in their positions to be able to take time off when they are unwell, preferring to come into work for fear of losing their job; a phenomenon known as 'presenteeism'. In 2015, a survey by Personnel Today revealed that 31 percent of the 600 employers that responded said that 'presenteeism' had increased over the previous twelve months with most also admitting to doing nothing to discourage it.[15]

Another aspect of workplace culture that affects people in insecure employment is bullying. The TUC reported in that in 2015 six out of ten workers had experienced bullying in their workplaces; with over a third of those workers having been bullied themselves. Furthermore, the problem of bullying affects some groups more than others. Women for instance are more likely than men to suffer bullying behaviour towards them, as are older workers. Although the perpetrators of bullying can be colleagues, they are far more likely to be managers. The effects upon the individual can be very negative for both mental and physical health. Job security and income can also suffer, as workers affected are more likely to take time off work because of having been bullied.[16]

Low pay leads to 'over-working' for many employees, as they take on more and more hours to make ends meet. Indeed, the number of individuals working for more than 48 hours per week has increased by fifteen percent since 2010. The TUC's 2015 report revealed that 3,417,000 workers were now in that position; an increase of 453,000 in just five

---

14 TUC (2015), '1.7 Million People Missing Out on Their Paid Holidays'. Press release, 30 July. https://www.tuc.org.uk/workplace-issues/employment-rights/working-time-holidays/17-million-people-missing-out-their-paid

15 Paton, N. (2015), 'Presenteeism Costs Twice As Much As Sickness Absence', *Personnel Today*, 27 November, http://www.personneltoday.com/hr/presenteeism-costs-twice-much-sickness-absence/

16 TUC (2015), 'Action Needed On Workplace Bullying'. Press release, 21 August, https://www.tuc.org.uk/workplace-issues/health-and-safety/bullying/action-needed-workplace-bullying

years,[17] the greater part of this increase being women working excessive hours. Working life for these workers, in what the TUC dubbed 'Burnout Britain' increases the chances of heart disease, stress, mental illness, strokes and diabetes as well as impacting negatively upon family life. Here the weakness of the European Working Time Directive was all too clear. The Directive stipulates a maximum of 48 hours working time per week. Over the years leading up to 2010, its effect in the UK was indeed to reduce the problem of excessive hours. However, the Directive also allows for individual 'op-out'. Increasing numbers of employers then made this a condition of employment leaving many workers with little choice but accept this condition if they were to obtain work at all.

The problem of excessively long working days and weeks is also compounded by increases in the travel time to work that, as we have seen, often result from restricted housing choice as house-prices and rents have risen. In just ten years the number of people travelling for more than two hours to and from work has increased by 72 percent.[18] The number having to travel for three hours or more has increased by 75 percent to 880,000 over the same period. Within this figure, the trend has been steeper for women workers than for men. The figures are also the worst in services compared to all other sectors.

Between 2007 and 2014, the numbers of employees who do mostly shift work rose by 5.2 percent; those who do regular night shifts rose by 6.9 percent. Although traditionally far more men than women did shift-work and night-work, patterns are changing rapidly. Over these same years for instance the increase in the proportion of women night workers has risen by twelve percent, compared to four percent for men. In the social and health sectors, most night workers are women. Black and ethnic minority workers are also more likely to work nights than their white counterparts.[19] The effects of night-work particularly

17 TUC (2015), '15 Percent Increase in People Working More Than 48 Hours a Week Risks a Return to "Burnout Britain"'. Press release, 9 September, https://www.tuc.org.uk/international-issues/europe/workplace-issues/work-life-balance/15-cent-increase-people-working-more

18 TUC (2015), 'Number of Commuters Spending More Than Two Hours Travelling to and from Work up by 72 Percent in Last Decade'. Press release, 5 November, https://www.tuc.org.uk/workplace-issues/work-life-balance/number-commuters-spending-more-two-hours-travelling-and-work-72

19 TUC (2015), 'A Hard Day's Night: The Effect of Night Shift Work on Work/Life Balance', p. 1, https://www.tuc.org.uk/sites/default/files/AHardDaysNight.pdf

can be very negative upon the person's health and upon family life. Cardiovascular disease, obesity, diabetes, breast cancer, stomach ulcers, depression, physical injury are all associated with working nights.[20] Reliance upon shift and night work can also be a cause of significant difficulties for child-care arrangements and costs, as well as being very disruptive of family relations.

Despite exhortations to the least well-off in society from successive governments since the 1980s regarding the virtues of work, the truth is that working life for the low paid has not become any easier; it has become harder—much harder. Nearly half of workers for instance, say their job makes them feel worried some, most or all of the time.[21] Annually, around 1.2 million workers suffer some type of illness they attribute directly to their employment; 700,000 who no longer work, are unwell because of their previous employment. The most common types of work-related illness are musculoskeletal disorders, stress and depression, accounting for 70 percent of absences from work due to ill health.[22] It seems clear; the combination of the trends and factors described here, means that over recent years the workplace and working life more generally, has become more tiring, stressful and unhealthy for many millions of working people.

Family voices

The importance of work

The employment experience of the families wasn't just about being low paid, it was frequently defined by poor working conditions and exploitative employment practices. For all this, the families were adamant about the importance of having jobs to provide role models for their children and because it was engrained into them by their own parents. The importance of setting an example for the children was emphasised by Janet.

20 *Ibid.*, p. 2.

21 TUC (2010), 'In Sickness and in Health? Good Work—and How to Achieve It', https://www.tuc.org.uk/sites/default/files/extras/goodwork.pdf

22 TUC (2015), 'Work and Well-being: A Trade Union Resource', https://www.tuc.org.uk/workplace-issues/work-and-well-being-trade-union-resource, p. 5.

> *It's important for me to have a job because I want my kids to follow in my footsteps, and I don't want them to* [think] *'It probably would be easier for me to go on benefits' or stuff like that. But no, I want to work. I want my kids to work as well. The amount of money I get paid and the amount of money I pay out! It's still not an excuse not to work; but I understand why people choose not to.*
>
> Janet

Eileen made a similar point.

> *The main reason why it's majorly important for me is because I need my kids to see me getting up and working for a living every morning. I'm leading by example. I think it's important that they know that you get nothing unless you get out of bed and earn it.*
>
> Eileen

Will and Sam had two children. Will worked full-time in the leisure sector. Despite this, their average weekly expenditure in 2014 exceeded their income by £59.52, and they were paying back debts of over £1,600. They were getting help from Sam's father and had also made use of pay-day loans. However, Will explained that he emphasised the importance of working to his children, just as his father did with him.

> *I mean, I've always worked. It's always been instilled in me that you work; even with my disability, you work. It's a pride thing as well. It makes you feel better if you work. I would never—unless my disability got so bad that I couldn't—I would never not work. My Dad had his own business for 47 years, so he says 'I don't care what you do, you work', and that's what I want to instil into my kids. I think it will be very difficult in the future; but I will instil it into them.*
>
> Will

Phil took the same view and also saw employment as making a contribution to society.

> *I do think it's important; it's a 'self-thing'. You need to work. And I like to think 'I'm working'; and then later on in life I can think 'I've put my fair share into the pot' type of thing and I'm expecting a fair share back. I don't have a pension at the moment. We've both worked. I've worked in various other jobs, from the age of sixteen. The only time I've been unemployed was for about four years; and then I managed to get back into work.*
>
> Phil

Even though Ruth wasn't much better-off in work, she nonetheless recognised its value in her own life.

> *It is very important to me that I have a job at the moment, basically for my children, to be a role model to them. I don't want them sitting on the dole, you know what I mean. Yeah, set a better example. It's good for myself, for my wellbeing; getting out. Yeah, basically at the moment the way my wages and everything goes, I am only about £15 better-off working.*
>
> Ruth

For Amy, working was about having a sense of purpose.

> *To be fair, I've always worked. I left school at sixteen; worked for the summer in a factory and then went back to sixth form; and then left school and went to the factory. And even in between the kids I've always had part-time work and stuff. If I didn't work I'd be absolutely devastated. I'd have to do something. But I always said 'If I came into money I'd still do voluntary work', because you need a reason to get up in the morning.*
>
> Amy

Carol was a lone parent with five children. The family were living in privately rented property. She was working part-time, but valued her employment because it reduced the social isolation she would otherwise have experienced.

> *Oh, yes, I feel better in myself; and I feel better than like when I didn't have any money. Before I was just stuck in the house with no money. Now, I've still got no money but I can go out and talk to my friends; you know my work colleagues. They always cheer me up.*
>
> Carol

Ali and Rabia had five children. Ali had been working full-time as a support worker, but had been made redundant. He was now working in a fast-food outlet and getting paid at about the minimum wage. He worked shifts and had to be on-call during night hours but wanted more hours because he wasn't earning enough. Normally he was only getting three days a week. Rabia stressed the importance of work even though she thought they weren't any better-off financially.

> *It's important because it gets depressing if you're both out of work. If you think about it, there's no future for the kids either. So it's like, it gives him a bit of confidence, thinking that he's always working. Occasions when we were both not working, it was hard. In terms of our abilities, we were thinking how can we both not have a job? Other people put you down when you're not working. I want to go back to work.*
>
> Rabia

Terri also knew that her partner Don would become depressed if he wasn't in work. They had two children and were living in privately rented accommodation. Terri had been forced to give up her job due to ill health. Don was working part-time and had experienced poor mental health.

> *He would get depressed if he was in the house. I know he would because he has worked since he was sixteen. Since I have been with him, which is sixteen years. He started work in* [a local company] *and then he started working for* [a different company] *that do the docks and the trains, and he loved it; and they laid him off.*
>
> Terri

Sian's mother hadn't been able to support her financially once she'd turned sixteen, and so she got herself a job. Like others, she made the point that she had always worked, often having more than one job.

> *I've always worked, and when I look at it I've had 23 jobs! I've never been sacked from them though; it was like natural progression really. Sometimes, I've had three jobs at once, like at a call-centre and an off-licence and a club of an evening. So I was single and I could work hard, always. I've always had a second job, like in a pub. I've worked for the minimum wage for most of my life and I think it's just atrocious. People work hard on the minimum wage, and the price of everything's gone up and everyone's struggling. Everyone's in the same boat.*
>
> Sian

Denise had also always worked since leaving school, mainly in shops and bars. She was a lone parent with three children and was living in social housing. She said that being employed gave her a sense of self-sufficiency; of 'doing something' with herself. But of course, it was also a necessity and meant that she wasn't dependent upon her family for support.

> *It gets you down, days that, you know, I'm working for nothing. Nothing* [is] *left, you know, but it's life. But I don't let it get me down; just got to get on with it. To be honest, it's a case of 'you have to', isn't it? Nowhere to turn to; can't keep turning to family members all the time for money. I have to pay them back, you see; so it's hard.*
>
> Denise

Apart from the financial necessity of working, Carol saw a moral aspect to being in work.

I don't know, I suppose it's a moral thing isn't it? It's a 'how you've been brought up' kind of thing, really. We've both been brought up in working families, so that's what you do. I wouldn't cope any other way, anyway. Somebody's got to work, that's all there is to it. To us it's important that at least one of us is working.

Carol

The impact of insecure work

Low paid jobs are also frequently characterised by poor contractual status, without fixed hours and with low levels of entitlement. They also often offer little protection from arbitrary lay-off or dismissal. In these circumstances employees find it difficult to become established in their working lives or even to press for the rights they do lawfully have. Job insecurity was the reason Colette hadn't done anything about joining a union or a pension scheme.

I keep saying 'I am going to join the union and the pension scheme'. But I keep holding back until they make me permanent, because I don't want to start paying into something and then they say 'No, you're not staying on'.

Colette

Ric's job was also insecure and was a cause of stress for his family. His partner Carol made the point that as a care worker the hours weren't guaranteed

Everything is constantly hanging on a thread; there is no permanency to it. Although it's a 'permanent' position, it could be swept away at any moment and again funding is being cut and cut and cut. There are other people, this has happened to them: their services have been cut and they've been left without. You're paid for the hours you work, and then you're basically relying on them. You haven't got the redundancy money. You're just left in a situation where you're picking up shifts that can't be filled, or somebody goes off sick or whatever it is, that's all you've got for the time being. It's no better than a zero-hours contract at the end of the day is it?

Carol

Changes in her firm's management and cost cutting exercises were sources of real concern for Joy.

It is permanent; I've been there twelve years. My new boss, to be honest, seems to go through staff a lot more quickly. We all worked for the same company for

years and she seems to be different. She's more cost-effective; so she's trying to employ trainees and apprentices who are on £2.30 an hour. We do often, myself and two of the old girls, think that we are at risk really on account of the wage bill. So it is always a worry. We try not to think about it really. There were times when there have been things getting said in work about the wage bill and she needs to get rid of the highest waged people. It's one of them really. I know she couldn't just get rid of us, but we're always thinking she could do things, like obviously change my hours so I couldn't work them. It is always a worry, but I try not to worry about it.

Joy

Liz was doubtful about keeping her job because of redundancies and closures.

They're closing branches down constantly at the minute. There's people getting offered redundancies left right and centre. We think it's going to close. They're only allowing two of us to go off at a time now because they've got no staff.

Liz

The charity that Luke was working for was having serious financial problems due to cuts in funding. Things were looking very uncertain for his job in the medium-term.

We have been told by the trustees that this organisation is only able to survive for another 18–24 months. So unless we can get a big opportunity or big funding comes in, the charity may be shut down. The money that we've been getting from government has been getting less and less. I can't guarantee after two years.

Luke

Amy was a lone parent with four children. She had two jobs that together amounted to full-time employment, and pay above the national minimum rate. Even so, she was in serious financial difficulty and almost a third of her income was going to pay back debts of nearly £9,000. She was anxious about one of her jobs with a Community and Voluntary Sector Organisation.

To be honest with you, up until a couple of months ago it wasn't 'month-by-month', it was 'six-month-by-six-month'. They'd say 'The funding runs out in July'; but then, it's from all different places. So the funding that was paying our wages would run out in July; then it would be the second week in July. Then they would say 'We've secured some more funding so you're OK up until December'. Then we'd go back, and they'd say they've got more funding until March.

Amy

Pensions

Contributing into a pension scheme is unsustainable for families in working poverty who are already struggling to meet their immediate financial commitments. Carol and Ric were among many in that situation:

> *Again, that's a concern. It's hard isn't it, because I know you've got to put something away for your future. But we're living hand-to-mouth, day by day. We have to start making some provision. It's like all those things we're really, really crap at. We've got no savings or anything like that; we've got no insurance, no life insurance, nothing like that because, as I say it's that hand-to-mouth, living day-to-day. We can't plan for the future.*
>
> Carol

Eileen was a single parent with three children. She had two jobs and so effectively was working full-time. Her combined hourly rate worked out at about £7.75 an hour. She was still paying back a loan she'd obtained from what she called a 'legalised loan shark' three years previously, to pay the deposit on her rented property. Her debt was over £3,000. She was aware of the introduction of a workplace pension scheme, but hadn't been able to afford to begin paying into it.

> *I've heard that it's coming in and it's starting soon. But I haven't got a pension and I'm 48 years of age. No life insurance; no insurance on anything at all, and no pension. But apparently they've got to have them by law. I want to work for as long as I can and it worries me that the day will come when I can't. My biggest concern is ever being a burden on my kids.*
>
> Eileen

Chang and Jiao were a couple with two young children. Chang was working long hours in a Chinese restaurant being paid about £200 a week. Jiao was paid £6.31 an hour working part-time and didn't get paid for breaks or lunch. The family's expenditure exceeded their combined wage income and Child Tax Credit and Child Benefit by £5.34 a week. Jiao had worked in the same supermarket for about five years. On returning to work after having a baby, she found her pay had been reduced. Chang recognised that he and Jiao should have pensions but these circumstances meant they hadn't been able to do anything about it.

At the moment, there isn't much thought on how to deal with this problem. At the end of the day, age is an issue. Even if you can work ten or twenty years more, you would get old, and your functions would deteriorate. Your hands and feet wouldn't be as fast as other people. It is still a problem.

Chang

Amy's reaction on being asked about the future and retirement was fairly typical of many of the families' reactions to the question.

You're joking aren't you? I don't worry about it at the moment. Maybe it's something I will be doing a few years' time.

Amy

For Emma, a self-employed cleaner on the minimum wage, retirement wasn't an option.

I'll keep working. I don't pay into a pension, so retirement is out of the question. I have thought about it, but I think for me to get any type of pension now I'd have to pay a big amount, to benefit.

Emma

'Don't get sick'

Those on low pay, unable to afford any reduction in regular income, are under serious pressure to work during bouts of illness because of the absence of sick pay. Phil, who is on the National Minimum Wage, talked about this problem.

No, I can't see no end to it at all. I really can't see an end to it. It's just the way of dealing with it. You've just got to try and carry on with what you've got. I know I can't take sick days and things like that, because obviously they don't pay sick days anymore. So you've got to come into work. Even if you wanted a little day off somewhere along the way, or to take a holiday, you can't do that. Working here you do see the people with the money. But I'm not a jealous type of person. I'm given what I'm given. That's how I've got to get by.

Phil

Liam was in a similar situation and couldn't afford to take time off sick as Grace, his partner, explained.

He's a proud man, and it's awful to see someone that works so hard get a pittance. No, if he's off sick, he doesn't get paid. To be honest, he's never been off, touch wood. Oh, he worked with his foot broken for six weeks, and didn't know it was broken. Then he couldn't get his shoe on so went to Whiston [hospital] *and they said it was broken. And when he had the operation on his back, he had an open wound. It wasn't like he was in bed with a cold. They were the only times he was off. Whenever he feels sick, it's always on his days off. But he's that exhausted lately he comes home and he's asleep on the couch; his hours are so long.*

Grace

Maternity and paternity leave

Pete was on a zero-hour contract and could only take the minimum time away from work for paternity leave. On top of that he had recently had to take unpaid leave to look after their sick child. Tammy, Malcolm's partner explained the problem.

The baby's due soon, so not long to go now. [Their son] *hasn't been well. Malcolm has been off this last week, so he won't get paid either, because of the zero-hour contract. He only took it off because, with me being the way I am, he's* [their son] *too much now. This last month has been really hard basically, and with him being sick. He's dead clingy to Malcolm when he's not well and Malcolm took the week off. They've rung up today to see why he hadn't rung in, and he's meant to have rung in every day; but why? You're on a zero-hour contract, so why do you have to ring in every day to tell them when you're going to be back? He leaves here at 6:30am and comes back at 7pm at night; a full day isn't it? He's taking a month off; he's already told them that. He should get two week's paternity leave because you're entitled to that aren't you; so realistically you should get paid for that. Then he's got two weeks' holiday that he's taking as well.*

Tammy

Micha couldn't afford to take paternity leave because of the rate that he would have been paid at when he was away from work.

He's not even going to go on paternity leave because when I looked it up online, it's £130 a week. So he said, 'Just forget about it, I'm not going to go on it'. Say if mine's going to be £100 roughly paid every fortnight, which is worse, and if he's going to go on it for £130, probably paid fortnightly as well because the jobcentre pay it. So that would be £230 a week for both of us. He makes more when he goes to work, and makes overtime as well. So he says, 'I'm not going to go on it'. He might just take a week off as a holiday rather than take paternity leave. It's a joke, £130.

Karolina

Jiao talked about how maternity leave was also a break in employment that affected pay progression negatively.

> *Because after giving birth to children, the period when I was off for my maternity leave was more than a year, so when I went back, it was to the minimum wage, which is the lowest wage that they can give you. When I worked there before, they had given me a pay rise. Because it is as if you're starting fresh in the job.*
>
> Jiao

Work-life balance?

The need to take overtime when it's available, so working long and often anti-social hours, limits the time families have together. With both of them working, Phil and Dot had to manage their time to have at least one parent home with their daughter.

> *Sunday, we don't see each other at all. She goes into work and as soon as she's coming home, I have to leave. It tallies out with our daughter, so we don't have to get people to mind her.*
>
> Phil

Amber was on her own with three children, one of whom had a chronic health condition. The family were renting from a private landlord. Child-care costs and rent of £600 a month were a major drain on Amber's budget. She had recently started full-time work, and was worried about the impact that her hours would have on the family. Full-time work, on top of the time the children spent with their father meant that she wasn't seeing enough of her children. One of the children had been particularly upset.

> *She* [one of her children] *was like, 'I hate your new job; we only get a weekend together'. They have access with their father and then they are back to me. Then they are gone again and it's horrible for me. I am getting quite emotional talking about it. I miss them loads. That's something that is going to impact massively on them; not having as much time with me anymore. But you know the price of living is going up and you just go to work as much as you can now to get enough.*
>
> Amber

Recently Micha had done eighteen hours of overtime on top of his weekly full-time hours. Karolina's comments written at the end of her spending diary captured both the financial pressures she and Micha were under, and the impact this was having on their family life.

> *For these 52 weeks that I had this diary there were a few changes: rent increase, Council Tax increase, our Child Tax Credit has gone down from £54 per week to £26 per week due to overtime that Micha was working last year which was necessary for our financial needs. Food has gone up; minimum wage has gone up from £6.31 to £6.50 an hour—which we are both getting—but that is a change that we can't really feel. Micha still needs to work hard and long hours and days to bring in just enough money to live; but we can't buy anything for the house or go on holiday for cash; it has to be on credit card. And we are having another baby very soon. It's going to make it harder. Instead of spending some time as a family and having fun, we spend it at work to provide for the kids. It is very sad.*
>
> Karolina

Grace and Liam had four children and were living in social housing. Family time together was limited because Liam had to work long, irregular hours in his job in the catering industry. He was being paid just above the National Minimum Wage. Even with the hours Liam worked, the family was struggling financially. Each week their average expenditure exceeded their combined income from wages, tax credits and benefits by £31.64. They were trying to pay off debts of over £6,000.

> *Well, to be honest, it is a struggle. It's a struggle, because* [for example] *the kids' shoes; they're growing fast. You find the shoes just don't last. The coats, the uniforms, everything, the food. I just find it's a struggle. A loaf of bread's a pound now* [...] *and I'm thinking, 'We work; my partner works his butt cheeks off; and we're always struggling'.*
>
> Grace

The flexibility that Fiona hoped she would gain by being self-employed, to give her more family time, wasn't working out at all as she imagined.

> *I did a fourteen-hour day. I did this whole thing so I could spend time with the children. It's just the way things fell. I went home and had a boring sandwich because couldn't be bothered to make proper food. I guess that's what I've got to do if I'm to pay myself money.*
>
> Fiona

Brenda explained how her working routine was impacting upon her family and personal relationships.

> *Basically, when I'm in work the kids are at home. So then I have to rely on their Dad to take over; and if he's not doing it now I'm just wondering if he'll do it* [at all]. *So, that's when my Mum comes into it. Sometimes, I kind of feel like I use her.*
>
> Brenda

Conclusion

The deregulation of the workplace environment and the growth of a permissive culture towards regulation avoidance with respect to hours, job security and health and safety has been entirely an employers' agenda. It has been accompanied by a legitimising government and tabloid rhetoric of 'cutting red-tape' and easing bureaucratic burdens for employers; especially small to medium-size employers.[23] This narrative has both reflected and supported an intensification of competitive pressures within specific employment sectors. In turn, that has resulted in significant deteriorations of employment conditions for those whose work situations were already amongst the worst in the UK economy. The growth in the numbers and overall proportions of workers who are on short-term, temporary or zero-hour contracts or in bogus 'self-employment' are indicative of this long-term degrading effect. The results for those workers and their families have been terrible on many different and interacting levels. There is one aspect of the experience of work for the low paid that is crucial to consider however, and that is stress: its causes; and its effects.

On the subject of working life, all of the families spoke directly about work-related stress or described experiences or episodes that had clearly been stressful to them. These experiences of stress resulted from the erosion of employee protection that has already been described, though in a range of different manifestations. Uncertainty about work continuity was one major problem for many of these working families, and with all of its implications for housing security and difficulties of debt management and financial planning. A lack of control 'on the job' combined with arbitrary treatment at work was for some a source of significant mental strain. Long hours made necessary by low pay and insecure contracts, had a huge impact upon family life and personal happiness for some. Worries that resulted from having to juggle more than one job, working unsociable hours that undermined family life and the absence of pensions for the working members of these families were also unremitting facts-of-life for many.

---

23 Small and medium-sized enterprises are defined within the EU as employing fewer than 250 staff and having an annual turn-over of less than €50 million.

The effects of stress were all too predictable. Overwork was a frequently reported problem with all the attendant issues of sleep disruption, irritability, insufficient time spent with children etc., and all having very negative quality-of-life consequences. The harmful effects upon mental health that have been widely documented in medical and public health research, were familiar to many of the families who took part in the study. Negative consequences for physical health were also in evidence in the families' testimonies. When this is put alongside the difficulties of taking time off work because of sickness, it is easy to see how vicious downward cycles begin and descend in the lives of working individuals, their partners and their children.

Despite the health issues that are associated with poorly paid and insecure work, and that were very much in evidence here, a commitment to working was a consistent and often emphatically stated feature of the interviews. All who commented along these lines believed in the importance of work for being connected to the world, for feeling 'a part of things' and for providing an example to children. Contradicting utterly the media stereotype of the 'feckless Scouser',[24] these families, despite every obstacle in their path, remained committed to staying in work if at all possible. Their reward however, was often exhaustion, constant fear of unemployment and problems at home.

24 'Scousers' is an honorific of both affection and pride, referring to residents of the City of Liverpool and its region; 'Scouse' being the distinctive accent of the area.

5. Meeting Basic Needs

Wolves at the door

Income insecurity and the increasing stresses of work make life difficult for low paid workers in many ways: some all-too obvious; some hidden from a casual view. Shortages of cash from month-to-month, as well the constant worry about 'keeping the job', lead to a host of basic problems of life for those in such circumstances. It is these problems, and the issues of personal and family survival they raise, to which we turn here.

Managing on limited means of course depends entirely upon the adequacy of household income measured against the costs of living. During the *Getting By?* research period, typical weekly costs as tracked by the standard measure of the Consumer Prices Index (CPI) were relatively low and stable. The CPI however, is an averaged measure, and as such is not 'equivalised' according to socio-economic class or specific social circumstance. So, whereas for example the CPI is based in part upon average supermarket prices, this means very little for those who cannot afford bus and taxi fares for shopping trips, and so rely instead upon corner shops with far higher mark-ups on their goods than high street chains.

Looking more closely at the CPI also reveals that the various consumption elements that contribute to the calculations supporting it, behave differently over time and affect different socio-economic groups unevenly. So, whilst the CPI was quite stable through the years leading up to and covering the months over which the interviews were conducted, with 'clothing and footwear', 'furniture and

 https://doi.org/10.11647/OBP.0112.05

household goods' and 'recreation and culture' costs all falling slightly, transport costs increased significantly.[1] We have seen already how the difficulties of travel for work have become greater for many people in low-income jobs. This element of the CPI will therefore have had a disproportionately greater affect upon those same people, than upon those for whom transport costs make up a far smaller proportion of their overall expenditure. Annually, and even from one monthly cycle to the next, these various elements behave differently and their effect upon households will vary depending on their relative importance in relation to specific economic circumstances. The CPI then tells us little about the real impact of consumer costs, until we factor in original consumption levels and overall consumption patterns for different social groups.

As a corrective to complacent assessments of living standards for the low paid in the UK, we can look to one crucial indicator of severely adverse changes for the poorest families; that is the appalling phenomenon of 'food-poverty'. In recent years, food-poverty has moved from being a peripheral social issue, occurring at the margins of society, to being very much a mainstream issue for many thousands of working families. In 2010, as the Liberal Democrat-Conservative Coalition Government entered office, the Trussell Trust, a charitable provider of foodbanks in the UK, were running centres in 29 Local Authority areas; by 2014 the Trust was active in 251 areas.[2] This meant that the Trust was operating more than 400 foodbanks, covering 1,400 food distribution centres.[3] The use of foodbanks since their introduction has increased dramatically. Figures from the Trust showed a trebling in the number of 'three-day emergency food supplies' between 2012 and 2013. A further trebling had occurred by the end of 2014. By the end of 2015, a nineteen percent increase on the previous year took the number of such emergency supplies over the one million mark for that year, with 396,997 of these being to children. For the year 2015–2016 the figure

1 Office for National Statistics (2015), *Statistical Bulletin: Consumer Price Inflation*. December, https://www.ons.gov.uk/economy/inflationandpriceindices/bulletins/consumerpriceinflation/2015-10-13

2 Loopstra, R., Reeves, A., Taylor-Robinson, D., Barr, B., McKee, M. and Stuckler, D. (2015), 'Austerity, Sanctions, and the Rise of Foodbanks in the UK', *British Medical Journal*. 2015: 350, https://doi.org/10.1136/bmj.h1775

3 Garthwaite, K. (2016), *Hunger Pains: Life Inside Foodbank Britain*. Policy Press, pp. 35–36.

rose by another two percent taking the figure to 1.1 million emergency hand-outs across the Trust's 424 foodbanks.[4] Whilst not every donation equates to an individual, as users vary in the frequency of accessing a foodbank, the Trust's statistics suggest that approaching half of these donations were indeed to 'unique users'.

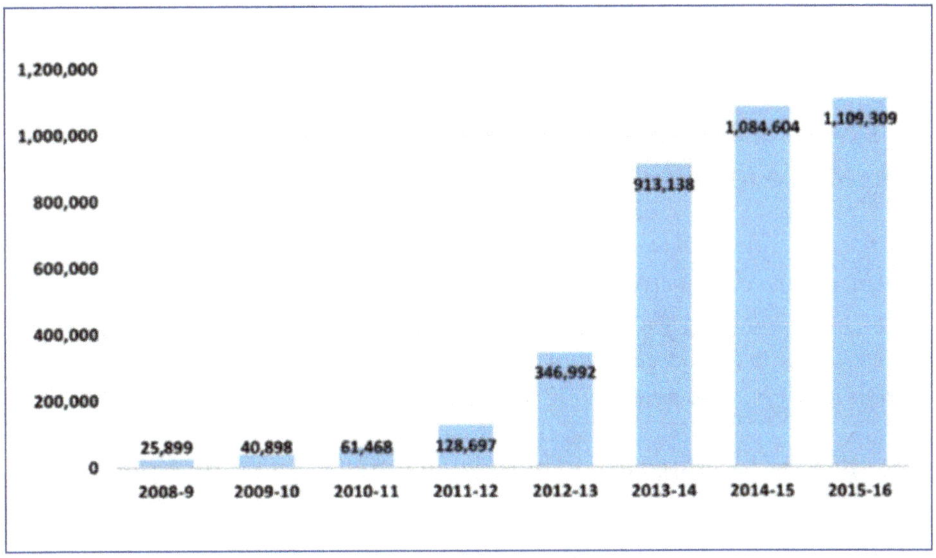

Three day emergency food supplies.
Trussell Trust 2017.[5]

The Trussell Trust's tracking of the reasons for people accessing its foodbanks is illuminating, providing a picture of the types of problem being faced by those struggling on low and insecure incomes. In 2016 for example, 43 percent of referrals to the Trust's foodbanks had arisen from delays in benefits payments and changes to the benefits system.[6] In the same year, as well as these causes, there had also been an increase in the numbers of referrals arising from sickness, homelessness, delayed

4 Trussell Trust (2016), 'Foodbank Use Remains at Record High, as New Data Mapping Tool Gives Fresh Insights into UK Hunger'. Press release, 12 April 2016, p. 1, https://www.trusselltrust.org/wp-content/uploads/sites/2/2015/06/Foodbank-use-remains-at-record-high.pdf

5 Trussell Trust (2017), https://www.trusselltrust.org/news-and-blog/latest-stats/

6 Trussell Trust (2015), The Trussell Trust's Response to Feeding Britain's Route Map to Ending Hunger'. Press release, 10 December 2015. Response to Forsey, A. and Mason, L. (2015), *Feeding Britain in 2015–16: A Route Map to Ending Hunger as We Know It in the United Kingdom*. Report for the All-Party Parliamentary Group on Hunger, https://www.trusselltrust.org/wp-content/uploads/sites/2/2016/01/Response-to-Feeding-Britains-route-map-to-ending-hunger.pdf

wages and unemployment. Receipt of foodbank donations by those who are in work but who are nonetheless unable to adequately feed their families, stood at 20 percent of all referrals in 2013–2014; this had risen to 23 percent by April 2016.[7]

A survey in 2015 found that the main causes of referral were "low income, administrative delays in paying social security benefits, benefits sanctions and debt".[8] Despite government denials that welfare reform has been a cause of the rise in foodbank use, the connection between them is clear, as Kayleigh Garthwaite (2016) discovered in her research conducted in a foodbank in Stockton-on-Tees.

> *The reasons why people used the foodbank were multiple and complex. Sanctions, benefit delays, debt, bereavement, low-paid jobs and poor health are all some of the factors driving people through the church doors. Almost 44% of people were referred to a Trussell Group foodbank in 2014/15 due to benefit delays and benefit changes, with a further 22% using a foodbank due to low income.*[9]

Where there is food poverty, there is also likely to be fuel poverty. Fuel poverty exists where more than ten percent of a household income is spent on fuel, including heating the home to a minimum standard of 21°C for a living room and 18°C in other parts of the home. Government estimates put the number of English households in fuel poverty at 2.38 million or 10.6 percent of the national total. The highest rates of fuel poverty are found in the privately rented sector where houses are more likely to be energy inefficient. Forty percent of homes in the bottom two income deciles suffer fuel poverty, as do least 30 percent of households with no-one in work.[10] Again however, working households now appear in categories of need formerly associated with more marginal social circumstances; so, 1.1 million in-work households are now in fuel poverty.[11] One-in-two low-income working households are not always

7 Trussell Trust (2016), p. 2.

8 Trussell Foundation (2015), 'Foodbank Use Tops One Million for First Time Says Trussell Trust'. Press Release, 22 April 2015, https://www.trusselltrust.org/2015/04/22/foodbank-use-tops-one-million-for-first-time-says-trussell-trust/

9 Garthwaite, K. (2016), p. 83.

10 Department for Energy and Climate Change (2015), *Annual Fuel Poverty Statistics Report 2015*, p. 17, https://www.gov.uk/government/statistics/annual-fuel-poverty-statistics-report-2016

11 Howard, R. (2015), *Warmer Homes: Improving Fuel Poverty and Energy Efficiency Policy in the UK*. Poverty Exchange, p. 12, https://policyexchange.org.uk/publication/warmer-homes-improving-fuel-poverty-and-energy-efficiency-policy-in-the-uk/

able to pay their energy bills, and 33 percent of those living in such situations have skipped meals in order to avoid going into fuel debt.[12] Each year 25,000 elderly people die as a direct result of being unable to heat their homes adequately. The charity Turn2us reported that during the winter of 2016 one in six disabled people had to wear a coat indoors to stay warm.[13] The problem however, does not only affect the old and the disabled. In 2013, research by the Association for the Conservation of Energy revealed that more than 1.6 million children were living in cold homes in the UK.[14]

The negative life effects of fuel poverty go well beyond day-to-day physical discomfort, distressing though this is for those who suffer it. Cold homes are also a cause of respiratory diseases and increased risk of heart attack and stroke. Children living in under-heated homes are more likely to develop asthma and bronchitis than children living in warm homes.[15] One-in-four adolescents living in cold homes will develop 'multiple mental health problems', compared to one-in-twenty of those living in warm homes. Being cold at home also negatively affects children's school attainment and their general well-being. Parents supporting families on the lowest incomes are forced to cut back on essentials including food purchases, to keep their homes warm.[16] Fuel poverty has a disproportionate effect upon the disabled as many health conditions are worsened by cold in the winter months. Disability means a more housebound existence for many. It also restricts options of moving to more heat-efficient homes given the high costs of mobility aids and home adaptations. Persistent cold also aggravates stress, anxiety and many mental health conditions.

Accessing and maintaining decent and stable housing itself is increasingly difficult for those on low incomes; and is impossible for more and more people at the lowest income levels. The 2011 Census

12 Motwanie, N. (2015), '50% of Working Households Struggle to Heat Homes', Turn2Us, https://www.turn2us.org.uk/About-Us/News/50-of-low-income-working-households-struggling-to

13 *Ibid.*

14 Guertler, P. and Royston, S. (2013), 'Fact-file: Families and Fuel Poverty'. Association for the Conservation of Energy, p. 2, http://www.ukace.org/wp-content/uploads/2013/02/ACE-and-EBR-fact-file-2012-02-Families-and-fuel-poverty.pdf

15 *Ibid.*, p. 7.

16 Barnado's (2012), *Priced Out: The Plight of Low Income Families and Young People Living in Fuel Poverty*, p. 5, London, http://www.barnardos.org.uk/pricedoutreport.pdf

revealed for example that the upward trend in home-ownership in the UK stopped and began to go into reverse for the first time since the 1951 census. The proportion of mortgage holders had dropped by fifteen percent since the previous census; whilst the proportion of privately rented homes has increased by 69 percent over the same period.[17] For millions of families, home ownership is simply not an option. With the social housing sector having nearly halved in size since 2002, private renting is the only option left to increasing numbers of families. Since 2002, the privately rented sector overall has almost doubled in size.[18] This includes an increase of nearly one million more households with children living in privately rented accommodation.[19]

The story however, does not stop there. The quality of houses in the privately rented sector is often poor: one third fail to meet the Decent Homes Standard. Complaints against landlords have risen significantly in recent years, with a large proportion of those being over matters that pose an immediate risk for tenants' health.[20] Housing insecurity is also a problem for increasing numbers of people. A 2017 analysis produced by the Citizens' Advice Bureau revealed that 39 percent of families with children in the privately rented sector have tenancies of six months or less. Over a third of the survey participants said that the period of notice they would receive to vacate their properties would not allow them sufficient time to find a suitable alternative. Nearly 80 percent reported significant deficiencies in the quality of their housing with problems of rodent infestations, poor heating and no hot water. Half said that their homes had mould, a third that their windows and doors didn't lock properly and a fifth that they were living with faulty wiring.[21]

---

17 Office for National Statistics (2014), *Households and Household Composition in England and Wales: 2001–11*, https://www.ons.gov.uk/peoplepopulationandcommunity/birthsdeathsandmarriages/families/articles/householdsandhouseholdcompositioninenglandandwales/2014-05-29

18 Foster, D. (2016), 'More Families Are Renting and Fewer People Ever Expect to Own a Home'. 25 February, https://www.theguardian.com/housing-network/2016/feb/25/families-renting-2016-english-housing-survey#img-1

19 *Ibid.*

20 Dorling, D. (2015), *All That is Solid. How the Great Housing Disaster Defines Our Times, and What We Can Do About It.* Penguin, p. 10.

21 Citizens' Advice Bureau (2017), 3 January, https://www.citizensadvice.org.uk/about-us/how-citizens-advice-works/media/press-releases/families-with-children-hit-by-insecurity-in-the-private-rented-sector/

A combination of shortages of affordable housing in most regions, rising average rent levels, decreasing employment security and the impacts of welfare reform have led to historic rates of evictions. The number of people being evicted from their homes in the privately rented sector has increased by 50 percent since the introduction of benefit cuts following the 2010 Comprehensive Spending Review.[22] Between April and June 2015, 10,361 households (more than 23,000 people) in England and Wales were repossessed compared to 7,072 over the same months of 2011. In 2016 government figures showed record levels of evictions of families with children.[23]

For households with children, child-care is a necessity without which parents and carers would not be able to work. For many thousands of families this is a major difficulty. One major issue is that the supply of child-care places has failed to keep up with demand. Under the Childcare Act 2006, English and Welsh local authorities have a duty to provide an adequate supply of places for the children of working families. In fact, the levels of provision have decreased in recent years. In 2015, just 43 percent of local authorities were maintaining an adequate supply of places; a drop of seven percent from the previous year. With respect to places for disabled children, the situation is much worse. Only 21 percent of English and seven percent of Welsh local authorities are providing sufficient numbers of places for disabled children; representing decreases of seven percent and nine percent respectively.[24]

Even where places are available, child-care fees can be prohibitive for those on low incomes. Despite much ministerial rhetoric maintaining a commitment to funding child-care as part of 'back-to-work' agendas, Government subsidies have not in fact kept up with the rising costs for families. In 2015, the cost of having a child under two part-time at nursery stood at £115.45 per week, having risen by 5.1 percent from 2014. Part-time care by a childminder rose over the same period by 4.3 percent

---

22 Gallagher, P. (2105) 'Number of People Evicted from Rented Homes has Soared Since Housing Benefit Cuts Began', *The Independent*. 13 August 2015, http://www.independent.co.uk/news/uk/home-news/number-of-people-evicted-from-rented-homes-has-soared-since-housing-benefit-cuts-began-10454150.html

23 Office for National Statistics (2016) , https://www.gov.uk/government/statistics/statutory-homelessness-and-homelessness-prevention-and-relief-england-april-to-june-2016

24 Rutter, J. (2015), 'Childcare Costs Survey 2015'. Family and Childcare Trust, https://www.familyandchildcaretrust.org/childcare-survey-2015

to £104.06 per week. These above inflation rises make it increasingly difficult for families to meet the full costs of professional care for their under school-age children whilst they at work. A 2014 report by the insurer Aviva, revealed that one-in-ten families has one working adult whose net income is nothing after travel and child-care costs have been covered. One-in-four working families have one adult who brings home £100 or less a month after these costs. The report showed also a median residual amount after child-care costs of just £243 per month for those on low incomes.[25]

With escalating costs of covering basic needs, come greater risks of descending into debt. Families on low incomes of course make strenuous efforts to manage within very restricted budgets by buying the cheapest goods. This is reflected in trends in retail patterns in the UK. Whilst retail outlets have reduced in number for most sectors over recent years, the single exception that has seen an expansion is the charity retail sector.[26]

Many thousands of families, along with 'make-do' strategies to stay on top of weekly expenses, are also more frequently accessing credit unions that require savings and provide short term affordable loans at favourable interest rates. By September 2014 figures, credit unions across England, Scotland and Wales had 1,173,299 members; a ten percent increase on the previous year.[27] Based on current trends in the UK, there will be two million users of credit unions by 2020.[28]

Still, the steady rise of the use of credit cards, store cards and loans in the UK has normalised debt as part of life for many low-income families. UK household debt has more than quadrupled since 1990. According to the government figures, by January 2017 the average household in the UK owed nearly £13,000 (not including mortgages).[29] Whilst the trend of rising debt is itself striking, it is the uses of debt that reveal the real

25 Monaghan, A. and Goodley, S. (2014) 'Cost of Childcare Cancels Out Pay for 1 in 10 Working Families'. *The Guardian*, 29 December 2014, https://www.theguardian.com/money/2014/dec/29/childcare-cost-pay-families-aviva

26 Armour, R. (2014) 'Charity Shops Buck Trend', http://thirdforcenews.org.uk, 24 March 2014.

27 Dobcheva, Z. (2015), 'Credit Unions in the UK—Balancing Social Benefit with Economic Viability'. Centre on Household Assets and Savings Management. Briefing Paper BP9/2015, August.

28 COOP News (2017), http://www.thenews.coop/100618/news/banking-and-insurance/end-year-review-2015-finance-credit-unions/

29 BBC (2017), http://www.bbc.co.uk/news/business-38534238

nature of the problem. Whereas personal debt might once have been associated with luxury consumption, today this is not the case; indeed, far from it. For those at the lower end of the income spectrum, debt more than ever results from the need to cover necessities, as income fails to keep pace with household costs.[30] Increasingly also, easy-to-access pay-day loans, provided at exorbitant rates of interest, are being used to buy essential weekly goods. Rather than being used for one-off and unpredictable expenses (the way such loans are often advertised), the most popular use of this type of lending is now for food and household bills. Forty-one percent of pay-day loans are used to pay for groceries; and 32 percent for gas, electricity and water payments.[31] The problem is that because such debts are a means of getting by from week-to-week, the surplus income required to clear the debt following the period or episode of need is simply absent. This leads to a rapid accumulation of even quite modest initial amounts of debt to uncontrollable and dangerous levels, as individuals and households are pushed towards financial crisis.

Family voices

Constant struggle

For these families, finances were a constant struggle. Family members explained the frequent predicaments they faced when having to consider how every pound was spent from one week to the next.

> *I just constantly feel I am on a treadmill. Keep saying to myself 'There is light at the end of the tunnel'. I just can't see it yet.*
>
> Colette

Indeed, the reality of this type of situation became all too evident during an interview with Sian, as it was being conducted. For Sian and Steve, weekly household outgoings were exceeding income by just under £11. They had started using a service that deals with individual and family

30 Osborne, H. (2015), 'New Consumer Debt Reaches Seven Year High in UK', *The Guardian,* 3 January 2015.

31 Coles, S. (2013) 'The Horrifying New Trend in Pay-day Loans'. *AOL Money,* 24 December 2013.

insolvency, to help manage and reduce their debts. They were trying to clear debts over £1,200. Their financial situation had become even more difficult when Steve was off work due to illness.

> *We genuinely are struggling; but I would have just struggled on. You just do don't you?*
>
> Sian

At this point the interview was interrupted by an urgent phone call from Steve. When Sian returned she was angry and flustered.

> *Sorry, sorry. He's saying he's just had a text from the bailiffs. The bailiffs are coming to remove stuff. I think it was* [firm of bailiffs]. *I can't really remember. The* [credit service] *people need to speak to them; but they're always texting. They've told me to ignore them but it gets a bit… you know.*
>
> Sian

The weekly shop

> *Everything's gone up; all the food's gone up; the bills have gone up. My wages don't go up.*
>
> Janet

Most of the families were clear that their financial situations had significantly worsened in just a very few years as a result of price increases, the failure of wages to keep pace with these and the impact of changes in tax credits. The weekly shop is always where the increase in the cost of living is most obviously felt. Just over twenty percent of Eileen's income was going on the weekly shop, with three-quarters of that being spent on food. She was keenly aware of just how much prices had gone up for the items she relied on.

> *Food's gone up tremendously. Electric, gas, massively; I can't believe it. I shop in* [a less well-known supermarket] *usually. That's the cheapest. So as to put stuff in the freezer and that. I know I could get a decent week's shopping four years ago for about £60–70; but its £110 now, for a normal shop. Not loads of treats, not loads of goodies; but a normal shop, you know with fruit and veg and all that. But sometimes it can't be done. So we do have a 'beans-on-toast' night and we do have 'cheese-on-toast' nights. That's the only way I can do it.*
>
> Eileen

Even though she was shopping very prudently, Eileen was still in debt. She was paying back over £3,000. That figure didn't include the bills that she was unable to stay on top of.

> *I haven't paid the TV license for twelve weeks. I've not paid the water rates for god knows how long; and when the 'Council Tax' catch up with me, I'm finished.*
>
> Eileen

The small annual increases in the minimum wage had made little difference for Karolina and Micha. Just over 23 percent of their income was going on the weekly shop.

> *I think first of all, the prices have gone up and I know the minimum wage has gone up every year, but by 20p* [...]. *Two years ago, the money was there and now all the money is just getting spent. The food and bills, everything is going up. I think that's the main problem, everything is going up, but wages are not going up in the same proportion as the food goes up.*
>
> Karolina

Sian and Steve had two young children. They were spending almost a quarter of their income on the weekly shop. They had almost nothing left after paying the bills and shopping to get through the week.

> *After we've paid everything out, we've got about £20 left spare for through the week. Out of what I pay, the rent and a few bills, like, I'm in so much debt. But then I've got £20, and that's for like a paper or milk or bread. There's always something you need a pound for. And when he gets his wages on a Friday, we go to* [a local supermarket]; *usually £40–60 on food and then gas and 'leccy. So it all adds up by the end of the week; and we just manage again.*
>
> Sian

As with all the other families, the children were the priority for Ali and Rabia.

> *We just have to pick and choose. Like we always feed the kids and clothe them, because they're my priorities; as long as we get the kids' stuff. I haven't got anything. I don't smoke. I don't drink. So I don't have a habit to give me financial problems. It's hard because you have to think about all the food and things. I have priorities; but every day at school they have to have like new things. But they don't get anything at school to help them, nothing; so it's hard. You have to buy your own uniform and shoes; my daughter's going on about her cardigan,*

school dress, summer dress. We can't afford holidays. We can't afford certain things; a car. It's just struggling. I just think as long as they get fed and they go to school and have an education, you know? I don't even have, like a carpet. We can't have mobile phone contracts; just pay as you go. The gas and the electric are on a meter. We just buy what we can afford.

Rabia

An observation made by Amber about supermarket packaging and 'two-for-one' offers, is one that many could identify with. It made things just that much harder for families on limited budgets.

Everything seems to have gone up in price, and smaller in packaging. Does that make sense? I have noticed like crisps and things the packets have gone smaller, but the price has gone up. Chocolate bars have gone smaller you know; even big food packaging like [well-known brand] *chicken fingers; there are only three in that, and there used to be four. Things like that have changed; and it's like you know* [well-known supermarket] *do these 'you pay £4 for one' or you can get 'two for a fiver'. So you end up spending more because it's on offer; you know what I mean.*

Amber

For many of the families, rising prices meant cutting back on basic costs. As Karen put it:

I just give them the bare essentials really; three meals a day. Sometimes I get things that are on offer.

Karen

Grace was spending thirteen percent of the family income on food. She found it hard to see how she was spending this much.

I mean we don't eat extravagant food; no takeaways. I mean the kids, we went to [well-known fast food outlet] *the other day; and it was the first time in like two months, which I don't think is like living beyond our means. It's a treat like. And I buy basic meat; I don't go and get the most expensive meat. I'm always buying basics. So I don't understand sometimes how I spend so much on food. But there's six of us.*

Grace

All of the families had become quite expert in getting their money to stretch as far as possible. This not only included shopping in the cheapest shops and looking for the cheapest items, but also, as Jiao explained, buying food near its sell-by date.

> *For example, when I'm buying things, when I see those approaching the use-by date and are reduced in price,* [or] *vegetables that are looking not too bad, then I would buy them. But for meat, I won't buy. Vegetables and fruits, I would buy some.*
>
> Jiao

On average Zoe was spending 15.4 percent of her income on food. She focused on buying reduced items and admitted to being 'almost obsessed' with trying to save on her weekly shop.

> *I just go for the reduced stuff and* [well-known supermarket] *like where everything is cheaper. I am obsessed with it. I am proud of that in a way. I do manage. I'm quite good at that; making use of reduced stuff. I never buy, you know, pre-packed. I am always making my own things.*
>
> Sue

Colette, who was spending just over twenty percent of her income on the weekly essential expenses, didn't go shopping without a list to stick to.

> *So definitely, I've found more so lately we are back to doing shopping lists and budgeting on things. You know, you don't just 'willy-nilly' go into the shops and pick stuff up any more.*
>
> Colette

The family weekly shop for Will and Sam was taking up just under nineteen percent of their income. Avoiding the temptations of the supermarket by shopping on-line was one of Sam's tactics.

> *I mean, every time I do shopping it's always more. I try to do mine online because once you're in the supermarket, it is tempting just to throw things in, even if it's just a pound. You know, it does add up. So I do try my best with little things and stuff, but even then, we have to cut down on other things just to live.*
>
> Sam

Planning meals and making extensive use of the freezer helped Terri to make savings. She was spending thirteen percent of the family income on food.

> *I pick chicken bits up or something each week, so my freezer is always full. I freeze bread; I freeze milk; I freeze butter so it's always in; I freeze soup as well. So I am quite nifty in my shopping. It's just my bills and everything else that's suffocating.*
>
> Terri

The costs of child-care

For many families the cost of child-care was the crucial factor in deciding whether mothers stay at home or return to work. For some, the only option was to go back to work and increase the hours worked if possible, to be able to afford care for children following their maternity leave. In practice, very few of the families were paying for child-care, relying instead on grandparents and other family members to help mind the children. When this wasn't practicable, the view was often that it simply wasn't worth returning to work or increasing hours because there was little, if any, financial benefit once child-care was paid for.

> *I can't really put on people to do child-care. It didn't work out. Child-care was costing £10 an hour and I am only getting paid £8; so it didn't work out.*
>
> Ruth

For the parents of older children, the costs of after-school care and school holidays were also very high. Amber with three young children explained the problem.

> *Just after-school care which comes to £108 a week. They have just been off two weeks for Easter and they were only in, what eight of the ten days; that cost me £360. Quite expensive! It's hard, and, as I say, with me and my partner working, and him doing shift work; he's never off on the same days each week. So I can't confuse the nursery by saying 'I need them that week, that week, that week. I just have to pay it and just let them go in. There is nothing really I can do.*
>
> Amber

Later in the year with the summer holidays approaching, Amber described how she felt about the costs involved.

> *I just want to highlight the cost of child-care. I think it's outrageous, and it needs to be regulated. I don't know how anyone is expected to afford it; especially me, and I've got multiple children. It's ridiculous. We used to live in a Sure Start*[32] *area so that nursery was reasonable; and we could afford that. But now because we live in* [area] *the only nursery linked to our school is a private day nursery, and it's £210 a week. It is just outrageous. I am worried genuinely about the six*

32 Sure Start centres provide community support for families living in deprived areas. Decreases in Central Government funding has led to the closures of hundreds of Sure Start centres in recent years.

weeks coming up; what is going to happen? I mean my partner's going to try and get his Mum to have them and stuff, because I can't.

Amber

Shortly after the family interviews, plans were announced for ten of Liverpool's Sure Start children's centres to close due to further reductions in Central Government funding. Liverpool currently had been providing fifteen hours free early learning for children over two, for parents receiving Working Tax Credit. Taking advantage of this had proved to be difficult for Jiao, due to the hours she works. At the same time, she couldn't afford to pay child-care.

I now go to work; and asking people to look after [the children] *would cost me £30. I only earn £50 a day.*

Jiao

Luke and Minnie had been talking with their parents about looking after their children, again because of child-care costs.

The places are available at nursery, but we're considering the cost, to be honest. If we put the kids in the nursery for five days, it means almost a full-time wage. That's why we were thinking that the first option was my parents looking after them, to be honest with you. It costs about £50 per day, or even a half day is £30. Because I'm still working full-time there's no help. We have to sort out our own, unless the kids reach three years old and then they're entitled to fifteen hours a week. That's still in one year's time for my first kid.

Luke

Malcolm was on a zero-hour contract with uncertain hours and that made it difficult for Tammy to get a job. Again, this was because of the sheer cost of child-care.

It's just hard with child-care and the only time I'd be able to go out and work is when [their son] *goes to full-time school. He could go to nursery; but your child-care costs are just horrendous aren't they. Then that's another expense you've got to look for throughout the month, isn't it?*

Tammy

Cath's situation was complicated by having a child with special needs who was refusing to go to after-school club. Even though she wanted to return to work, she would have to wait until her son went to senior school. She also felt that it wouldn't have made financial sense, especially as the youngest would have had to go into nursery.

> *Yes, even going to work is tricky, like with three children. The cost of nursery for the youngest ones pretty much rules out working, because I would probably pay more for nursery than I would get in income.*
>
> Cath

With a new baby and having to work shifts, Brenda was faced with the prospect of having to pay the costs of all-day nursery-care. She was reluctant to do this, not only because of the costs involved, but also due to her poor experience of nursery care with one of her children.

> *Lilly went back to nursery. She started at the age of one, and when I look back I think it was too early. Because the nursery that she was in, there were a lot of kids in there, a lot of babies. I remember going to pick her up, and she'd be in a part of the nursery, but on the floor, on like baby mats and then, like, at the time, I thought, 'It is what it is, I have to do this'. And now when I look back, I go, 'No, I don't want to do that with the baby'.*
>
> Brenda

Grace felt that working night-shifts seemed to be her only option if she was going to return to work.

> *I mean I want to go and get a job myself, but we're really going to struggle working round my partner's hours and my hours; and then if I pay for child-care, what's that going to cost, for four kids? I can't leave an eleven year old. I've looked for jobs to do of a night, to try and work it around the kids; because there's no job you can get from 9 o'clock to 3 o'clock.*
>
> Grace

With no family in this country, Karolina had limited options when it came to child-care. She saw the cost of child-care as the biggest barrier to mothers returning to work.

> *Child-care, cheaper child-care. I would say that's the most important. Because once someone's got a baby, it's not as easy as it was before to find another job; especially people like me when they haven't got any family to help them with the child. I was looking for a place for* [her daughter]*; it was about £33 a day. And that wasn't even like eight hours; it was a six or seven hour day. If I go for six hours even at that time, that was still minimum wage, that would be £36. So it would only be a few quid left for me. So what's the point? Getting the bus pass for that few pounds left; working for nothing.*
>
> Karolina

Cutting back

The only option for the families when faced with an escalating cost of living combined with falling wages, was to cut back on spending. For Gaynor, who usually had just £10 left at the end of each week, everything to do with family finances was a struggle. She was having to cut back everywhere she could, except for spending on her daughter.

> *Virtually everything; everything. Oh, clothes shopping; I haven't been clothes shopping for a very long time. Hair doesn't get done very often; maybe once every six months. It's hard; like* [her daughter] *gets everything. What she needs she gets; and if there's anything left, I might go and get my hair cut, or get myself a new pair of knickers or a bra or just something.*
>
> Gaynor

In the same way Zoe, with nearly £4,000 of debt and less than £10 left in her purse at the end of the week, had been cutting back on weekly spending, and on just about everything else.

> *Yeah: petrol; shopping; the bills in the house; heating; social time. We don't go the movies anymore. We don't go for a meal, nothing like that. That's like gone. Holiday. The TV package: that's something I've got to ring them up about. I've got to cancel it and buy a little box now.*
>
> Sue

Ruth was spending more each week on household bills and shopping than she had coming in. Like the other families she'd had to consider where she could cut back. She had recently cancelled her household insurance.

> *So it will be saving me another £30 a month. I have cancelled insurance on the house. I haven't got any house insurance now. Yeah, I have had to cut back on lots of things. Me and my daughter were going through it the other day, and we worked out what we paid the window cleaner; and she said 'Maybe we get shot of the window cleaner and clean the windows Mum?'*
>
> Ruth

With two new babies, Minnie and Luke had spent £1,357 on nappies and baby items over the course of the year. The family were having to cut back on spending and were looking to make savings.

> *There's quite a lot we've had to cut back on, like clothes. In the past I could just buy what I liked; but at the moment I need to keep considering every item. So we*

spend less money when we buy clothes, also maybe, we consider our food more; we buy cheaper products and that type of thing. We have broadband but we need a cheaper package. In the past we could spend quite a lot of money on it; and the mobile phones of course.

Luke

Emma had stopped using her credit card and was cutting back wherever she could, including on food items.

Now I've had to cut back on food. I used to save up for social, leisure money. It's not for me, I don't do anything. But I used to save it up, and now I'm going to have to use that to buy important things; or as a fund for unexpected things.

Emma

Keeping something back

None of the families had savings and most relied either upon help from their families or upon borrowing from wherever they could obtain credit, and often at high rates of interest. Carol couldn't remember a time when she'd had anything left at the end of the month that she could save. Joy had wanted to save to go on holiday with her daughter but had found it impossible. Denise's situation was also typical.

Don't really have any money left by the end of the week, or the end of the month. I've just got to budget all the time. Make sure I've got money put away to do something; especially like they're on half-term next week, you know. You've got to find the money then to do things with them. Sometimes I just haven't got it. So it is hard you know. It's just hard, very hard.

Denise

Over the course of the year Janet was spending an average of £138 more than she had coming in each week. Not surprisingly, she was finding things very difficult and was in a significant amount of debt.

No, probably about the second week of the month it's gone. That's once you've got a big shop in and stuff like that; paid all your bills.

Janet

Coming from Poland, Micha and Karolina needed to keep something back for an emergency in case they had to return home urgently. During the year they had also had to make proion for the arrival of a new baby. On average they had a surplus of about £44 a week.

> *So I can't let myself or my family have any money at all, because the way that I'm thinking is maybe one day we will need to go back, all of us. So I need to have the money just to buy the tickets, and get us ready to go back if something happens. I know it's not right; it's a pessimistic way of thinking. But what happens if someone dies? I've got a Nan; she's 84. So, I'll need the money to go there for her funeral and get back.*
>
> Karolina

Over the course of the year Liz had nearly £3,000 of unexpected expenses recorded in her spending dairy, or almost fourteen percent of her total income. With a weekly deficit of £27 she had found it extremely difficult to stay on top of unexpected costs. She had tried to manage things by using her overdraft. In the end, she had turned to her family for help.

> *Cry to my Dad, that's usually what I do. Go to my Mum and Dad. To be honest, not really; it's only if something goes really wrong. If something breaks, that kind of thing, I'd go to them then. But most of the time, to be honest with you I'd just use my overdraft. I'm always in overdraft, always. But 'touch wood', nothing has ever gone majorly wrong. Things like my washing machine broke, and Dad bought me a new one. I wouldn't have been able to just* [buy one]. *I probably would have had to go to one of those places where you pay monthly.*
>
> Liz

Without savings and with an average weekly deficit of over £30, coupled with debt of more than £6,000, Sam and Will were having to wait until they could get enough money together to get some important household items fixed or replaced.

> *There's things that we can't* [get fixed], *like my tumble drier. We're really lucky to have my tumble drier at home; a lot of people don't have one. I use it when I'm trying to get the kids' things dry, or in an emergency. But I just can't afford to get it fixed. It's things like that. We can't do that this month, so we'll have to wait until next month and see.*
>
> Sam

Unexpected costs such as having to replace domestic items, coming on top of debt repayments, were causing some of the families serious difficulties. Ric and Carol were having to contend with nearly £3,000 of recent unplanned expenditure. So when the washing machine broke down for example, they couldn't afford to get it fixed.

> *It broke down just before Christmas and I had nothing. I was washing; doing all my washing in the bath and basically asking round if anybody had a washing machine that they didn't want. My auntie had just bought a new one, so she gave me her old one; so I've got that. The tumble drier was my birthday present last year—no, it was my Christmas present. My birthday present was the printer I needed for* [her son's] *school.*
>
> Carol

New and old

Clothes shopping was frequently an area where families tried to cut back on spending, sometimes by using charity shops. Cath and Nick were spending a little under £1,000 a year on clothes and shoes, or 2.4 percent of the total family income. Carol was spending a bit more at £1,369, or four percent of family income. Terri and Don also were spending four percent of their budget on clothes and shoes. All were making use of charity shops.

> *Well, we shop in all the cheap shops; and definitely cut back on clothes. A lot of my friends like myself, we go to charity shops. You know, for us. For the children, they get new clothes; but we go to charity shops and we'd rather do that and buy second hand.*
>
> Terri

> *A lot of my clothes come from the sales. I either buy in the sales or the charity shops, or whatever I'm donated, basically.*
>
> Carol

> *Well, I have put it down in here* [spending diary] *just to show you. I think one month I spent £150 for the school uniforms which was skirts, jumpers, shirts and PE kit and trainers. I think I put I got their blazers in a charity shop.*
>
> Terri

Sian had recorded almost no expenditure on clothing and shoes over the year.

> *I've looked at myself and, it's like, 'Oh, I've got a hole in my shoe!' And one of my friends, she's the same; she goes 'The kids are all walking round in their*

> *trainers and I've got holes in my shoes!' You literally have to wear your shoes out; and then you have to go and buy a new pair.*
>
> Sian

Emma had also spent very little on clothes and shoes over the course of the year. She explained that she had stopped buying clothes for herself. Instead, now she gets her daughter's cast-offs.

> *Like stuff for myself, clothes for myself, I don't really.* [Her daughter's] *stuff gets passed down to me. Luckily we're the same size and height and so on, so stuff comes down to me.*
>
> Emma

Grace couldn't afford to go the hairdresser to get her hair done and so she did it herself. She was buying clothes through a catalogue as a way of getting credit. But, as she admitted, this is an expensive option in the longer term.

> *Well, we have to look at catalogues and things like that; and then you get penalised for using them. Then that costs more, so it's just like a vicious circle. It's the only way you can do it; that or get loans. But then again it's going worse* [into debt], *so it's a vicious circle.*
>
> Grace

Budgeting

Budgeting is especially important for low-income families. Zoe, who was spending over fifteen percent of her income on the weekly shop, explained how she tried to budget.

> *I was trying to keep to a budget of £50; but then other weeks I would only spend £40. I do struggle with food you know and household stuff; trying to keep to the £50 because that's what would keep me even.*
>
> Sue

Emma whose weekly shop was accounting for over 22 percent of her income, had switched to shopping at one of the discount supermarkets. This had resulted in a big saving on her weekly shop. Later in the year she had reduced her spending further.

I got my shopping down to £50 per week which is not as bad as I thought because I'm making things like soup. So, what I'd spend on soup, I would spend three times as much on a whole chicken. I've sat the kids down, we've talked about it and they are fine now.

Emma

Chang and Jiao had a very tight budget that they were trying to stick to.

Usually, our income is divided into different portions. One portion, no matter how much would go into saving for their [children's] *education fund. Then a portion is some money, when necessary for use in an emergency. Some parts go into living cost say 'daily living'. Some parts for insurances or so forth that definitely have to be paid.*

Jiao

Even though their sofa needed replacing, Karolina explained that she would rather budget to save for a replacement than get a new one on hire purchase.

As you can see the sofa is split in places. It's time to think about getting a new one; but that has to be well planned. We could get one but that would be where you pay some money and then you pay monthly; and I don't really like that. I would rather prefer to put £10 or £5 away each week and then pay the cash. Because you never know these days; if my husband lost his job there wouldn't be the money left to be paid.

Karolina

The exercise of keeping the spending diary had helped Brenda see where her money was going; but it had also been depressing to her for what it revealed.

I've been looking through it and thinking where can I pull back to save money here? But I'm kind of 'There's nothing that I can pull back on'. It's helped me see where my money goes; but nothing's really any different. It's kind of depressing when you see your outgoings and you try and think where you can pull it back. Should I starve the kids this week, or can I save a little bit? It's just getting by, isn't it? You see it coming in on one hand and then it goes the next. But at the same time you get by, you make do, you have to.

Brenda

The spending diary had helped Carol in a similar way. However, she made the same point about the difficulty of budgeting when the money simply won't stretch. She was spending nearly a quarter of the family income on the weekly shop.

> *The diary definitely has heightened my awareness of what I spend. But it's finding places to make the changes. That's my big one; the food. It's having the lump of money to be able to do that. It's all very well to be able to say 'I pay my bills'. It goes through my head, if everything is paid, what I've got left. I then have to divide between four weeks. It doesn't work like that because things come up constantly. Schools are terrible for constantly wanting money off you; money for this, money for that.*
>
> Carol

Fuel poverty

> *Well yesterday, because it was really cold I went home and washed the girls' dressing gowns. And so, as soon as they came in, they put on them onesie things, so they keep them warm. And we all try to huddle. It sounds stupid in this day-and-age that you've got to do it; but you have to.*
>
> Terri

The efforts the families were making to reduce their domestic fuel bills showed just how strained their finances were. Liz was spending nearly £1,400 annually on her domestic fuel bills for herself and one child, or 6.5 percent of her income. On top of that had come a large and unexpected energy bill.

> *Last year I found it really hard with my gas and electric, because they hadn't been taking out enough on my direct debit. So, I got hit with a whopping bill that I was devastated about.*
>
> Liz

The amount Brenda was spending on her domestic fuel was similar at nearly £1,200, or 6.3 percent of her income. Even though she had tried to save on energy use, she was struggling to pay her bills. She had also been told that she had long-standing arrears with one utility company.

> *Don't talk to me about my gas and electric. For some reason, I don't know why, but £200 came out this month. Maybe it's me or the household, maybe we're not budgeting. But I always switch everything off and try and manage it as much as I can. But for some reason it just seems to be really expensive; everything though, not just your gas and electric. I mean I've got the water company*

coming to me from years ago saying 'You owe us this much'; and it's just one thing after another.

Brenda

Jenny was typical in trying to reduce her heating costs to a minimum, especially if her child wasn't at home.

I don't put the heating on if [her son] *is not here. I won't have the heating on. Like if he goes to visit my Mum for the night, I won't put the heating on if he is not here.*

Jenny

When the children were at home Carol did much the same thing to keep warm.

Sometimes we get the duvets down because if you've got the heating on all the time, it's at least £5 a day; so that's £35 a week on the gas which is something. So, there are odd occasions when I say, 'Come on, get the duvets down' and then we all get snuggled under them and then it's actually quite warm. That's the truth that! We've done it for years to be honest, to save on the gas.

Carol

Terri had managed to get her domestic fuel bills down to just under a £1,000 a year, or 4.8 percent of the family income. Her strategy had been simply putting on extra clothing to go to bed.

I went to bed last night in a jumper. I took my jeans off, put my 'jama pants on and went to bed in my jumper I'd been wearing all day; because it was so cold.

Terri

Cold homes

People living in privately rented accommodation have the highest rates of fuel poverty. Gaynor pointed out that the poor insulation in her privately rented property added to her fuel bills. She was spending £2,155 on her domestic fuel bills, over ten percent of her total income, for just herself and one child. Not surprisingly she only put the heating on when it was absolutely necessary.

I am going to be moving out of this house. It's just costing me a fortune in gas and 'leccy bills. It's more gas really, because my house just has single pane windows. It hasn't got double glazing. I just feel like I'm throwing money out

> *the window. Just like 'Go on, here you are, here's twenty quid, you spend that. Here's twenty quid'. So really I can't really afford to put my central heating on. Sometimes the gas is £40 or £50 a week if I put the central heating on. It just swallows it.*
>
> Gaynor

Denise also had a poorly insulated home. As she put it, it cost her 'a fortune' to heat. She had recently received a fuel rebate.

> *Yeah, don't know why, someone said to me that the 'leccy companies are doing this now, people are being paid back. They've been paying through their noses and now being paid back. But I don't know, will they find out and take it back? I don't know. Well I just know I put £15 on the card and they gave me £140. It's a four-bedroomed house, and it's constantly freezing, constantly. I mean I have to have the heating on day and night.*
>
> Denise

Ruth was living in social housing with her partner Mark and their four children. Her domestic fuel bills accounted for 5.3 percent of the family income. She explained that she would always delay putting the heating on.

> *You know, I'll say 'Put a house coat on if you're cold', you know when the kids are sitting 'round. Well I am always moving, so I am always warm anyway. But they can just sit there and they go 'Put the heating on Mum' and I go 'No'. Well, I sort of say 'No' to them. Now we don't put it on as much; but you've got no choice when it's freezing though.*
>
> Ruth

Pre-payment meters

Although the families were usually aware that pre-payment meters for domestic fuel cost them more than monthly or quarterly meter readings, many still had them. Some had not been given the option because of previous arrears. Others preferred to have a pre-payment meter for the sense of control it gave them for their budgeting. Which was the better option in reality was a calculation that the families had to make very carefully. Nick and Cath had a pre-payment meter, but they were getting it changed.

> *We've gone on a meter; pre-payment meter. But we're getting that changed because, well you know there's been a mild winter; but we've still had to keep*

putting money in. And then it runs out; and then everything cuts off. Not ideal! Now I tried to explain it to my husband but he believes 'Well it's a good pay off, because in the winter you pay, but then in the summer when it gets warmer you don't pay at all'. But I tried to explain that it's set higher anyway; so you are paying more. Maybe he's listened to me, because we're getting a meter now.

Cath

Liam and Grace were spending over £1,300 on their domestic fuel bill, or 5.7 percent of the family income. Grace was firmly of the view that the higher cost of using pre-payment meters was unfair.

We're on those meters. I have to have a meter because you know where you're going; and it's dear. You get penalised because you're poor. Yes, you have a card and you go to a shop and you put say 'a fiver on' or 'a tenner'—a fiver lasts for hardly anytime at all. You're just putting money into it constantly.

Grace

A key reason for choosing pre-payment meters, where the choice existed, was to avoid a large quarterly bill that the families knew they wouldn't be able to pay. Pre-payment meters also enable people to see exactly how much they are spending.

I try my best. I don't like having direct debits going out of my bank because I just can't control them. I'd rather have payment cards for everything now that I am in this house. I have payment cards for them all.

Jenny

Amy was spending over £1,200 on her domestic fuel bills. The ways in which she managed the heating was typical of many of the families.

I'm on a meter; so usually when I get paid, I get £60 each for both [electricity and gas] *at the start of the month. But I usually have to top up about £20 towards the end of the month on each. I think my kids aren't very cold kids anyway. So they're quite happy to sit on the couch with a blanket rather than putting the heating on. If it's not too bad, we'll sit with blankets rather than putting the heating on.*

Amy

Karen and Steve also had a pre-payment meter.

It's a meter. We put about £15 a week; but we need more in this weather. Its central heating, but the radiators downstairs don't work, so the heating has to be on for ages before it heats up. The only times we have it on is of a morning and then when the kids come home from school for a little bit. It's not on all the time, I couldn't afford that.

Karen

Phil revealed that he and Dot were falling behind on their fuel bills, even though they had been keeping their heating down to a minimum, trying to have it on only when their child was home.

We're on quarterly meters; we're paying £30 every two weeks to 'the electric', then £30 every two weeks 'to the gas'. That's what we have to pay and that's all we can afford; but they would like us to pay more. Because the bill's going up we're starting to owe them money and we can't afford to pay them more, because we haven't got the money. What they generally do is cancel the payment card, then they write us a letter saying they've cancelled it. So you're forced then to phone them up and then you've got to explain to them why you can't pay any more; and that's how you get another one. It's not right.

Phil

Because of the problems she had been having with her supplier, Colette wanted to stop having to use the pre-payment cards.

I am having all sorts of problems with [well-known utility company] *at the moment. When I moved in, in September, I gave them meter readings from August and said, 'This is what I am paying on my property at the moment'—which was £50 gas and £30 electric. 'Can I carry on doing that?' They were like 'Yeah, that's fine'. They sent me two payment cards, one for gas and one for electric. So I have been paying £50 a month. Then a couple of weeks ago I got a bill saying I owe £203; 'Pay immediately' sort of thing. So, we are going through a lot of problems with them. It turns out they never actually set up an account to pay £50 a month. They are acknowledging that I have been paying, but they never set up an account for it; so I am trying to go on to direct debit.*

Colette

Switching supplier

Those families who had tried to switch suppliers to get a better deal were sceptical of government recommendations to 'shop around' to make savings. For instance, the annual domestic fuel bill came to nearly £1,300 for Will and Sam, or 8.6 percent of their income. Switching utility company had made little difference to the cost of their bills.

We pay a month £115 for gas and electric. Now I think last month I looked online at our account. I don't do it every day, obviously, but I looked back and they put it up without telling me to £175 a month. I went 'Nah, I can't afford that!' We'll get our next bill and I'm fully expecting that we'll pay out more then; a lot more. What I do get quite annoyed about is you keep switching to save money; but when you look into it, it's 'Nah, they're all going to make money aren't they?' The hassle it is to switch! And the savings you get from it are negligible. It's just repackaged in a different way.

Will

Jiao and Chang also had a similar view about switching energy supplier.

There isn't a solution. Sometimes the electricity rate is more expensive in comparison to other providers; but their gas rate is cheaper than others. So, it compensates on each other.

Jiao

Public transport

Over the course of the school year the weekly cost of bus tickets mounted up for the families. Liz was spending nearly £22 on average a week on bus fares, amounting to 5.4 percent of her income. She was walking her son to school when she could, even though it was a good distance.

I pay weekly for my bus pass for work. It would probably be better if I could pay a yearly pass. It's the same with Sam; his school is like a 25–30 minute walk. Now, in the summer I don't mind doing it; and when it's nice, it's lovely. But in the miserable weather, when it's raining and stuff, his favourite words are 'Can we get a taxi,' to which he's told 'No, we can't'. But I will get a bus with him. But then, in the last few weeks he's wanted bus tickets. But the other day I was like 'We're going to have to just walk'; or we get the bus 'round the corner that's like the cheaper bus—the little one, called the Comfy Bus—because the other buses are too much. It's like £1.40 for him on the bus now. It used to only be 19p when I got it. It's like, I can't expect him to walk in that weather so I have to [pay]. *When I get him a weekly bus ticket and me a weekly one, it's like £25 a week; and that's just the bus, so it's not cheap.*

Liz

The cost of getting children to and from out-of-school activities also adds up. Liam and Grace were spending nearly £30 a week on bus fares, or 6.5 percent of their income.

> *You're trying to get the kids to do activities after-school, which all cost money. You have to get a bus to get there, because there's nothing in this local area. So then you're spending again. But you don't want the kids to be sitting at home; you want them to be socially active and fit. So it is it's a vicious circle.*
>
> Grace

Eileen was spending over £30 a week on bus fares, but getting a weekly ticket was helping.

> *Bus fares, you know, £9 for a weekly bus ticket; for the two kids its £18! We have to* [pay]; *it's far, so we have to. So, I have to give them a weekly bus ticket, because it works out a lot cheaper.*
>
> Eileen

Terri had noticed that even the small savings matter and mount up over the year.

> *I'll buy Saveaways—cheaper than bus tickets. Bus tickets are £10 and a Saveaway is £7.80.*
>
> Terri

Cars

For working families with children, a car is often a necessity. Both Phil and Dot worked and needed to run a car. Phil explained that it was as cost effective as using buses.

> *We're buying it in instalments. That's £132 a month; about £35 a week. The insurance stayed the same which we were really made up with, because that's the biggest one. It's a second hand car, but it's only had one prior owner and it was low mileage as well. I work up to 11:30pm of a night and the last bus is like 11:45pm, and there's no chance of running for that. And if not, it's a taxi or walking. When we looked at bus fares and things like that it would cost us £30 a week for both of us to travel on a bus; and that's just a weekly pass. So obviously it's just 'Get the bus and pay the £30' or 'Have a car and it's a bit more comfortable'. It works out more or less the same.*
>
> Phil

Brenda was working shifts and couldn't do without a car. Allowing for the costs of taking the children to school and after-school activities, a car often worked out cheaper than public transport. Both Carol and Cath saw having a car as essential because they each had a child with health problems. In Carol's case, she and Ric were spending eight percent of their income on transport, most of it going on running their car. Sam and Will were also spending over eight percent of their income on running their car. Sam explained why they needed one.

> *My husband is disabled and he can't walk very far and so does need the car; so things like that play a big part in it* [the weekly costs]; *and even more so if it breaks down or whatever.*
>
> Sam

Buying and running a car is of course a significant expense for those on low incomes. Luke and Minnie were spending nearly six percent of their income on transport, mostly because of the costs of having a car.

> *Because of the two babies I needed to change my car. I changed my car and so I have some expenses for my new vehicle. I used some of my savings for a deposit and also I paid by loan for the car. I part-exchanged my old car so got a bit of money towards it, the new vehicle that I bought. The situation is the tyres aren't that good; so I have to spend more than £250 to exchange old for new tyres.*
>
> Luke

The costs of car ownership for Mark and Ruth in the end became unmanageable and they were left reliant on public transport once more.

> *No, it was just costing too much basically. It was costing insurance and it was costing everything: petrol; diesel. So, the car has gone.*
>
> Mark

Debt: how it happens

Nearly all of the families were in debt. In some cases, the debts amounted to several thousands of pounds. These debts had normally been incurred simply by being unable to manage on inadequate incomes as opposed to any type of unnecessary expenditure. Without savings to fall back on, meeting unexpected costs left the families few options but to turn to various forms of high-cost credit. It then became a case of borrowing again from another source to pay back the original loan. For many families, the accumulation of debts created a situation of having to juggle one against another, to decide which to pay at any one time. This stressful situation was made worse by the sense of being in a debt trap, which the families saw no prospect of escaping. Two of the families had agreed to an Individual Voluntary Arrangement (IVA)[33] with their creditors. However, the consequence was then being blocked from access to any new forms of credit.

The arrival of unexpected utility bills was one of the most common causes of debt amongst the families. For Liz, who was spending 36 percent of her income on rent, the problem started after she had moved house.

> *It's just when things hit you all at once. Like it must have been coming up to a year ago and apparently they hadn't had the original meter readings when I moved in. And it turned out that I owed them about £500 to £600 in gas and electricity, because they hadn't done the meter readings properly when they first came out, or the landlord hadn't given them the proper readings or something. And so I was devastated, because I hate the idea of being in debt. There's nothing worse. So I've had to struggle, trying to pay that back, because for the last few months I've been having to pay £167 a month gas and electric; and it's not the easiest thing to do when you're on your own.*
>
> Liz

Ruth and Mark were paying back over £5,500 of debts, or twenty percent of the family income. Ruth was clear that the changes to Working Tax Credit were having the biggest impact on the family's ability to cope with the cost of living, and that this had dragged them into debt.

> *I am not 100 percent sure, but I think it was when the government come into power; when I lost the money* [Working Tax Credit]. *That made a massive impact on our lives because that was when* [the problems began]. *For a while you just cope without it. But I didn't realise I was spiralling into debt.*
>
> Ruth

Family bereavements and associated costs were the principal reasons for Steve's and Sian's debt situation. The fact that Steve was being treated as 'self-employed' by his employer and so did not get paid for holidays, or for any other time he took off, had added greatly to their difficulties. These problems were compounded by a long-standing television licence fine.

33 Individual Voluntary Arrangements are a legal alternative to personal bankruptcy. Regular payments to creditors are agreed by mediation via an insolvency practitioner.

> *Over the last year we've had a couple of occasions with family tragedies, loads of things. He's had to take time off; so we've got a bit in debt over the last year or two, over, you know, with our bills and stuff. With one wage coming in the house it is hard. Obviously we get Working Tax Credit; only £15 at the moment. And I haven't paid the school dinners for ages. I need to do that and there's load of things, like over Christmas he doesn't get paid. So we didn't pay the rent over Christmas so we got more in arrears. So it's always 'catch-up' really.*
>
> Sian

Their situation had recently become especially difficult following a family bereavement.

> *We're all grieving, and in November we had a bailiff turn up; put his hands on the car and said he was seizing the car for the TV licence fine that we had in 2005; and we had 24 hours to get that. We got it off his brother, but then obviously before Christmas we had to get that back to him. So it's a constant challenge.*
>
> Sian

Gavin and Phoebe were paying back nearly £4,000 of debt, and that accounted for eleven percent of their income. Whilst Gavin was off work due to illness, the family were sinking even further into debt.

> *I fell behind with the rent last week because, I just basically didn't have the money; things crop up. Gavin was off work for a few days. He doesn't get paid when he's off sick; so they sent me a letter straight away because they didn't get paid on the Friday. And I was just like, 'Urgh'. So then it was like juggling. Rather than getting all the letters and getting the hassle, it was a case of 'We'll just buy the shopping on the credit card. And then what shopping money we have we'll pay the rent'; and that's how we worked it, but again it's just getting deeper and deeper into debt. We owe £3,800 on one credit card; and now with everything breaking and stuff in the house, we're back up to £4,600.*
>
> Phoebe

Joy's debts partly went back to when she had moved from a furnished house to an unfurnished one. She'd had to raise the finance for furniture. This had added significantly to the running costs of the house.

> *I have got quite a few debts; like something from Christmas. I'll get stuff from catalogues or stuff on finance. When I moved house, I've had to get stuff on finance. It's like an ongoing problem trying to pay them. Or I'll ask family members. If I'm struggling for bills I'll go to family members, and ask them for money.*
>
> Joy

Denise was in long-standing arrears with her Council Tax and didn't know how she would be able to clear them.

> *Last week I had a bailiff's letter for Council Tax* [arrears] *I had about six years ago. I haven't paid it because I can't afford to give it them in one go. So, they're waiting for a payment now; threatening me with letters. But it's scary, though. I haven't got it to be honest, it's been that long. Then you've got to find it. But they're saying to pay and I don't think I can. They say I could go bankrupt; but I don't know about that, how it would work.*
>
> Denise

Sian and Steve were also in Council Tax arrears dating back over several years.

> *I had quite a few bills from 2010, for my Council Tax. I have actually paid that. I had letters from three different bailiffs; and from ten years ago and eight years ago. So what I've done is, I've asked for an attachment of earnings. I felt a little bit embarrassed when a letter got sent to my workplace explaining what it was for. But at the end of the day, I'm quite an open person; So, I'll probably make a joke of it when I go up to HR.*[34]
>
> Sian

Banks and credit cards

The families often had to make of use of high-cost credit simply because they had no access to the services that provide financial products at lower rates of interest. These are normally available to people in better paid employment. Those without bank accounts and using credit cards are often at the limit of their borrowing and overdraft facilities, and are managing only interest payments. Emma had a high level of debt on her credit cards. Nine percent of her income was being spent on debt repayment.

> *To be perfectly honest with you, I use credit cards an awful lot. So, say something breaks, I'll use my credit card to replace it, or clothes for the kids and stuff like that. I usually get my shopping on my Visa card as well, most weeks. I've got debts on my credit card; about £7,000. It's not going up and it's not coming down to be honest. It's just the interest rate is really high. Each month the interest is about £80 a month; so I'm only paying literally £20 off what I owe and the rest is the interest.*
>
> Emma

34 Human resources.

Karen had been left with £19,000 of debt by her ex-partner. After ten years, she was still paying back that debt. She had obtained an Individual Voluntary Agreement to reduce what she had to pay back on her credit cards.

> *I've got my credit card debt. I think it's about £400 or £500. Since like August I haven't been able to make any payments.*
>
> Karen

Ruth had seen her overdraft steadily increase, with little prospect of reducing it in the immediate term.

> *Now I live on my overdraft. I'm not in credit. I don't ever credit my bank any more. Do you know what I mean? It's gone from being a £200 overdraft to being a £900 overdraft, in the space of two years.*
>
> Ruth

Amy was also relying on her overdraft and 42 percent of her income was going on paying back debt. She was aware that she needed help to manage the situation.

> *I've got an overdraft of £1,250. I live on my overdraft. Basically, as the money goes in, it goes back out. There is a charge on it, but it's about £12 a month or something like that; basically if my wages went in and I didn't live on my overdraft I wouldn't have any money for the week or the month. So, that then pays for the month; credit cards, the likes of* [a credit service] *I had to pay. Water rates and Council Tax, I'm still in arrears with. I keep hiding from them because it scares me, that debt. I think it's about £4–5,000.*
>
> Amy

Phil and Dot had a permanent overdraft and were only able to pay the monthly interest.

> *I've got a bank overdraft; it's just an overdraft of £750. They charge me £20 a month to maintain it. It just stays the same, there's nothing I can do about it. So, I think that's just going to be there until we can manage to save something. I can't foresee that.*
>
> Phil

Over thirteen percent of Brenda's annual income was being spent on paying back debt. She couldn't increase her overdraft anymore and was now paying charges on it.

I've maxed it out. I arranged a £1,500 overdraft but it's gone. So, every month I'm getting charged £1 per day, and I've been doing that for a month or two.

Brenda

Joy had taken some action to try to get on top of her bank debt.

I had my overdraft sometime last year. It was going up and up and up. I was getting bank charges and it was just like never-ending. So eventually I got a loan to pay off the overdraft, which I pay each month. And I have got quite a lot of credit which I have to pay, with my bank.

Joy

Pay-day loans

Jenny's experience illustrated the consequences of there being no cap on the amount lenders can charge for their loans. She found herself struggling to pay her bills, trying to defer payments on some debts, whilst paying others. She had been constantly moving payments around to find a way to get through the month. Then she got behind with her rent.

It was through [a credit service]. *It was only £80 I took out and it's now gone to, I think £700, because I haven't paid it* [the monthly payment]. *What it was, I was on the internet in my Mum's, trying to do it because I was in a bit of a panic about this rent situation. So I was applying for a few on-line and they were all coming up 'decline', 'decline', 'decline'; and I thought 'There is nothing I can do now'. So, I left it. The next day I went to check my bank and my rent had gone out of my bank, and I was thinking 'That's strange'. Didn't realise and I thought 'I must have miscalculated the rent; it was in there and it's all alright'.*

Jenny

In fact, her bank balance had been increased by a pay-day loan payment she wasn't aware she had actually been given.

I was just relieved seeing that my rent had gone out OK. I didn't even look into it, which was my own silly mistake. That was in the September; and then it was around Christmas time. I got a letter to say that I owed this £700 and odd; and I was thinking 'Off what?' So I phoned up and I was like 'I never got a pay-day loan off you, I asked for one and I got declined'. They said, 'We will give you the bank account number it's been put in to, and then check it against yours. If it is not yours we can rectify it'; and I [checked] *it and it was mine.*

Jenny

A pay-day lender had also taken money from Eileen's account without her having knowingly entered into an agreement with them.

> *I tried to get a pay-day loan, like an idiot, and they took nearly £200 out of my account; and I never got nothing. Apparently, they're legal if you search and look for one on the internet. And my son had got one many moons ago and swore that he would never do it again and they used his bank account. So* [a well-known credit service], *I think it was; they still had his bank account details and sold it to the ones I was looking at—and they're entitled by law; they can take up to £100 out of your account just for you looking. So it's an absolute nightmare. You just go 'Where has that money gone?'*
>
> Eileen

The stress caused by getting into debt with a pay-day lender was evident in what Eileen went on to say.

> *I've got about seven letters sat on my back kitchen worktop and I haven't got myself to open them, because I know what's in them. I know I should go for help, I know. This is why I'm thinking, I could phone these loan people and say 'There's no way'. There's no way they're going to take me to court, because a judge will say 'Why did you give it to a single mum?' I'm going to have to reduce that loan over the next week or so. The Council Tax has to be sorted. I'm still catching up on Christmas, that's why. I was just blinkered and stupid.*
>
> Eileen

Sam explained that they had only turned to Will's father as a last resort. Normally, rather than doing that they have opted for pay-day loans.

> *We have used a few pay-day loans, and at the time it's good, because it's instant money and we can deal with our bills or whatever we need it for. We have to pay double or whatever it is, so we try and avoid them where possible; but it's not always possible. We try not to get into debt, it's really hard; but we try.*
>
> Sam

Amy's experience showed just how easy it is to access pay-day loans; even when the person applying already has a number of other debts. She owed over £10,000, a significant part of which was debt left behind by her ex-partner. As we have already seen, more than forty percent of her annual income was being spent servicing debt.

> *I'd managed to spend all my wages; took out a loan and then had to use the catalogue as well. Then I had to take out a pay-day loan at the end of the month to pay my bills that were due. I got that online, I think I got £700 all-in-all, and*

> *I think it worked out to just on £900, and something to pay back. So what I've done is I've split it over three months; so it's about £350 a month to pay it back. I think it's something like a one thousand percent interest rate. I've used them before.*
>
> Amy

She was also very unhappy about her thirteen year-old son being offered a pay-day loan.

> *Three messages came up on his phone for pay-day loans. Now my son's thirteen, so obviously someone's selling the numbers onto these companies. I get quite a lot of text messages about pay-day loans. In my son's case, I don't know how it's happened because obviously he's never had a pay-day loan.*
>
> Amy

Gaynor had fallen into debt initially due to a wages overpayment that had to be repaid. That led in turn to her getting into difficulties caused by the reduction in her Housing Benefit that followed.

> *I had to do one with* [well-known credit service]. *Yes, last year. I've took one out with them; and still I'm paying it back, only because Liverpool City Council overpaid me. Yes, not once, twice. Once in August 2013, and once three months later in October 2013. It was their mistake. Then because of the overpayment, my rent got stopped. So from August to December, where my landlord would normally get £103, he wasn't; he was getting £74. So there was a shortfall. So, from now, I'm £305 in rent arrears.*
>
> Gaynor

Amber was finding that she couldn't afford to pay back her loan.

> *I did go to the* [well-known credit service], *but they were just being outrageous. So, I just didn't pay them. I said 'Look I can't pay on this day; you are going to have to wait'. It was like 'Oh well, you are getting charged £30'; something like that. I can't remember now because it was a while back. So, I just said 'You are putting me in a position where I can't pay you back, so you are going to have to take action against me now'. But they haven't bothered.*
>
> Amber

Door-to-door lending

Door-to-door lending makes borrowing very easy, with collectors often arriving on the doorstep each week and building up a friendly relationship with the client. A company like the Provident will charge interest from between 170 percent to 500 percent. Amy had not appreciated quite how much she was paying out in total, until she started using the project spending diary. Because she kept up the repayments, she was regularly offered top-ups, which she said were difficult to refuse because she was always 'broke'. She described how door-to-door lending works.

> *My collector is like a family friend now, he's been coming that long and that's why. I think they get something like ten percent of what they collect, or something like that. So, I didn't want to* [not pay] *because obviously it would be a reduction in his wages. I used to pay him every week religiously. Whether I had the money or not because I did see him as a friend rather than a debt collector. But obviously with the reduction in the tax credits, I thought 'I really couldn't afford to pay it'. So, the payments I've reduced by over half. Obviously, they just said to me, if my circumstances change I can go back onto* [higher payments]. *But then I thought, if I do reduce the payments then they're not going to offer me anything else. So, I'm not going to get myself further and further into debt with that.*
>
> Amy

Eileen was also in debt to a door-to-door lender.

> *I've also got a* [credit service loan], *which is the same. They're all posh words for the* [well-known credit service]. *They all change their name, disgusting interest; but great, as I say, when school uniform time comes up, or Christmas comes up. And I go 'Oh yeah, go on'. It's there and I'll just get it and regret five days later ever getting it; and it's gone. And a catalogue; I've probably got £7,000. I pay one £40 a week, and one £70. They're lovely, in all fairness, the people who come, they are lovely. They're on commission on what they collect, aren't they? It's just a big vicious circle though, isn't it? You find yourself on that wheel and it's very difficult to get off.*
>
> Eileen

Cash conversion and pawning

Pawn brokers or their modern high street equivalents such as Cash Convertors, were another means by which the families obtained access to ready cash. When it was something personal that had to be pawned this was an upsetting experience. That was especially true when the money wasn't available to get the item back.

> *I have put things in, things that I don't use, like necklaces and that, that my Mum had bought me for my birthday; and things like that. I pawned all of them.*
>
> Jenny

Terri and Don hadn't been able to get credit elsewhere and so had pawned items.

> *No, I've tried; but in the long run I think it's better they've said 'No'. If we struggle, my partner's Xbox goes in. Yeah, on 'buy back'. So, what we tend to do is put it in there if we need it at the beginning of the month; and then when the wages come in, go and get it back. That's what we try to do.*
>
> Terri

Amber had been doing the same thing.

> *Plenty of times, yeah. Not recently, but I was doing it with the kids' computers and everything because I just didn't have any* [money].
>
> Amber

Catalogues and shop credit

One way around a lack of access to credit is to get things that are needed using a family member's name. Amy had done this to buy children's clothes, furniture and a washing machine. Because the debt was in her mother's name, the repayments were a priority.

> *It's in my Mum's name, but I pay the bill. I think that's about £1,200 outstanding; so it's about £200-ish a month. But the kids needed new bedroom furniture, new beds, so I got that.*
>
> Amy

Terri had used a friend's name to get a mobile phone contract for the same reason.

> *I mean I've got a mobile phone in my friend's name, because I can't get credit.*
>
> Terri

Credit unions

Credit unions do provide a source of low interest loans. However, only a few of the families were members of a credit union. In part this was because up until quite recently at that time, saving with a credit union had been a condition of borrowing from it. Credit unions in fact can now offer loans to people who haven't been able to save. However, Ric and Carol were unaware of this change.

> *We used to have a credit union when Ric worked for the council. But again I can't afford to pay into a credit union to borrow from it.*
>
> Carol

Phoebe made a similar point.

> *I've actually got a credit union, but I've never got any money. I used to use it all the time. I used to save up and then at Christmas, I'd take a loan out; and then throughout the year I'd pay the loan back off; and then the following Christmas I'd do the same. Last Christmas there was no money to save. Now that I can't, I couldn't take a loan out because I wouldn't have had the money to pay it back. So therefore, 'No'; that's totally cut off from us.*
>
> Phoebe

Amy had used a credit union to cover the costs of Christmas.

> *I've got credit union loans. I topped it up at Christmas, and I think it was about £1,600. I don't know exactly what it is; but I know how much I pay them—£80 a week off one loan, and a monthly one of £160. I think I've got four on the go with them.*
>
> Amy

Eileen was getting a credit union loan for Christmas, while still paying back pay-day loans and other debts.

> *I've just put in for a credit union loan that will see me over Christmas. I've still got one outstanding with them, and I owe £300 and something on that. But when I say 'That will see me over Christmas', it won't do Christmas. And I've got loans for home, I think its* [well-known credit service] *under a different name; and I pay that £70 a week. I'm constantly turning that over. In fact probably, it only gets to about half of what I owe, and then I'm getting it back; and usually I'm getting it back* [the debt] *for shopping.*
>
> Eileen

For Gaynor, the credit union was the only option for a loan.

> *I've got a credit union, and I've had catalogues; but because of having no money, I've got no credit now. But I use the credit union. I go to them now.*
>
> Gaynor

Individual Voluntary Arrangements

Carol and Ric had obtained an Individual Voluntary Arrangement (IVA) with help from their local Citizens' Advice Bureau. Steve and Sian had also chosen this option as they had no other way of dealing with their debt, given its size.

> *I've got all types of bills, so I've decided to go for an IVA. I'm in the process of getting it through now. I've got about £9,000 of debts since last April when I came off benefits. I have stuff coming from 2005; Council Tax that that I wasn't aware about, I forgot about. So they've crept up. The bailiffs have crept up about them. It's just an ongoing battle at the moment. So what they've said is that, if I could pay £100 a month for sixty months, my debts will go down to £6,000 from £9,000. I've got what they call a practitioner; they get around £200 to set it up but then after that is all goes to the debts.*
>
> Sian

With no other way of paying off her debts Emma had also signed up to an agreement. It did mean however, that she was blocked from any type of credit for the future.

> *First I have been accepted for an IVA which is an Independent Voluntary Assessment* [sic], *which is regarding my Visa cards because I couldn't afford to pay them. So now I have one payment per month of £100 which lasts for five years and in five years the debt will be written off. It's a lot less because I don't think I would ever have paid it off, and the minimum payment I was making was £280 per month. That was the minimum and out of that I was only paying about £40 off the actual debt. So, I'm quite pleased with that; but I've been to the bank to try and pay my mortgage today. But my account has been blocked by the IVA so I couldn't pay my mortgage and because the account is in joint names you can't use the credit cards. You are not declared bankrupt. But it comes up on every computer. I can't buy anything on credit until five years is up.*
>
> Emma

Families on low wages, unable to manage on their incomes, often find that they are forced to spend beyond their means. Whether that means taking on high-cost loans or going for an IVA, the consequence is an all-too-predictable downward spiral of debt. Moreover, there are no escape routes which don't themselves add significant further strain to personal and financial circumstances in the short, medium and sometimes very long term.

Extra costs

We have already seen how difficult it could be for some of the families to keep their homes warm. Where families had very young or sick children however, having the heating on continuously was unavoidable. This was the case for Amber.

> *My other son is asthmatic, severely asthmatic, and so I have to have the house warm. So the heating is normally on all the time, however much it is going to be. As I say it's outrageous. It's not normally that high* [the most recent bill] *but the past few months, with winter, it has been. But it's what I have got to do for him. I can't not have the heating on and him being freezing. He goes blue round the mouth; all of that.*
>
> Amber

With a baby at home, Fiona also had to keep the house warm.

> *The utility bills, even though it's a shared house and we share bills, they are ridiculous; they're very high at the moment. I think having a baby in the house, even now she's over one, we can't sort of skimp on it the way you would at other times of your life. Even though our energy use on the little graph on the website says it's about the same as last year, some of the bills are nearly a third higher than last year. There doesn't seem to be any reason for it other than gas prices.*
>
> Fiona

Chang and Jiao also prioritised having the heating on because of their young children. Their domestic fuel bills came to over £1,700 a year, more than nine percent of the family's income.

> *For some things savings really cannot be made. For example, like now the weather is so cold, your heating in the house. Your children are so young, so you must have to have it on. I won't save on those things. If it has to be used, then it must be used.*
>
> Jiao

Sian and Steve's domestic fuel bills came to £2,340, or 9.5 percent of the annual family income. Sian had been trying to save on the cost of heating the bath water.

> *The kids share a bath anyway, but I get in now; when they get out I get in. You know I'm not dirty. But he* [Steve] *has to have a bath every night after work, because he does ground works. Pity we haven't got a shower.*
>
> Sian

Conclusion

Managing on low pay combined with the many pressures of working life for all of the families, meant a constant struggle to balance basic costs against income. Across the range of family interviews, there were stories that involved being unable to cover the essentials, debt, outstanding utility bills, Council Tax arrears, problems paying the rent and bailiffs. As we have seen, a 'stable CPI' notwithstanding, the standard cost-of-living measures do not meaningfully index the complex challenges of surviving and supporting a family on low pay in the UK today.

A striking aspect of the families' stories was the ease with which many had slid into debt. An unexpected extra cost to do with domestic utility bills, a benefit overpayment, a mistake with a pay-day loan and so on, were the sorts of pressures that had forced these families into having to borrow, and often at the highest rates of interest. Once in debt of course, and particularly considering the disadvantageous ratio of interest payments against capital repayments, escaping it was a long and difficult (and for some, impossible) task, the final costs of which by far exceeded the original loan.

Although debt was frequently the result of additional costs over and above normal financial commitments, the reason that these had such a disproportionate effect was because of the underlying pressures of those routine living costs. Where families were just surviving from week to week, with little or no surplus to cushion against contingencies, even a relatively small extra burden could wreak havoc with the most careful budgeting.

All the families reported that basic costs had risen in recent years. Food costs for example, were described as having become more difficult to meet. Many were struggling with the cost of heating their homes. Expenses to do with transport of all types, though essential, were described as placing an increasing burden upon already strained family finances. Frequently, the participants talked about their various ways and means of making ends meet. Pre-payment meters, though more expensive in real terms, provided one means by which bills could be avoided. Budgeting down to the last pound was crucial to managing everyday domestic expenses for all the families. There were examples of pawning anything of monetary value, including items that were precious to the family. The use of credit unions had been important to some of the families in recent years. Two families had resorted to IVAs. And yet still, despite the most stringent efforts to keep afloat financially and to avoid debt, many of the families had found that they'd had no choice but to succumb to 'plastic', shop-credit and door-to-door lenders to cover extra costs and even sometimes quite basic family expenses.

Finally, the account that Terri gave the researchers, of her and her children huddling together for warmth, to avoid turning on the heating, provided a vivid image of the combined real life-effects of low pay, welfare cuts and rising costs for the lowest paid workers and their families.

6. Home and Family Life

A roof over your head

A sense of struggle pervaded the accounts that were given of working life and the need to 'hold down the job' by the families. Nowhere was this 'sense of struggle' more keenly expressed however, than when the families spoke of 'house and home'. Indeed, the home was often the place about which the families conveyed the greatest sense of effort and commitment. Home and family after all are the things that people will usually invest the most in, materially, emotionally and psychologically for themselves and for their children. For the same reasons, they are also the things also about which people can feel the greatest frustrations and disappointments.

A home must above all feel and be secure and stable, for family life not to be filled with uncertainty and anxiety. For that, housing status is of critical importance. In the UK, unlike many countries in Western Europe there isn't a culture of, or legislative framework for long-term rental letting. Normally, contracts are of no more than six months' or one year's duration. Contract security was also reduced with the introduction of the 'assured shorthold tenancy' by the 1988 Housing Act. This created a type of tenancy that removed minimum time restrictions upon landlords if they wished to evict occupants, and reduced the notice period for termination.

The impermanence of housing tenancies for many thousands of families in the UK, is unconducive to maintaining a happy and stress-free home-life. Considering the importance of home stability, it is a

 https://doi.org/10.11647/OBP.0112.06

concern now that there is a marked increase in the proportion of families living in the privately rented sector. Along with the problem of having to move far more frequently than those on higher incomes who can maintain home-ownership, these families have also faced difficulties caused by rents that have risen significantly over recent years. So, whilst home-owners have benefitted from historically low interest rates keeping mortgages relatively stable, the growing numbers of families who rent have not been so lucky.

House prices have continued to rise annually for more than a decade. Over the same period the supply of housing provided by local authorities and other social landlords has become more limited. One reason for this is the long-term decline in house building by local authorities. Another has been consistent policy shifts by successive governments towards the marketisation of housing provision that began in the 1980s. The 1980 Housing Act introduced 'right-to-buy' under which council tenants could own the property they had previously rented. The 1988 Housing Act made possible the large-scale voluntary transfer of tenants over to housing associations following a ballot. These measures, combined with the removal of rent control, the erosion of rent subsidies in relation to market values and the diversification of tenancies away from long-term and life-time tenancies, have conspired to significantly reduce the protection that social housing historically represented for families living on low incomes. So, in 1981, 5.5 million households (32 percent) were in the socially rented sector.[1] By 2014, 2.3 million (ten percent) were renting from a housing association, and just 1.6 million (seven percent) were renting from a Local Authority.[2]

The result has been a spectacular expansion in the number of households in the privately rented sector, the proportion rising sharply from 2003 onwards. The financial crisis of 2007 abruptly halted easy credit, resulting in greater difficulty in raising deposits and borrowing for many who otherwise could have afforded to buy their own homes. From the early 2000s to 2016, the numbers living in privately rented homes more than doubled to 5.4 million, or twenty percent of the total. This figure is likely to rise to 7.2 million, or one quarter of the total, by

1 Department for Communities and Local Government (2015), *English Housing survey-Households 2013–14*, Chapter 1: 'Trends in Tenure', p. 23. https://www.gov.uk/government/statistics/english-housing-survey-2013-to-2014-headline-report

2 *Ibid.*, p. 27.

2025. Within this trend it is younger households, especially those in the 20–39 age range that are the most affected. By 2025 more than half of those in this age bracket will be renting.[3]

With this trend comes a turn also in the statistics for 'floor-space-per-person', that started to decrease for households in the privately rented sector during the 2000s, as overcrowding began once more to characterise home-life for many in the worst financial circumstances. Alongside this, there has been an increase over the last decade of more than a third in the numbers of multiple family units sharing the same household.[4] Since 2013, these trends have intensified with the introduction of the 'bedroom tax' that means cuts to Housing Benefit for those who remain in properties with one or more 'spare' bedrooms. Overall, the combined effects of rising total costs of renting a home, downward pressures and caps on benefits and the erosion of security of tenancies has resulted predictably in soaring rates of eviction.

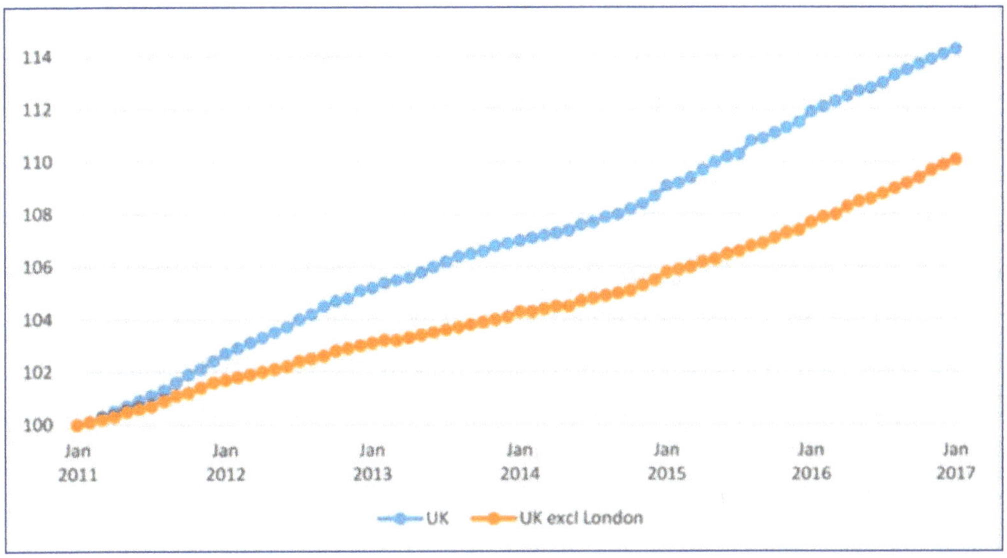

National average rental prices since 2011.
Office for National Statistics.[5]

3 Pricewaterhouse Coopers (2015), UK Economic Outlook, 'UK Housing Market Outlook: The Continuing Rise of Generation Rent', July.

4 Belfield, C. Chandler, D. and Joyce, R. (2015), 'Housing: Trends in Prices, Costs and Tenure', Nuffield Foundation and The Institute for Fiscal Studies, February, p. 2

5 Office for National Statistics (2017), https://www.ons.gov.uk/economy/inflationandpriceindices/bulletins/indexofprivatehousingrentalprices/jan2017

A historic high for eviction rates was reached in 2015. During that year 42,728 households in rented accommodation (170 people a day) in England and Wales were evicted: the highest figure since records began in 2000.[6] Driven by steadily rising rental prices and cuts to housing benefit support, another historic high was reached in 2016, when record numbers of families lost their homes with nowhere to go, each following the end of an assured shorthold tenancy.

Paying for the kids

Whilst maintaining a secure home for the family is a constant challenge for low income families, the financial burden of raising children has also become heavier over the last decade. The costs of school uniforms, sports strips and school dinners are things that those on the very lowest incomes can obtain support for. However, with thresholds set low, those who narrowly miss eligibility struggle to meet these costs. Specifically, in relation to school uniforms a government-funded survey in 2015 found that eighteen percent of parents said they had suffered financial hardship because of purchasing their child's school uniform.[7] Another survey of parents conducted the same year by the National Association of Schoolmasters Union of Women Teachers found that school trips were too expensive for more than a third of parents.[8]

For those in work, breakfast club fees, after-school club fees and items with school-logos, often add significant extra financial difficulties. In its 2014 report, the Children's Commission on Poverty concluded that the combined effect of these and other types of school-related costs means that 'free education' is far from being the reality for the poorest families. The Commission's research showed that more than two thirds of families struggle to afford the costs of school; rising to 95 percent of those who were 'not at all well-off'. More than half said they had cut back on clothing (47 percent), food (27 percent) or heating (29 percent) to meet these costs. A quarter of parents, and more than half of those

6 Foster, D. (2015), 'Eviction is the Last Refuge for Poor Tenants', *The Guardian*, 18 February 2016.

7 Davies, E. (2015), 'Cost of School Uniform 2015', Department for Education. June, https://www.gov.uk/government/publications/cost-of-school-uniform-2015, p. 11.

8 Knight, K. 'Forget the Local Museum! How Far-flung School Trips Costing up to £3,000 are Leaving Parents Broke—and Fuming'. *Mail Online*. 25 June 2015.

who were 'not at all well-off', said they had borrowed money to pay for school expenses.[9]

With respect to 'clothing the kids', the intense influences of advertising and celebrity culture upon children and their demands for brand named goods only add to the problems faced by working families; bringing also the psychological strain of trying to meet children's expectations. These pressures become particularly intense on the approach to Christmas. In December 2015, research by the Money Advice Trusts National Debtline revealed that 23 percent of parents felt under pressure to spend more than they could afford for Christmas. Thirty-five percent said that they would be relying on borrowing to cover their Christmas costs.

Staying healthy

Whilst the corner-stone of the National Health Service (NHS) is its commitment to health care that is 'free at the point of use', a range of essential care services are subject to charges. Prescription drugs, sight tests, prescription glasses and dental treatment (in three bands of treatment type) all bring a cost to the user. A range of exemptions protect school-aged children, young people up to the age of eighteen years in full-time education, the over-60s, pregnant women, those on benefits and those on very low incomes. Some items are always free, for example: medication from an NHS walk-in centre; medication to treat a sexually transmitted disease or tuberculosis; prescribed contraceptives; and medication for mental disorders.[10] Specifically with respect to income, full exemptions apply for treatment and essential travel where the costs of required care or treatment exceed income; or where income exceeds the costs of care by no more than half of the standard prescription charges.

Under the NHS Low-income Scheme costs may be partially covered with eligibility broadly following the criteria used for means-tested benefits (but also considering housing costs). Those who do not fall within the very narrow qualifying thresholds however, must pay. So,

---

9 The Children's Commission on Poverty (2014), *At What Cost? Exposing the Impact of Poverty on School Life*, October.

10 NHS Choices (2016), 'NHS in England—Help with Health Costs', http://www.nhs.uk

whilst children, pregnant women, state pensioners and other groups don't have to pay for their prescriptions, this is not the case for many working adults on low pay. Although prescription charges have been done away with in Wales, Northern Ireland and Scotland, they still exist in England. Prescription charges increased by 20p in April 2014 to £8.05, with the cost of an annual prescription plan going to £104; or £29.10 for three months. At the same time, dental charges increased by up to £5.

Public health information from the NHS promotes healthy lifestyles that reduce the risks of health problems. The importance of 'eating-healthy' particularly is a central message. However, repeated government campaigns (and celebrity chef exhortations) notwithstanding, the truth is that many millions who live in the lowest paid working families, cannot afford a healthy diet. Supermarket 'healthy options' are consistently more expensive than less healthy alternatives. Moreover, the gap between the price of a healthy diet and that of an unhealthy one, continues to grow wider. The greatest gaps exist at corner shops, where many poorer families will shop for food because they cannot afford the transport costs of travelling to supermarkets. These trends clearly raise concerns for long-term structural health inequalities.[11]

We have seen that the stresses of maintaining a stable and secure home as well as meeting the costs of raising children, place an enormous strain on parents. For many this strain reaches the limit of what can be sustained without beginning to affect the health and wellbeing of family members; and for some it becomes intolerable. In her research into the lives of families living in poverty for her 2014 book *Austerity Bites*, Mary O'Hara discovered just how harrowing the experience was for many. O'Hara commented upon the emerging crisis being caused by the strain of struggling to cope for those most affected by government cuts:

> *Throughout the time I was interviewing people, news reports of mental distress, suicides or attempted suicides connected to austerity and cuts came thick and fast. Even taking into account the necessary caution about exaggerating causal links, it seemed that something extreme was happening as individuals affected*

11 Jones, N., Conklin, A., Suhrcke, M. and Monsivai, P. (2014), 'The Growing Price Gap between More and Less Healthy Foods: Analysis of a Novel Longitudinal UK Dataset', PLoS ONE 9(10): e109343, https://doi.org/10.1371/journal.pone.0109343

and their families called on the government to acknowledge the pressures pushing people to a mental edge.[12]

Each year around a quarter of the UK population suffer from mental health problems, with 'mixed anxiety and depression' being the most common type. The statistics for mental illness took a sharp turn for the worse following the financial crisis of 2007 and the introduction of 'austerity' by the 2010–2015 Coalition Government. In 2011 alone, the prescription of anti-depressants rose by 43 percent on the previous year. In the same period, mental health help-line services reported that calls citing debt rose significantly.[13] There is a strong correlation between household income and the risk of mental illness. This link is especially pronounced amongst men; men in the lowest income group being three times more likely than those in the highest income group to have a mental health problem (23.5 percent and 8.8 percent respectively). A link also exists between mental illness and housing tenure. Those renting their homes are 50 percent more likely to suffer poor mental health than home-owners.[14]

For those living under the kinds of pressure described here, one source of personal resilience is their network of family and friends. The social relationships upon which people depend for comfort and material and psychological support however, are not themselves invulnerable to the harmful effects of those same pressures. During times when money is short, the use of the 'family bank' is a necessary fall-back for many who are struggling to survive. This inevitably puts added pressure on family relationships.[15] Considering the costs of child-care, couples living on a low income and unable to afford nursery fees, will often use 'tag-parenting' between their periods of work, which then places strain on their relationship.[16]

---

12 O'Hara, M. (2014), *Austerity Bites: A Journey to the Sharp End of Cuts in the UK.* Policy Press, p. 215.

13 O'Hara, M. (2015), 'Cut Off: How Austerity Relates to Our Mental Health'. *New Statesman*, 6 October.

14 Mental Health Network (2014), 'Key Facts and Trends in Mental Health: 2014 Update', NHS Confederation, Fact Sheet, January.

15 Hall, S. and Perry, C. (2013), *Family Matters: Understanding Families in an Age of Austerity.* Family and Childcare Trust.

16 Hannon, C. (2013), *Living Precariously: Families in an Age of Austerity.* Family and Childcare Trust, May.

In a large-scale survey the personal relationships service Relate found that 93 percent of respondents said their relationships with their partner and family were important when times were hard, and 59 percent said they turn to their partner to share their worries. However, 52 percent said that they were worried about having the money for everyday costs (food, housing and household bills) and 38 percent said that their concerns had a negative impact on their family relationships. The report also identified a 'sandwich generation' of those in the 40–59-year age range, who find that they must support both children and elderly parents as life-expectancy increases, and suffer high levels of stress as a result.[17]

The stresses of working and family responsibilities combined, can have a terrible impact upon the stability of family and social relationships and overall quality-of-life and the stability of relationships.[18] The strain of never being able to relax about money and constantly having to manage bills and debts whilst on a low and often insecure income, can affect all family members. When these pressures are compounded by complications such as illness, loss of full-time employment or paid hours, unforeseen expenses and so on, the toll they take can push those affected towards personal collapse. That scenario of course also brings frightening potential consequences of family breakdown, mental illness, distress and psychological harm to adults and children alike. For many of the people who took part in the research, their struggle in life was precisely to avoid this eventuality for themselves and their children.

Family voices

Rent

Amber was living in a privately rented property. She didn't have a tenancy agreement and her landlord had recently told her that he was

17 Relate (2013), *How is Austerity Affecting Our Relationships? Relationships: Our Support Systems in Good Times and Bad,* https://www.relate.org.uk/policy-campaigns/publications/how-austerity-affecting-our-relationships-relationships-our-support-systems-good-times-and-bad

18 Power, A., Willmot, H. and Davidson, R. (2011), p. 177.

putting the property up for sale. Over a short period, she had seen her rent increase from about £400 to £600 a month. She was very clear why this has happened.

> *There's not been much social housing available; so I think it's like people are forced into not buying* [but] *renting privately. And the private landlord knows this; and they bump their prices up.*
>
> Amber

It isn't simply the high cost of rent that's an issue for families in the private sector. Joy for example was spending more than a third of her income on rent; over £6,500 a year. She'd had to find a large deposit when she moved into her property and now the landlord was pressurising her to sign and pay for a new tenancy agreement. She was reluctant to do so because of his failure to deal with the damp and repairs that the property required.

> *I haven't got £50 to pay at the moment, just to pay out for paperwork; but even when I moved in I had to pay for all the checks. It ends up as well over £1,000 before I can move in. And that was what got me in debt with my overdraft, because I had to pay my rent a month in advance, and then all of the paperwork costs as well which was a ridiculous amount. And now they want £50 each time they renew it. So, every six months they want £50 just to sign a piece of paper. I've been here for eighteen months and there's things that I've asked for. So I'm not going to sign any more until they've done the work that needs to be done. It's just been like ongoing problems like damp in my bedroom. I'm not going to sign another contract; plus I haven't got the £50.*
>
> Joy

Eileen was spending over a quarter of her income on her privately rented property which was costing over £7,000 a year. She had struggled to find the deposit and this resulted in a debt that she was still paying off.

> *I've always been chasing that deposit ever since, because I had to find £1,100 to move. I borrowed it from a glorified loan shark. Well, legalised loan shark, a Provident organisation. So, I've been chasing that ever since.*
>
> Eileen

Living in overcrowded conditions, Amy had been trying to move from her social housing to a privately rented home. However, the costs involved had been too high.

I was looking at 'private', to move, because my landlord's saying that my house is too small a size for the five of us. But the rent was just too much. It was like £1,100, and that was only a parlour house.

Amy

Carol's and Ric's rent had doubled in the seven years they had been living in social housing. Their conditions were also overcrowded but they didn't feel they could afford to move to a four-bedroom house; particularly as one of the children was possibly about to leave to go to college. There were also the up-front costs of moving that the family would have had to cover.

Even just to hire the van to move, if I was offered somewhere. Apart from anything else, you've got to rely on friends and family and things like that. The place needs decorating right through. It needs painting and as long as I've lived here we've never even had a carpet in my bedroom. The kids have got theirs; but I've never had a carpet. I've got rugs down; bits of old rugs, because I can't afford to buy a carpet. Things like that; and again it's not something I want to get in debt for. All my furniture, everything you see in the room, apart from the telly which we've just bought, has been passed on from my Mum and Dad. Nothing, not one item here have I actually gone out and bought.

Carol

Security of tenure

Housing conditions for the families in privately rented property are generally of poorer quality than those in social housing, and their tenancies are less secure. Eileen had been having difficulties with her landlord which highlighted the housing insecurity that private renters can face. The family had lived in their home for more than four years, and had never fallen into arrears. However, the landlord now wanted the property back. To terminate the tenancy, he only had to declare that his 'circumstances had changed', without providing any further explanation. Eileen believed that the real reason he wanted to sell the property was to take advantage of a dramatic increase in the value of local housing.

I got an email saying basically the landlord wants his house back so 'Get out; and you've got two months!' That was four months ago; so things are getting a bit fraught. I'm getting a few knocks on my door. I wouldn't go as far as to say

> *heavies; but it's getting a bit threatening. You know, 'You need to get out'. I did explain to them that I did have rights and I knew what my rights were, and they laughed and walked away; which is a bit threatening and a bit intimidating, I believe. It's two men from the letting agency that look after the house and, quite frankly, they're gangsters. They only deal in cash; you have to go to a shop front with £550 in an envelope; your rent every month. If you're two days late, you get a threatening phone call; and, when I say 'threatening phone call', it's: 'Where are you?'; 'You should have been here with your rent'; 'If you're not here by the end of the week, we'll be looking for your house back'.*
>
> Eileen

The tension and anxiety this was causing affected the children as well as Eileen herself.

> *The kids are upset. 'Mum there's a knock; there's a knock'. I said 'Don't worry about it; answer the door'. But when I come in, if they're home from work or school, they come in and pull the blinds straight down and won't answer the door to anybody. And I hate them being like that; but I can understand why they're being like that. I keep telling them not to worry, and yet I'm not sleeping at night. I probably had about two hours sleep last night, worrying about it myself. But I'm trying to keep upbeat.*
>
> Eileen

Housing conditions

Families in privately rented accommodation sometimes struggle to get the landlords to do necessary repairs. Terri's house had a hole in the bedroom ceiling, as well as damp.

> *I have just had a text message, and I am getting my repairs done. He said 'I'll be out the next day to do that'; and he hasn't. It is still like that now. So, I showed him that* [the damp] *and then he came to see the leak in my bedroom. It's still like that in my bedroom* [a hole in the ceiling and damp].
>
> Terri

Colette's landlord had told her that she would have to pay him to get the damp treated in her rented property.

> *My house is damp. I have got damp patches in my kids' room that are growing. I've got to pay him before I can get out. He's given me a new boiler only because last winter I was left without heat for two weeks; and that wasn't my fault.*
>
> Colette

Tammy and Malcolm had repeatedly raised several issues with their landlord over the condition of their accommodation. They had been left waiting for repairs to deal with problems such as the spread of green mould throughout the property. They believed the landlord to be living abroad and were having to deal with a letting agency.

> *We've got the Environmental Health coming out because the landlord is doing nothing. Someone said that if we report it to the City Council they'll do something about it, and come out and do all the jobs that need doing, because it's a massive priority with having kids, and they'll send him the bill. They'll give him the option first to do the job within seven days. In the long run, he is better-off doing the job himself.*
>
> Tammy

Social housing

Eileen had been offered social housing, thanks to the intervention of her local councillor. Things went wrong however, when she mentioned that in the past she had been subject to a Housing Benefit investigation.

> *It's now gone to the CEO*[19] [of the housing association] *and he's going to meet with me and my local councillor; it was a huge mistake. I mentioned that fact, and because of that I was refused the house—by a social landlord! I don't think so! I showed them the letters and one said I owed £8,000 and two days later I got a letter saying 'It's not £8,000, it's £800'. Then the week after they said 'You owe £249' and stopped my Housing Benefit. I've had no Housing Benefit for three months. I wouldn't go near them. I would rather struggle.*
>
> Eileen

Eileen had by this point signed the contract for a privately rented house. The property had no floor coverings and she was going to have to find the money for carpets. The rent, however, was considerably more at £550 a month, compared to £313. She pointed out the obstacles caused by debt for those needing to rent.

> *Them* [a social landlord] *doing credit checks! Who's going to get a house if they are doing credit checks? Very few people haven't got debt or problems with debts; surely then they'd buy their own house.*
>
> Eileen

19 Chief executive officer.

Liam and Grace had found their social landlord to be far too ready to take court action for rent arrears. Liam was being paid monthly; however, the rent had to be paid weekly and Grace was finding it difficult budgeting to do this.

> *October was the worst month ever, it was five weeks and it was a terrible struggle, and what it was, she'd* [a social landlord officer] *come 'round and said I hadn't paid it; but I had paid it and it doesn't clear on their account until the next week. But she still put court proceedings through, even though I'd paid. She wouldn't take my word for it that I'd paid. Now if I'd ever owed money at the most it would be £300 and then it gets cleared. But I pay it; it's never left to mount, never. But she still put court proceedings through. Now I could have been evicted and I thought 'Why have you done that?' So, I got a letter and I phoned them up and put in a complaint.*
>
> Grace

The condition of their social housing, and ongoing problems with damp particularly, had been an issue for Micha and Karolina. Karolina believed the social landlord had been reluctant to do necessary repairs because of the expense involved.

> *The house that we moved into, there was damp previously; we knew there was. It's been treated but we only moved into this house 4–5 months ago; but it's started to show up even in the kitchen, in the cupboards, damp, black spots, where I've got my plates. As far as I know, for now, the landlord doesn't want to do anything about it; and my daughter has had a cough for a month.*
>
> Karolina

The neighbourhood

The families had contrasting views about the neighbourhoods in which they lived; and different experiences of the level of community support around them. Amy and Sian's comments captured this contrast.

> *People have been trampled on and finding it hard to come back. Where I live, people are community-minded and pull together. They have swop-shops; people coming in who can't afford to buy clothes. It's like a jumble sale. But it shouldn't have to be like that. You've got your foodbanks, and people shouldn't be living like that. The communities have pulled together to make sure that the service is there for people who are struggling.*
>
> Amy

The old community spirit's gone. People are really negative, and they're down; don't know where to go. How do you turn that round?

Sian

There was more agreement amongst the families over the impact that cuts in community services were having on working households. Gaynor had seen a decline in her area, and blamed the Government.

Yeah, like the Sure Start centres; most of them have gone. They've just cut the resource centre where the adults with learning difficulties go every day. The library's going; they're trying to get rid of the lollipop ladies and men; trying to get shut of them. But these are things that people need. Like there used to be a group I used to go to: it's like confidence building and health and well-being for women. Just little groups like that that they used to put on. They used to be free, but its £25 a session now, which is quite expensive. They used to have sessions for like post-natal depression and stuff like that, for people who would self-harm. They used to do relaxation classes, and some people need that. Some people need to get out and maybe talk to someone, and these are the type of groups that we need around here. There's nothing like that around here anymore. Yeah, they just keep taking things away and people put forward ideas, but they just keep getting knocked back all the time.

Gaynor

Denise was aware of services that were under direct threat due to the cuts in her own area.

Yes, well the baths was threatened to be closed down, but we've turned that round and it's being kept open. Schools and everything were getting threatened, weren't they? But they seem to have not done it; they all still seem to be open.

Denise

Sue's neighbourhood had lost a local library and a swimming pool and had seen cuts to projects supporting young people, including one that helped one of her own children.

They have just closed down all the Connexions[20] *haven't they? That was like a service for young people. It helped me with my girls getting apprenticeships. Yeah, yeah there were a couple 'round here, and they were brilliant. That's gone and I do think it's the government* [to blame].

Sue

20 A government funded agency supporting young people into the world of work.

The medical centre that Luke's mother had been using had stopped providing an interpreter. This was causing problems for the family because the alternative—a phone-based interpretation services—didn't work for them.

> *The hospitals still have interpreters, but the GPs don't provide that anymore; only a 'language line'. So maybe my Mum sometimes needs to see a GP; I need to take time off my holiday, to take her or my grandmother to see the GP.*
>
> Luke

Like many of the families, Grace directed her anger at the Government.

> *The children's centre is getting closed down; it wasn't generating enough money. But they don't have anything on for the kids to generate any money. They just want to take everything off here. They're not pumping any money into anywhere. It's like the Government are just taking and taking, and giving themselves these pay advances.*
>
> Grace

The 'bedroom tax'

Denise and her three children had been living in the same four-bedroom house for four years. She had to pay the 'bedroom tax' and had been unsuccessful in getting a discretionary housing payment towards this. She knew that she would have to find a smaller house. However, with two boys and a girl she was also aware they would need their own rooms as they were getting older, and so was reluctant to move. Even though she was in receipt of Working Tax Credit and Housing Benefit these did not make up the loss from the under-occupation charge reduction on her Housing Benefit, and so found herself in arrears.

> *Well just at the minute, I've been put back and don't have to pay until March. I just have to pay the housing arrears. I was like £700 in arrears with the housing, so I couldn't get any repairs done, nothing at all. Now I've paid them, well I'm paying a fiver a week, bit by bit. I could have been homeless to be honest.*
>
> Denise

Denise was by this point paying her rent arrears off at the rate of £18.50 a week, £13.50 of which was for the 'bedroom tax'. She'd been successful in getting the payments postponed. She explained that moving to a smaller house wasn't an option because she couldn't afford the costs of the move.

> *You know they want me to move, but it's not as easy as that. I said to them 'Are you going to give me the money for the move? You going to get me the money for all the furniture, new carpets? No, so I'm not moving then'. So, I have to struggle and pay that. Now I'm glad that I've won that little bit of appeal back; only until March, but it's something isn't it? You know, they're going to want it again in March; but I'll just have to work my way 'round it somehow. It's a lot of money. Basically, they've said I've got to start paying it again in March. That's all I know. Every little helps in the meantime. Don't get me wrong, it's helping me quite a lot. But I don't agree with it. I think it's disgusting. I really do.*
>
> Denise

Clothing growing children

Like most children as they grow older, Ruth's children wanted to be wearing the same styles and brands as their peers. At the same time, she had to find the money for clothes for an activity one of the children was involved in, and 'proper' shoes for another child's first job interview. Nearly ten percent of the family income was spent on clothing and shoes.

> *Well, basically we've been going without. At the minute we will go without, you know. Where previously, I have just gone out and bought my kids' shoes, if they needed a pair of shoes. Now I'm having to wait until I get paid. I can't just go and put it on my card, you know what I mean. Normally, I would just go and take my bank account card and put it on my card. But at the moment I can't. I've got to wait for money to go in before it's available to spend.*
>
> Ruth

Children's clothing and shoes were two of the things that Sian and Steve were having the most difficulty finding the money for.

> *So we don't really spend that much; it's food really, or something happens. They need shoes. Our* [daughter] *needs a new 'pinny, a school 'pinny, she's grown already. So it's stuff like that. The white shirts constantly; my little boy's always rolling round in the mud, and you can't get the stains off the white shirts. So constantly those things you've got to buy.*
>
> Sian

The speed at which children grow out of their clothes was something that Colette knew only too well, and something she couldn't afford to deal with.

> *The biggest demand at the moment actually is that I can't really afford clothes and shoes. They have both had a growth spurt. Unfortunately, they are both going to have to wait a couple of weeks, you know what I mean, until I can put a bit of money from this week aside for the following week, to then go to the shops. I just haven't got it spare at the moment.*
>
> Colette

Amber's children had also recently gone through growth spurts which meant a big expense on top everything else.

> *I have had to replace the children's clothes. As I say, they're at an age where they just suddenly grow, and I have had to do a full wardrobe revamp on the three of them. It cost about £600 for all of it.*
>
> Amber

Denise had three young children and keeping them properly clothed was a continual struggle.

> *Well they always need something; if it's not shoes or a coat, it's clothes. It's awful.*
>
> Denise

For Luke, the expense of having two babies and his wife being on maternity leave meant using what savings remained to buy things the children needed.

> *I did not realise that I had that many expenses. I spend quite a lot on the food and on the babies, their clothes, and so that's a bit of a surprise. Because I'm not in that much control of my budget, maybe sometimes I overspend my money. It's quite difficult because for the kids, you've got to spend it, there's no choice. That's why I said in the last two years, because of the two children, all my family's savings will be gone. So maybe it's a difficult time if my wife doesn't get a job in the future.*
>
> Luke

Chang and Jiao relied mainly on getting hand-me-downs from other family members.

Buying? I would rarely buy for her [their daughter]. *But if it's her birthday, or if her clothes don't fit anymore, then I would buy one or two for her. Normally, they are relatives' sons and daughters whose clothes don't fit anymore, and save for her* [to wear].

Chang

School uniforms

Many schools still require their pupils to wear expensive badged uniforms. As Ruth explained, she could have purchased relatively inexpensive items of school uniform from the local supermarket. However, she had to buy the specific items the school required. She also had to buy the correct, and so more expensive, items of sports-kit.

They are the ones that have been like catching me; because I have to go out and I have to get new shoes for football, because he can't go to football if they don't fit him. So it's £17; I think it is £17 for a school jumper also.

Ruth

Chang and Jiao had been able to buy school uniform items from a supermarket for their young child.

But for buying uniform for her; I'm really embarrassed to say that I have never bought a proper one; a proper uniform for her. Now maybe this school isn't very strict and the supermarket does sell uniforms; and the school haven't requested you have to have their school badge. So buying is relatively cheap.

Chang

Terri was having to find cheaper options than the uniform requirements stipulated by the school.

It's so hard. They have school polo shirts with an emblem. I haven't bought them because I can't afford them. So they've got a black men's one from [well-known low cost clothing store] *for £3. It's terrible, finding the cheapest of everything.*

Terri

The cost of shoes for school had been a problem.

I mean, my daughter came in the other day and her shoes have cracked right across the sole; and I went to her 'Have you got a pair upstairs you can use?' She'll be getting black ones for Christmas, which is only in two weeks' time. So, she found a pair and I said 'Wear them, because I can't afford now and Christmas'. She said, 'OK Mum'. They are so good like that.

Terri

Grace made a similar point about the expense of shoes.

> *The shoes are £40 each. So, by the time you get them, before they go back in September, in the holidays I go and get them all their school shoes to go back to school. They need to have shoes. The shoes fall apart after a few weeks; so, I had to go and get them black trainers then, because they last a bit longer. And one's in a size four which is adult prices for shoes; and he's only eleven! So, you can't win, can you?*
>
> Grace

Phil and Dot were finding it difficult to meet the cost of their child's new school uniform as she moved to senior school.

> *She's going into seniors' this year, in September. We've just been told there's another expense coming in now, of a school uniform. That's about £200-odd; we don't get any help for that. Generally we'll try and go to charity shops; things like that; maybe the* [well-known supermarket] *as well. But we don't go to any of these upmarket things. We can't afford to do that.*
>
> Phil

Janet had been fortunate that her mother could help.

> *My Mum helped me out a little bit; uniforms. That was a big part as well, because I had to come home to make sure all the uniforms were there; money I haven't got.* [Younger daughter]*'s was easy*: [refers to two well-known supermarket chains]. *But it cost me over £300 for* [older daughter]'s *uniform; bearing in mind it's her last year as well. I could have done without it. She was trying to wear her old shoes to go back to school, but she got new ones in the end.*
>
> Janet

School dinners

School meals were just one of the expenses that Amy was struggling with. She missed the help that the School Uniform Grant had provided to families on low incomes, before it was cut. Now, the loss of the support the grant had provided added to the financial burden of other school-related costs.

> *They stopped the 'uniform grant'. It costs me £5 a day to send* [daughter] *to school at the moment; so, it will cost me £10 a day. She gets a bus ticket, which they've recently reduced. They do a £2 ticket now, whereas she used to have to get a weekly bus pass from* [the bus company] *which was £11 a week. But*

again, the £2 a day-ticket and £3 for her dinner; she has school dinners. I'm going to try and look into whether they are eligible for bus passes. I actually went into it. It was a couple of years ago actually, when they were in junior school. And I went in and asked them and she said 'Do you get Working Tax Credit?' And I said, 'Yeah', and she said, 'They've changed it all. If you get Working Tax Credit you're not entitled to free school meals'.

Amy

Janet was also struggling with the costs of school dinners.

I can't afford the school dinners anymore; so it's trying to put them on packed lunches. But by the time you do for two or three of them, it works out the same anyway. So you've got two kids saying 'I don't want packed lunches; I want hot dinners'. That's £16, then you've got one saying 'Oh I don't like the school dinners, I want packed lunch'.

Janet

Out-of-school activities

Families in low paid employment are restricted in what they can do with their children out-of-school, as well as during school holidays. Sian explained how this limited the options for the family.

So our days out are kind of 'go for a walk around Sefton Park', rather than going out to spend money on any type of shows and activities. It would be literally after tea going out for a walk and get their scooters.

Sian

Similarly Carol and Ric would always try to do things that were free with their children.

We'll go and do something with the kids, but it will mean that we'll have to go somewhere that's free basically; go to the museum or something. I couldn't afford to take them bowling or anything like that.

Ric

Denise's children were all involved in out-of-school activities and she talked about how the costs add up.

The kids have all got their hobbies, and they cost a lot. By the time you've bought their kits. They do majorettes the girls, and the boys do football. At the moment it's not too bad as there's no dancing on until April. Then there's twenty weeks when the girls dance out; and then you're talking coach fares and stuff like that. Thirty pounds to let them go dancing. So, every week for twenty weeks. That's really horrendous that.

Denise

After-school activities can represent a significant cost. Phoebe's children were members of sports teams, but they wouldn't have been able to participate without sponsorship.

The membership for them was £60 a month for the three of them. Luckily we've just been given sponsorship for the three kids. Otherwise we would have had to pull them out.

Phoebe

Liz was finding it difficult to meet the costs of her child's out-of-school activities.

His after-school clubs; they're the only other things, but they're not cheap. They say to you its only £40! Only! You have them for an hour after-school! I don't put him in anything like breakfast club. But in the half-terms he goes to Little League. So I have to pay for that; because my Mum and Dad would go grey if they had him for a week; because he's hard work. So he goes to Little League for three days; and that's £25 to £30.

Liz

Fiona was being helped by her parents.

I'm very lucky because my Mum and Dad pay for a lot of activities for the girls as presents and things. But it's not money that comes from me. But it makes you feel quite bad actually, that you can't afford to give them the opportunities. But I know I'm lucky to have that.

Fiona

Brenda was struggling to find the money to pay for her children's out-of-school activities and was also relying on help from her family.

My son, you know he's doing more activities and he does basketball and he's got fees. So I'm just kind of 'robbing Peter to pay Paul' kind of thing. I can't afford to do anything really. Maybe just go to the park for days out; things like that. I'm going to be struggling with child-care over the summer holidays. I'm struggling with child-care as it is now. You know I'm having to rely on the family to be able to look after the kids.

Brenda

For Karolina and Micha, taking time off work with their young daughter was the problem. Their daughter was attending a Sure Start Children's Centre.

> *She just missed a trip on Saturday because there was a trip for dads which was good. So, I said to Micha 'Just don't go to work on Saturday, just take her for a trip'. I've booked a place, because it was only for dads so I couldn't go anyway and I was in work. Because you know, he's working that many hours, so he doesn't spend much time with her. It was a trip to the farm. But then because she wasn't well, I just had to cancel it. So, I've missed my overtime on Friday.*
>
> Karolina

Pocket-money

The families found it hard to afford pocket-money for the children. Janet explained how her family helped her.

> *They just have to save, my Mum and Dad kind of give. She's got a godmother who gives her some money. So, she tries to save her own money. My other daughter gets some money from my Mum and Dad. They don't get pocket-money; they just get what they need, if they need it.*
>
> Janet

It was a similar situation for Carol and Ric with their children.

> *No, nothing at all. The jar of coppers; the coppers go in and my Mother-in-law and my Mum both do the same; put the coppers in the jar. And they go to the kids when its summer holidays and things like that.*
>
> Carol

Sian also couldn't afford to give her children pocket-money and was helped out by the children's grandparents.

> *My Nan spoils them rotten. She gives them pocket-money. I don't give them pocket-money. My Nan gives them £2.50 a week; we haven't seen her for a fortnight so it's going to be £5 each; so, then we're going shopping. I can say, 'That's your money. I'm not giving you a penny more!' So, in the end they do get money.*
>
> Sian

Phil and Dot were having to find more for their daughter's pocket-money each week since she had moved to senior school, and was wanting to buy things herself.

She gets £2 a week pocket-money. Obviously that's going to have to go up soon. She complains about the money; she wants things. We'll be in the shopping centre and she sees something, and we have to say 'You can't have that'. So, what we'll do is pass it off with some sweets or something, but that's instead of what she wants, you know what I mean.

Dot

Don and Terri's children knew that their parents didn't have money to spare.

Other than that they know we struggle, they know. I mean the kids ask for a pound every morning. I have a moneybox and I say to them 'See what you can get out of that. If you can get a pound each, have a pound each'. Some mornings they only get 50p but they are made up. I don't know many kids that are made up with 50p.

Terri

The TV

Televisions that operate with a pay-as-you-go meter provide an alternative to having to pay up front for a set. However, this is an expensive option. Over the previous year it had cost Eileen £800, whereas the cost of buying a set would normally have been half that figure.

It was somebody who came knocking at the door with a brochure; and you know when your kids have only got a small portable telly in the corner and you think 'Yeah, sounds great'. The meter's on the back of the TV so you get four hours for a pound (can you believe that still goes on?) But they wouldn't give anybody in my position credit. So I couldn't go to [well-known retailer] *and go 'Give me that TV which is only £300 and I'll pay for it monthly', because they just wouldn't. You've got to go and pay the top whack.*

Eileen

Family occasions and Christmas

Family occasions and religious celebrations (Christmas in particular) brought an additional strain to budgets that were already overstretched. Jenny was trying to save for Christmas, but found each year to be more difficult than the last.

> *Well, any money that I do have left like, if it's one week and I have like £5 or £10 left, I have got a post office card which I go and put on for Christmas. Like last year and the year before, and all the years before. I've got myself into a big mess over Christmas; and it takes me forever to try and get myself back out of it.*
>
> Jenny

Jenny was trying to limit the cost of presents by just buying for the children. She also was also keeping festive costs down by staying at her mother's house over the Christmas period. Her uncle helped by buying clothes for birthdays, some of which could be held back for Christmas.

> *I go to my Mum's. Things like her* [daughter's] *Christmas clothes and things like that. It's her birthday in October and my uncle always buys her clothes for her birthday because he never buys her toys. So I always keep two sets of what he buys her for her birthday and for Christmas.*
>
> Jenny

The pressure of costs associated with Christmas made it more a 'season of dread' than celebration for families like Amy's.

> *Christmas is horrendous. It costs me about £10–12 per child for different activities: the pantomime; Christmas parties; Christmas lunch. There's quite a few things, and it's very expensive.*
>
> Amy

Joy's experience of family occasions and Christmas was similar.

> *I do find it a struggle, especially for things like birthdays, Christmas and buying clothes and uniforms for school. Trying to do things in the school holidays, fun things for my daughter really. I find it a bit of a struggle sometimes; and just keeping on top of the Christmas bills.*
>
> Joy

Tammy and Malcolm only bought Christmas presents for the children and not for each other.

> *As I said to him because there's nothing that I need; there was nothing that he needed. So, we just told family and that 'Don't buy us nothing and we won't buy you nothing. Just buy for the kids.*
>
> Tammy

Terri also was struggling with the cost of Christmas.

> *I've struggled; but I have had to do it. When they open their presents they won't get what other kids get. I mean my daughter came home the other day and said*

> *'Mum, there's a coat; it's called Moncler'. I think* [they're] *skiing coats. Four hundred and odd* [pounds]. *I said You can't have one of them'. So, I went to* [well-known retailer] *and bought her a £20 coat, which is the same with a furry hood.*
>
> Terri

Joy had been lucky in receiving a generous contribution to her Christmas costs from her son's grandparents.

> *They said they are sending him a £100 for Christmas, but also said they are sending me a £100 for the Christmas dinner; which I thought was lovely. I've ordered meat today on the back of that. That was lovely. Christmas dinner has been sorted; and now I've only got to be Father Christmas.*
>
> Joy

Brenda had made regular savings to cope with Christmas, but it was money she couldn't really afford.

> *We saved each month with a savings, like a hamper-type company. My sister does it, and we put away £20 a month. That's really hard; it's really, really hard. That means then at Christmas we've got £200. It means the kids can get something nice at Christmas. It means it is a big chunk out of the costs. But we wouldn't be able to find that money at Christmas. You know, we miss it so much that money, each month; but then we've got this lump sum that we can use at Christmas.*
>
> Brenda

Like some of the other families, Sian and Steve had saved for a food hamper and were limiting what they spent on presents.

> *I do* [a hamper savings company]. *So I pay £7 a week; so I get about £300 that helps. Just takes a bit of pressure off. What we buy each other is only a couple of quid or whatever. This year we went to his Mum's for Christmas Day. Just play it by ear really. We do what we can.*
>
> Sian

Some families, like Denise's, had been able to save for Christmas with a credit union.

> *I didn't really cope, but I managed in the end* [with] *the credit union. I get loans off them every year. I would have been lost this year. But I managed; just paying it back now. That's nice. But we managed to have a nice Christmas. That's the main thing.*
>
> Denise

Gaynor was struggling also and had gone to her parents for Christmas to cope.

> *Christmas was OK. We got by; didn't have any food* [laughs]. *So we went to my Mum's; and his Dad helped out. But we can't keep going to him for stuff really. So yeah, I went to my Mum's for dinner, like all over the Christmas. I even stayed there a few nights, because I didn't like want to be in the house on my own at Christmas time.*
>
> Gaynor

"Children can't understand"

These parents worried constantly about the impact of money problems on their children. Gaynor was aware that she was continually having to say that she couldn't afford to do things. The family hadn't had a holiday for four years. Her daughter would also get upset when she couldn't have something. Although Gaynor did think her daughter was understanding of their situation, she was also aware that it was having an effect on her.

> *My little girl, it does affect her. I think, it does. She goes on about her friends 'have got this' and her friends 'have got that', and I'm just thinking 'Well, I'm not her friend's Mum, sweetheart, I can't. I haven't got it'.*
>
> Gaynor

Amber's small children couldn't understand why their mother never seemed to have any money.

> *The kids have this attitude when I say 'There is no money'; they just say 'Well go to the bank'. They just assume that there is never-ending money just coming out that bank. They don't really understand. I have never really involved them in stuff like that. I don't want them to worry.*
>
> Amber

Ruth knew that her eldest child was aware of the family's lack of money.

> *Yeah, my eldest daughter, she knows now. She is old enough to sort of understand. She's like 'We're poor; why couldn't I have been born to a rich family?'*
>
> Ruth

Denise could see that the family's financial situation was affecting her children as they got older.

I mean, it doesn't affect them all the time. But there are times when it does affect them. Especially as my eldest daughter's getting that bit older now; she likes to go out more and socialise. Sometimes I have to go 'I haven't got the money for you to go there', and it does put a bit of a downer on her because she thinks 'well, why? You work; what about the money'. I just have to explain to her, you know what I mean.

Denise

Amy thought her children appreciated what they get and that they also realised that, while they were not as well-off as some of their friends' families, things could have been worse.

They do realise that I work hard to bring money in. And like I say, if they want to go to the pictures at the weekend, 'the money just isn't there'. So I get a bit of 'Oh, it's not fair', and stuff. But then on the other hand like, little things will trip them off to be really thankful. But I just want to instil in them, they've always seen me going off to work and hopefully, like, I keep talking them into getting better jobs. So they can look after me when they're well off!

Amy

Eileen was aware of the effects of peer pressure on her children; but was also grateful for their understanding attitude. Her daughter had obtained a part-time job whilst she was still at school to help out. She appreciated the problems her mother was dealing with and would often say that it didn't matter that she couldn't afford things.

She knows everything's a struggle and very rarely asks; but being in the sixth form there was an eighteenth birthday party every other week. She couldn't to go to them all because of outfits, shoes and that. But there was one she really had to go to; and I usually borrow the money or beg steal or borrow and buy her a cheap dress from [well-known retailer] *and give her money to be able to go. And she was always really grateful. I felt really awful and I would have loved her to go to every one of them. But if I was that sort of a mum, she wouldn't have turned into the lovely girl she is. I don't believe they should get everything they want. If* [her daughter] *gets money the first thing she does is give* [her brother] *money or buy him something and she always buys me something.*

Eileen

Grace's son was much younger, but still showed understanding about the family's circumstances. Grace found this upsetting.

It comes to the point where your seven-year-old son's going 'I know you haven't got any money Mum'. So, it's a bit upsetting because you don't want them to go without. It's heart-breaking hearing your seven-year-old worrying if we can afford something.

Grace

Mental health

The continual worry about paying bills and the stress of dealing with mounting debt undermines the psychological health of many people. This may be compounded by family tensions caused by financial pressures, partners working long hours and anxieties about the impact on children. Potential outlets for the pressures created are limited by the social isolation that working poverty creates.

I had a really bad, like, anxiety breakdown. It was horrendous. I was backwards and forwards to 'A&E'[21] because I was just convinced that something else was wrong with me. It was generalised anxiety.

Amber

Terri had been working as a cleaner but gave it up due to ill health. The family was relying on Don's earnings which were just above minimum pay level. Debt was a constant worry and the family had been dealing with bailiffs over rent and Council Tax arrears. Terri talked about the effects upon her own health.

I suffer from depression and anxiety as well. I was off my tablets and the doctor has put me back on them. When I was first on them, it was one and then two and now it's three a day. It's the worry of the money; and I am not sleeping. But my Mum says she's finding it very hard. So everybody, no matter who you speak to, whether they are in work or on benefits, they are all struggling. But I find it terrible, sometimes I just go to bed and shut myself away.

Terri

Terri had been diagnosed as suffering from anxiety and recounted what happened on one occasion.

And then my Mum gets a phone call from my children and it was 'Nan we can't wake Mum up'. But I hadn't taken anything. I was awake but I couldn't open my eyes; I've had a panic attack. I thought I was having a heart attack.

Terri

21 Accident and emergency.

Struggling to stay on top of her three jobs, Gaynor hadn't had a holiday for four years. Council Tax and rent arrears to a private landlord, and a pay-day loan she had been paying off for a year, had all heaped pressure on her.

> *But even though the stress I'm going through, I've never been on anti-depressants. But now I've had to go on anti-depressants; just because of the stress that they've* [debts] *left me in.*
>
> Gaynor

On top of finding work very stressful, Jenny was finding that managing the family budget was a continual worry.

> *Constantly, constantly worry about money getting into the bank, and money coming out; and paying my money into the post office. It's a constant worry of when it's coming in and when it's got to go back out.*
>
> Jenny

The sense of having nothing to look forward to came through in Emma's comments about her routine.

> *It's been a really bad year. The other day I got dressed, did my hair (first time in ages) and put my make-up on. It was only a hospital appointment to get her* [her daughter] *finger checked; and then we did the school run and I didn't want to go home. Because I know as soon as I go home, it's tidying up, it's dinner, it's tea; and then we are in bed by 7pm. There's nothing to look forward to.*
>
> Emma

When Eileen collapsed at work she was taken to hospital for tests. She had never previously had high blood pressure, but as she said 'It was through the roof'. She attributed this directly to the stress she was under due to her debts and harassment from her landlord. She was aware that many people are developing mental health problems because of financial pressures.

> *So sometimes when I am worried I just go to bed, and that way I don't force the worry on the kids then. It's that bad though, it seriously is that bad. Thankfully, I'm a strong person, so as for mental health, I've not felt anything give yet. But anyone with a weaker disposition would have gone under if they'd been me, by about twelve months ago. But it's depressing because I can't see a way out in the near future; and I'm in that state, not because I'm a habitual drug taker, or not because I go to the bingo five nights a week. I like the odd bottle of wine, don't get me wrong. But I'm in that state, literally, for keeping a roof over my kids' heads*

and feeding them and clothing them, you know what I mean? I don't know how people who have got problems manage, I don't know. I'm actually looking for a night job in a chippy or something. That's what I'm looking for at the minute; for regular cash coming in, maybe weekly and I've been looking round. My eldest son came down and said 'Don't you dare; you do enough'.

Eileen

Liz's child had serious health problems and was going to need an operation. Her financial situation, on top of her worry for her child was very stressful.

It does stress me out sometimes. I get dead upset; I'm a crier. I'm dead emotional about things, I am. But then, I'm like that anyway. I wouldn't say I was like 'depressed'. But I have been really down about stuff in the past.

Liz

Two of Amber's three children had health problems. Because of her financial situation she couldn't justify spending anything on herself, for example for a night out with friends. Whatever money she had left over after paying her bills was spent on the children. Anxiety about her finances had impacted upon her health just two years previously.

I got diagnosed with OCD.[22] *It was like constantly being anxious, and then having panic attacks on top of that. It was horrible. I still get them now, but not to the same extent.*

Amber

Sue was continually stressed about money.

We used to go out a bit more. I am always stressed a bit and always like trying to cut corners: 'Don't get that, get this one, it's cheaper'. It's like obsession. It's shown me that in order to get a nice calm manageable life which I want, I have got to watch my spending because it causes me stress. It makes me feel so insecure, you know. Then I think 'No, you can get on top of this if you plan'.

Sue

Joy also felt that financial worries becoming too much for her to deal with. She couldn't see a way to get on top of her money situation and felt like she was doing nothing more than working to survive.

There have been times when I've been stressed or really down; just like with bills getting on top of me and stuff. When I've got a few to pay and I just haven't got

22 Obsessive compulsive disorder.

> *the money; and I've been getting phone calls saying I owe money. It's been quite stressful. It seems like the same every month. I can't really get out of it because I've got all these payments. It's just hard to get on top of. I'm not going to over-exaggerate and say 'Oh, you know, I'm really down'. But I do feel like all I do is work to pay bills, to support the kids. Then when I'm not working, I'm kind of at home, trying to make a home kind of thing. I just feel like I've got no life. I'm just there doing what I need to do to get by and pay my bills and look after the kids. That's how my financial situation makes me feel.*
>
> Joy

Denise had experienced similar feelings.

> *Yeah, it gets you down. The days that you know, I'm working for nothing; nothing left, you know. But it's life; but I don't let it get me down; just got to get on with it. To be honest, it's a case of you have to, isn't it? Nowhere to turn to; can't keep turning to family members all the time for money; have to pay them back you see, so it's hard. So I just try to avoid it if I can, you know, getting into debt. I try to budget. But it's not easy.*
>
> Denise

Partners

Both Carol's and Ric's two children had health problems and most weeks they had to take them both for essential treatments at Alder Hey Children's Hospital. There was never money to spare at the end of the month and they always had to borrow something. Carol had become depressed about their situation. She was also very worried about the impact that Ric's long working hours and shift work were having on his health.

> *Ric was worried because he was off with stress for a week this month. But he had to go back in; basically had no choice about it. He's got to go back in. We can't afford for him to be off work for any length of time whatsoever. Statutory sick pay is really bad; and then he was worried sick that when he goes back in: 'Am I going to have a job to go to'. That kind of thing.*
>
> Carol

Karolina, who was having her second child, was also worried about her partner, Micha, and the long hours he works.

> *I do get stressed, especially now with being pregnant. When I found out I was pregnant, we'd just been talking with my Micha all about it and the first thing that hit me, it wasn't the 'Whoo, I'm pregnant!' like I was with* [her daughter],

> *I mean I was happy; don't get me wrong. We are happy that were going to get another member of the family and all that. But the first thing that hit me was 'How are we going to cope? How are we going to manage?' But then I felt 'If we can manage with one, then we're going to manage with two'. It's going to need some cuts, but we'll get there somewhere. But now I can see the bump growing, I don't really much think about it. I just think more about the baby than the financial thing. But that was the first reaction: 'How are we going to manage?' Micha said 'Oh, I think I'm going to have to find another job'. If there was another week, another few days in the week maybe yes, it would be possible. He's just over-tired. He does work such long hours. Sometimes he comes home dead frustrated saying 'I don't get that I'm working that many hours; where is the money? What am I working for?'*
>
> Karolina

Grace had the same worries about her partner, Liam.

> *Well his hours are really long. He doesn't get a break. As you know he's a chef so he gets no break. I've noticed the last few years where he's working now he comes home and he's absolutely knackered. It's not fair to be on your feet all day, especially in the summer; the heat was unbearable. He had a lot of trouble because he was sweating so much. He got like an infection on his back and we thought maybe it was cancer. He's been really stressed out. He went to see a specialist yesterday and he said 'No, it's fine'. But he is under a lot of stress as well. You know he works hard and he gets paid a pittance really.*
>
> Grace

Cath's worries about her partner Liam, were also about the excessive hours he was having to work.

> *He was on nights last night and this morning. He didn't get home until about quarter past eight. It's exhausting for him sometimes; just getting home. He's such a hard working guy.*
>
> Cath

The stress of money problems had been causing arguments between Phoebe and her partner Gavin. Phoebe was also anxious about Gavin's health. He worked full-time in manufacturing and rode a bike twenty miles to and from his job each day. He didn't have proper weather-proof clothing and would often get wet. Gavin left each day for work at 6am and normally didn't get home till 7pm. He often didn't feel like eating a proper meal when he got home and had been losing weight.

> *He's 50 next year and again it's good for his health, riding* [his bike]. *But the stress he's under! No, you know what I mean? It's horrific: he's not eating properly; he's not sleeping properly because he's worried constantly about money; and 'How am I going to save money to do this, that or the other?*
>
> Phoebe

Sick children

Having a child who is ill or has a long-term health condition, increases the stress of trying to get by on a low income. On top of trying to make sure that the children have the correct diet for their condition, there are many other practical and financial difficulties ranging from the costs of regular visits to hospital, additional laundry costs and the need to make special provision for holidays and child-care.

Rabia normally used the bus for her regular visits to the Alder Hey hospital. Sometimes however, that wasn't possible and she would then have to take her child by taxi to her appointments.

> *One of my kids suffers with asthma, and so we're often spending time in Alder Hey. So we've got to ride the buses. If we have to take a taxi, then it costs me £10; and it can't wait because you've got kids. We've got no car and sometimes people can offer you a lift to Alder Hey. But it's a distance isn't it?*
>
> Rabia

Emma also had to deal with the costs of frequent hospital visits with one of her children.

> *Sometimes I was going up twice a day. I tended to go straight from work, so that I could pick* [one of her daughters] *up from school. I couldn't do it that way. I would go up in the evening when* [a relative] *could mind her for me. Parking was £3 each visit; so it was working out on average about £20 a week. I borrowed, like a lump sum off my Mum which I'm paying back now.*
>
> Emma

Liz also had to manage regular hospital visits on top of the pressure to be in work.

> *With* [her son], *he's got arthritis, so I've got a lot of hospital appointments with him and that costs; going up to Alder Hey hospital and stuff. We have to get the bus and then we'll wait; and if you're waiting and you've got an appointment,*

and the bus doesn't come, it's like £10 in a taxi up there; and it's like 'Oh God'. But it's something that I've got to do, because he's got to be seen and he's got to be up-to-date with his consultations and things. After that I know he's going to be sick for two or three days; but I'm expected to be back in work the next day, so he's going to have to go to my Mum and Dad.

Liz

The main reason Carol and Ric paid to run a car was to manage the routine of hospital visits for their children.

We've got a car. It is essential at the moment, for getting [their daughter] *around more than anything, because her health is not great either. She's asthmatic but she's also had a chest infection that will not go away for the last two years; so she's under Alder Hey. We're there nearly every week and she's just in and out of hospital like that, basically. My son* [...] *has got health problems as well. He suffers a lot from anxiety, so sometimes he has vomiting issues and things like that. We're going backwards and forwards to Alder Hey.*

Carol

One of Eileen's children had developed asthma, and she was having to work hard to make sure that the home environment was free of dust.

I'm washing a lot more; changing his bed every other day instead of once a week. He's developed severe hay-fever and asthma. So I said to the consultant 'I just need to know why, with a perfectly healthy thirteen year-old?' He's got a brown inhaler of a morning, and of a night. He's got to carry the blue one around and he probably uses it twice a day; and he's on antihistamines twice a day, so it's really bad. That's another big thing that's happened since February. And it put a bit of a jinx through me to be perfectly honest. That's a lot onto my electric. The electricity has gone up fourfold.

Eileen

Eileen also had worries about her daughter, who was trying to help with the family finances on top of school work.

She worked every Saturday and Sunday for about eighteen months in town, and it became far too much for her. She was going out of the door early hours, seven days a week. Her school work suffered a bit. To be fair she got a bit depressed. I had to take her the doctors as she was under too much pressure; and the doctor said 'Maybe the job is too much with all the school work'. So that stopped. And I did explain to her that I just wouldn't have the money to give to her. She doesn't go out much; she's a very good girl. I'm lucky.

Eileen

One of Nick's and Cath's children was autistic and could be violent and aggressive. Cath was conscious of the increasing pressure she had been under. Coping with the school summer holidays and not being able to have a family holiday together had been particularly upsetting.

> *So, I do struggle, really struggle, to find something suitable. So most of the time we split up* [for holidays]. *It's hugely stressful; more than usual compared to the average family. And all of us going away together? We can't actually afford that type of holiday.*
>
> Cath

A healthy diet

At least four of the families had been using foodbanks over the course of the year. Grace was too embarrassed to talk about it at length, but did explain that she had resorted to them when she'd fallen into arrears with her rent. Sian had serious debts and was having to make use of a foodbank when there was no alternative. Denise and Carol also both briefly talked about when they had used a foodbank.

> *I have struggled. Getting foodbanks for myself for my children, and I'm a worker. I shouldn't have to do that, but sometimes I struggle that much I have to. It's hard.*
>
> Denise

> *Well, every now and then, as I've said, I rely on the foodbank. But I still find, well, I'm just going to have to go to one of them. It does help, it's a meal.*
>
> Carol

Amber found providing her children with a healthy diet to be real challenge.

> *Obviously the price of food now is just outrageous; to feed a family, you know, on a healthy diet. Not only that, my son has autism so he will only eat certain foods. So I'm having to have a separate shopping budget for him.*
>
> Amber

There were some weeks when she could barely afford even the basics, and had to cut back on fresh fruit and vegetables.

> *Beans, spaghetti, and we will just have beans-on-toast, noodles, small little teas you know. I'd literally just go to the* [well-known supermarket] *and*

spend about £15 and just get nuggets and chips. I don't cut out fruit-and-veg completely during that week; only when I can't afford it. It's literally a bag of cornflakes. It's all 'smart price' and it will literally be cornflakes and bread.

Amber

Phoebe was spending over fifteen percent of the family income on food. The cost of fresh food was too high for the family budget and she found she was having to buy more frozen food, which wasn't good for the children's health.

I've always tried to give them healthy fresh food; whereas now I'm thinking 'Oh, God'. So I'm buying more frozen stuff. I've noticed the difference in them because they never used to get sick. Now all of a sudden, they're catching every cough and cold. And it's just horrendous, the price of the shopping that's coming and it's, as I say, it's just too much. But it's a case of 'the kids eat fresh and I'll eat a pack of noodles'. As long as they're eating healthy, that's my priority. That's why I do get sick all the time; that's why I mustn't lose weight. Then I get even more sick, because I can't afford to eat healthy.

Phoebe

Grace's spending on food was nearly thirteen percent of the family income. She had been buying a lot less meat because of the expense, and was avoiding ready meals.

I did buy the really cheap stuff once, but it was disgusting. But what can you do? And I cook all my food from scratch. I don't buy all ready-meals. The only thing they have that's bad is once every couple of weeks, they'd have a pizza; and one of them doesn't eat that because he's allergic to dairy. I used to buy the cheap noodles, but then I found out they're really bad for you; so now I just get the plain egg noodles. They're dearer, and I put a bit of soup in.

Grace

Carol's own health problems meant that eating a correct diet was a priority. But it was something she was struggling to do. The family were spending over seventeen percent of their income on food.

Every time you go the supermarket prices are going up, and going up before your eyes. And I do have to shop around and basically get the cheapest of everything; and I check everything on the shelves. I just have to get the cheapest. That's all I can afford.

Carol

The loss of Child Benefit has caused Eileen to cut back on her food budget. Over the course of the year she had still spent over fifteen percent of her income on food.

> *I've definitely noted I am spending a little less on food because I can't afford as much as I could. I try to do the fresh veg and meat thing once a week, but it doesn't always work out like that. I'm spending less on food now than at the beginning of the year. But that's because my money has gone down with* [her daughter] *leaving school. I'm losing benefits I was getting for* [her daughter].
>
> Eileen

The NHS—free at the point of use?

The cost of prescriptions, dental work and optician's costs can be significant for families in working poverty. Financial problems can and do lead to people neglecting their own health. As we have seen, concerns about the health of family members in many cases were adding to the anxiety and stress caused by money worries.

Phoebe had been in poor health for a number of years and should have been taking various medications for serious health issues. However, she couldn't afford the prescription pre-payment plan and so was either getting pain killers from family and friends, or going without entirely. The prescription for her eyesight had also changed and she'd had to find the money for new glasses.

> *The likes of prescriptions; I've had really bad health over the last five years and it's a case of 'I can't get my tablets', so I've had to stop taking them because we can't afford the prescription. So even getting the yearly one, we literally can't afford it. Since I went back to work, I've actually been getting prescriptions every month; well trying to get them every month. Sometimes I leave the painkillers off. I was getting to the point where wrong thoughts were coming in: like I didn't want to cook; didn't want to go out. I do work full-time. I get exhausted and I end up collapsing anyway. I just don't see a way out unless I get another part-time job of a weekend.*
>
> Phoebe

One of Phoebe's and Gavin's children had developed bad eczema and the medication prescribed by the family doctor hadn't worked. Phoebe had asked the doctor for a different treatment which a friend had introduced her to; but had been disappointed.

> *I took him to the doctors and asked for it, and got told 'We don't prescribe that because it's too expensive'. I said 'Are you messing? He's ten years of age and if it is something that actually works, why can't we have it?' We argued and argued with them, but they wouldn't give it us because it costs them too much. I was fuming over it. He was upset as well. It took my friend to go back to her doctor's to get this tape and she gave it me. Otherwise it is £30 odd to buy.*
>
> Phoebe

Janet was aware of the anomalies in prescription charges around the UK, and the difficulties involved in paying them.

> *When are we going to get free prescriptions as well? Scotland do it, Wales do it, any chance that we can? Wales have had it for years haven't they? They don't have to pay for theirs. I'm lucky enough that I don't have to pay because I'm on Working Families Tax Credit. That's why I don't pay for my prescriptions. But if you're not, then you're snookered aren't you? I think it's about nine pound something. It's bad, isn't it? That's for everything that you're getting, every prescription that you get. I've got a friend over the road and his wife's really poorly at the moment, and she has to get six or seven items every month. That's like £60, that's terrible.*
>
> Janet

Carol had given up her job up due to illness and was continuing to have health problems. However, her entitlement to free prescriptions was about to run out due to an improvement in one of her multiple long-term conditions.

> *I'll no longer be eligible for my free prescriptions and I do have quite a lot of health problems and numerous deficiencies. So I have God knows know many items each month on prescription and, again, I don't know how I'm going to pay for them once the free prescription runs out.*
>
> Carol

Both Grace and Liam had suffered poor health. Although they could get free prescriptions for their four children for minor ailments, Grace said she would rather pay over the counter even though family finances were very difficult. She explained why.

> *Well, honestly, I don't know how we manage. It cost me the other week £25 for prescriptions. Me and my partner have to pay, but it's something that could go on gas or electric. Cost-of-living just keeps going up, doesn't it? But his wages*

don't keep going up. I never want anyone to think I won't make an appointment for my kids to get them medicine; but I buy the medicine over the counter. I don't go to the doctor and say 'He needs Calpol', I don't. I go and buy it. I use that 'Care in the Chemists'. But I just get like you feel like you're begging for stuff; and I'm just not into that. I'd rather just pay for it.

Grace

Grace and Liam had also been through a fight to get their youngest child diagnosed with a speech impediment. They'd had a similar experience with their eldest child and thought it made a difference if you can pay.

It's like with his speech. I've had to fight all the way. His speech isn't clear, and I've waited since last year and it's infuriating. Like if you've got money you'll get seen. If you blend in the background like my eldest son, all the way through I've had to fight for him to get proper tests to see what learning disabilities he's got. They just said now 'He's dyslexic'.

Grace

The cost of dental care was also a significant expense. Karolina talked about this problem.

So I went to the dentist and I've asked if he would have to pay, and she said '£18 for a test and then about £33 to take it off' [remove part of a broken tooth]. *So it's like for £50 to take it; only a tiny bit of tooth; but it's still £50.*

Karolina

Pressure on relationships

Most of the families described the ways in which financial difficulties put pressure on their relationships. When long hours of overtime are needed to pay the bills, there is even more strain, as Karolina explained.

I was complaining, moaning to him about him working a lot and I'm always on my own. When he comes back after working eleven hours he just wants to sit down quiet. I'm on my own and so I'm talking and talking and talking. Sometimes we have an argument about that. I said to him 'If we could just have two days to take [her daughter] *somewhere, or just stay in the house.*

Karolina

It was much the same for Phoebe and Gavin.

We used to get out once a month and make time for ourselves, but we can't do that. He's working longer hours. We don't see each other; and then we are arguing all the time. The stress of Christmas means it's going to come to a head. We literally cannot afford to carry on like this.

Phoebe

For many years Phoebe and Gavin had not lived together. Phoebe explained that financially they were better-off when that was the case, although she also felt it was important for the children that they live together. She was now thinking that it might be better to go back to a previous arrangement when he had just stayed twice a week at the family home. This was something she has seen other couples do.

I know loads now; they've actually split up. They still go out, but they don't live together. They've both got the separate houses. They go out with the kids; they do everything with the kids. They just don't live together. They've got their house, or the fellas have moved back home to their Mum and Dad's. They're better-off; they just come and stay now and then. It's tearing families apart because no one can handle it, no one can.

Gavin

Phil and Dot had experienced the same difficulties.

We actually split up one time because of it, and when we did split up we found that we were actually better-off, when we split up. That wasn't last year, but the year before. We lived separately. I went into a room accommodation, like a hostel type of thing; she stayed in the house. She was able to claim then, her Housing Benefit and whatever else and tax credits, Council Tax benefit; she was getting a lot of help with that. We were a lot better-off. I would say we were apart for about nine months. Then we realised that, there's more than the money at the end of the day, you know. When we were with each other then, there was so much happening at that time and, as I say, we've got back together. And the first thing that's gone is the tax credits. When they heard we were back together everything got stopped.

Phil

The fact that Mark couldn't find work was causing arguments between him and Ruth. She had been trying to hide the pressure she was feeling, but it wasn't working.

When you are more stressed out about money it comes out in the family and people pick it up. My partner picks up on it all the time: 'You are stressed'. He can see it. I can see him stressed as well. So, I have sort of put a mask on, because I don't want to put my stress on to him.

Ruth

Brenda's partner hadn't been able to get work either, and this was one of the reasons they weren't living together and always argued about money. The arrival of their new baby had brought things to a head.

> *Things are not going to change with me and the kids' Dad. That's getting worse. We can't even talk to each other. Any time we are together, we are at each other's throats. I'm saying 'You are not doing this' and he's going 'Leave me alone, stop moaning'. When anything happened it always fell to me. I was the one who paid for everything; sorted everything out. I was out at work while he was in the house with the kids. If I came home from work and the place was a mess I'd be saying 'What have you been doing all day?' We are still in the same situation. He's not better-off financially. It is a big part of it. He said 'Let me, be me'. He wanted me to apologise because one day I just exploded. I'd worked ten shifts back-to-back. Next thing he just walked out and it just carried on from there.* [If he had a job] *I would stop saying 'You are not giving the kids a future'. He's just surviving and has been for a long time.*
>
> Brenda

Another of the mothers[23] wasn't living with the father of her children anymore because she felt he wasn't responsible enough with money. She was also aware of how it would affect her financial position if he did live with them.

> *Well, for financial reasons I can't live with him because he's not very sensible with the money. So I've got the kids to think about really; they come first. I'd lose a lot of money if he moved back in anyway; and I don't trust him enough to be wise enough with what he does get. He does work, but he's not very sensible. So, it's not fair on the kids, to be honest. Obviously, I still love him because it's gone on for years and years and years. But I think until he grows up—he's 35—and unless he grows up, I can't* [be with him]. *I'd lose a lot of money if he moves back in anyway.*

Sam had recently separated from her husband. She didn't feel it was particularly due to financial pressures. However, she was aware of how money worries can lead to couples separating. The sudden change in her own situation illustrated some of the difficult consequences of separation for parents forced onto benefits.

> *So I went from living in a house when we were on a low wage and living with my husband and two children. I've actually had to move, and me and the two*

23 A request was made not to attribute this comment, even using a different name.

children are now in rented accommodation. I have had to put in a claim. I'm on income support and I've got my tax credits and my Child Benefit and everything. So it's sort of, it's hard for me, because I'm having to deal with money. I was used to not dealing with claiming benefits.

Sam

Reliance on family

Parents, brothers and sisters and extended family were a vital source of help to the families. This spanned from emotional support to financial assistance and practical help, and especially child-care. The difference that having a family makes is something that Joy really appreciated.

I just do find it a struggle, and obviously there must be people worse off than me as well who must find it even harder. And I think it must lead to other problems; if people can't get money or don't have family who can help. I mean, I've been quite lucky that my Mum and Dad can help me. Not that I like to ask, but sometimes there's no other option, and I have to ask.

Joy

Denise's feelings about having to get financial help from her parents was typical of what many of the families felt on this issue.

They do; they do help me a lot. Like my Mum and my Dad help me quite a lot. But sometimes I'm like a let-down when I can't give it them back. And they're like, 'Why? Why? Why?' And it's because I've got to pay for this, and pay for that, and it gets me down that I can't pay them back. I wish I could, but then I haven't got any spare to give them back. My Mum's very good. She's always coming round with a bag of shopping or stuff for the kids. But she's a pensioner; it shouldn't be like that. It should be the other way 'round. I should be going 'round taking stuff 'round to hers.

Denise

Gaynor felt much the same way.

My Mum gave me some money; me and my sister and brothers; some money to get a start on Christmas. But really it shouldn't be down to my Mum. It should be down to myself really. Oh my Mum's wonderful; she's my little guardian angel. But she shouldn't be; like she's getting on now; a pensioner.

Gaynor

Amy's father used to help by taking out loans on her behalf. Since his death, her mother hadn't been able to help financially. However, she did help in other ways.

> *She's in a worse situation than me I think, but she has borrowed for me in her name. I've got a catalogue in her name. I don't know if it's a good thing or a bad thing. But it's helping me out. I mean obviously I pay it. She only works part-time. She's sixty this year. She works as a cleaner, but she's got osteoarthritis and she can't get any benefit top-ups or anything; so she struggles. Occasionally, she will help out with babysitting.*
>
> Amy

Ric and Carol were finding that they needed to rely on both sets of parents. Ric's parents were helping by buying groceries for the family; Carol was borrowing money regularly from her parents, who were pensioners. They had help with other things also.

> *I don't know what I'd do without my Dad quite honestly. I just, well my Mum and my Dad, I borrow off them every month; and the guilt that goes with it! I'd love a new suite, even down to things like bedding and towels; all those sort of things. I just haven't got the money to go out and buy all that stuff new. So I feel like I just live off hand-me-downs basically, still. Rapidly approaching fifty and still living off hand-me-downs from my Mum and Dad and Ric's Mum and Dad. It's like I still don't feel like we're self-sufficient.*
>
> Carol

Feeling guilty about asking for help was a common experience, as Colette described.

> *I try not to, and I absolutely hate asking for anything, you know what I mean. But last week I had to borrow £40 off my Mum for her* [daughter's] *birthday. I will give it back to Mum today; but I absolutely hate it. As long as I have got enough food in for them, I will go without rather than ask.*
>
> Colette

Sue came from a large family. However, many of the family members were themselves in financial difficulties. She felt guilty asking her father for help.

> *Well I do feel guilty, because my Dad's getting on you know. I did ask him and he said 'Look, I've just lent to this one and that one; but I will be there for you in a real emergency. But for now try and do it yourself'.*
>
> Sue

Brenda estimated that over the years she must have borrowed thousands of pounds from her mother, given the number of times she'd had to ask. In fact, she didn't always have to ask for help; it was often just volunteered.

> *I've been doing as much as I can. Sometimes if she goes shopping she'll buy the kids clothes or she'll buy the food, and I'll go 'Are you sure, Mum?' And she'll go, 'Yeah'. The kids' uniforms cost me; it cost £300. But my Mum paid £100 of it. When we got to the till she's thrown her card in and I've gone 'Are you sure, Mum?' And she's like', Yeah'. You don't get anything for school uniforms anymore; and* [her son] *is a size ten in shoes. So his shoes are like £60-£70. It's non-stop isn't it? Constantly.*
>
> Brenda

Cath's mother also helped with shopping for clothes for the children.

> *I'm very fortunate, I've got a wonderful mother. She doesn't buy shoes, but she'll buy some clothes quite regularly. Several times a year she'll buy them clothes, and she'll pay for a meal out, and without that I would struggle even more. Not everyone's in that position; not everyone is that lucky.*
>
> Cath

Like many of the parents, Karolina was taking up a friend's offer of help on a regular basis with child-care. She said she would feel differently if it was her mother she was asking. Her mother however, lived in Poland.

> *I think it's very nice of her; but I wouldn't ask for help. I would rather she say 'No, I can't help', because I don't think it's right asking people. I don't think it's right to drop your child to a friend to go to work, even if she's only there for two hours because Micha is then going to pick her up. But no, I don't really want to do it, not every Friday. But say if my Mum was here, I'd have no problem.*
>
> Karolina

Since Ali had been made redundant, he and Rabia had been having to manage on the irregular work he was getting in a fast-food outlet. As a result, they struggled and Rabia's family weren't in a position to help financially.

> *No, because my Mum is on a pension herself and my brothers and sisters, they struggle themselves. It's hard, even for the ones that work.*
>
> Rabia

Helping with child-care was often the most practical form of support that the wider family was able to provide. As Ruth put it:

> *She* [her mother] *takes my son to school for me; things like that, all sorts. She will cook a leg of lamb and give it to me to take home. She is great. Yeah, I don't want to exploit her, and I am conscious of that. Do you know what I mean?*
>
> Ruth

Emma's mother was there to look after her children if they were ill.

> *My Mum, she helps out a lot if* [her daughter] *is off sick and I have to go to work, she'll look after her.*
>
> Emma

Brenda stressed the importance of social support and the fact that, even though she didn't live with her partner any more, he was there to look after the children.

> *I think social support is really, really important. I couldn't afford to do child-care. Because it's shift work, sometimes I have to be in at 6 am. So I rely on the children's Dad to have them in the morning, and pick them up from school and just be there with them. He doesn't do as good a job as I do, but he's there; they're safe, so, yeah, I think it's really, really important. If I didn't have him and my Mum, my sisters, I'd be really buggered.*
>
> Brenda

Luke and Minnie had been relying on Luke's parents for help with child-care.

> *I really rely on my grandparents, because my wife, she's only got two hands, so two babies is a bit heavy. They're both really small at the moment, so we quite rely on my grandparents. They give a hand during the terms, but we try to really be independent on the financial side; so, we don't ask for any money from them. They are retired; they've got more time than we have. Because we can't afford the full amount when the children go to nursery, if both of us are working. We've negotiated with my parents. They are happy to help us out three days a week and then we put the kids in the nursery for two days, and then we still have to look after them over the weekend. That's what the family plan is after Christmas.*
>
> Luke

Living in a shared house with her parents meant that Fiona did have ongoing support and child-care.

> *My Mum's fantastic. She supports us, not quite financially* [...] *and my Dad watches the baby once a week. It's good to have them. I couldn't see my way out of a low income without that family support.*
>
> Fiona

Support from ex-partners

The difficulties faced by lone parents struggling with sole responsibility for their children, were exacerbated where their ex-partners were not providing any support. In some cases, they also had to carry responsibility for debts that had been taken on before the separation. This was Amy's situation and her ex-partner couldn't make any financial contribution to the family, only picking the children up from school twice a week because of the long hours he was working.

> *Most of the bills and the debts were all in my name, because when we first registered I was the first person on the tenancy agreement. So I got stuck with all the debt. It was all left to me. That was, I think, at the time I had to go to court, not long after we split up, because I was getting evicted from the house. I thought he'd been going to the meetings and stuff like that to make arrangements because there were rent arrears. The arrears were £3,500, nearly £4,000 at the time. I thought he was dealing with it, and then I found out he never* [did]. *So I had to go to court and make arrangements to pay it, which I've paid off.*
>
> Amy

Janet was in a similar situation, but with even more debt.

> *I'm completely blacklisted. He's left me about twenty grand's worth of debt. Just all the Visa bills and all that stuff. So it was all left to me because it was all in my name. So I'm completely blacklisted. So I've got nothing like that; no back up at all. I've never taken a loan out; maybe a good few years ago in my other place. That was completely paid off. I'm still paying all of that back. He can walk away scot free. It's all in my name. I don't know how long that's going to take to pay off, probably ten years or something.*
>
> Janet

Social life

Going for a meal as a couple or for a drink with friends was seen by all the families as a luxury, and something that had to be calculated against other bills or expenses. Grace and Liam didn't drink alcohol and said if they did have any money spare, it would always go towards paying a utility bill or buying shoes.

> *We can't; we've never been out. We've been together fourteen years and since we've had the kids, we've never in eleven years, we've never been out. If you go on a family trip, that costs us about £100. We went to Chester Zoo that cost us £100, plus our travelling which was £30. That's a week's shopping just for a day out.*
>
> Grace

As money had become tighter, Phil and Dot had increasingly cut back on their social life.

> *I've packed in the cigarettes, which is a good thing probably. We used to enjoy a glass of wine at the weekends; but we can't do that anymore. It's just like pleasurable things that we used to be able to do; they've all gone. Even, like, we used to be able to go out at the weekends; we used to be able to visit somewhere. You had £30–40 over, so you could put a bit of petrol in for the distance to go somewhere. But you can't even do that now.*
>
> Dot

It was a similar story for many of the other families. As Ruth put it:

> *Socially, going out and things, I have not been out for ages because we've got no money basically to go out now.*
>
> Ruth

Other couples never went out and relied entirely upon the television as their sole source of entertainment. Some families had internet-television packages. These were often the main source of entertainment for families, and compensated for a social life to some degree.

Some of the families also saw the fixed costs of a television package as one means by which they could keep control of their spending on recreation and leisure time.

> *I don't really go out, not really. I mean, I go out, I take Luke out. But I don't actually go out in the evening or socialise. My Mum will babysit;* [two relatives] *are really*

good. But then I think, well if it's going to cost me £40 to do something, I'd rather spend that on my shopping or my Visa card or things like that. I just watch the TV. We've got Sky; that's within the phone bill. I think its £45 a month. It's just so I don't get overdrawn with the bank, because then you have to pay bank charges.

Emma

Liz explained that she would sooner spend money on her child than go out for an evening.

To be honest, most of my money goes on him. It's not like I go out drinking every weekend or anything like that, because it's just not an option. It wouldn't be an option, even if I did have the money. I can go out for someone's birthday; but I still have to budget and make sure I've got the money for everything else.

Liz

Having friends who could afford to go out was a cause of social embarrassment for people like Carol and Ric.

Ric hasn't heard from his friend from a while and he's thinking 'He's fallen out with me'; but it's because every time he phoned him it was 'Come for a drink, come for a drink'. And he can't. He says 'I think he's got to the point where he's that pissed off with me he doesn't phone anymore'. The same myself, I haven't been out for months; months! People go 'What's up with you?' You're being antisocial' and you go 'Oh yeah, I haven't been in the mood lately', or whatever. Because you don't want to turn round and constantly go 'I'm skint', you know what I mean'. It's embarrassing as well, because you almost feel like you're inadequate because you can't do those things.

Carol

Holidays

Holidays were an expense that all of the families struggled to meet. Whilst the parents could have time off work, stay-at-home holidays were the norm and involved having low-cost days out, as Rabia explained.

We can't afford holidays. We can't afford certain things like cars. It's just struggling. I just think as long as they [the children] *get fed and they go to school and have an education, you know? We haven't been on holiday since before I had kids* [seven years]. *The places where I have taken them are just to the park and places like that.*

Rabia

Jenny also struggled to afford holidays.

> *It's a lot more stressful, like when it comes to taking the baby on days out and things like that in the summer. When she is off school obviously you want to do something with them. Money, the way it is, it's going to be very tight at the minute. When she's coming home we are staying in because it's so cold. But when it gets warmer we just go to the park. There's like a Sure Start we go to. We go swimming there once a week. It's only £2.50 to go in the swimming baths for an hour. So I take her there and do things like that. Even if it's just like going to my Mum's or my mates coming down with their children.*
>
> Jenny

In the same way Colette did things over the school holidays that wouldn't cost anything.

> *I'd love to take them on holiday. We sort of choose to go to the park rather than a play centre where you have got to pay. You know what I mean. We obviously go for the cheaper options all the time. Every now and then you'd love to just splash out. But at the end of the day things like that aren't really important. It's just about spending time together isn't it?*
>
> Colette

Ruth described how not having money for family holidays affected her.

> *Sometimes it makes me feel, how can I put it? I don't really know how to explain it. I don't feel I am able to express it, you know. Like, I have not got the funds to be able to do what I would like to be able to do at the moment. You know, when people are saying to me 'I am booking a holiday' and 'I am going here, there and everywhere'. I do feel a tinge of jealousy towards them. I want to go away. I want to go on holiday with my kids. I want to do that as well, you know. It is just a case of, right now, we have not got the money and that's it.*
>
> Ruth

Joy didn't see any prospect of being able to save enough to afford a holiday.

> *No, never any savings or anything. I wanted to save for me and my daughter to go away on holiday. But there's just nothing at the end of the month to save, to put away.*
>
> Joy

Parents often felt guilty about being unable to afford to take their children away on holiday. Phoebe hadn't had a break away with the children for four years.

> *My brother, he said to me last week 'I've got a caravan for a few days, do you want to come up with the kids?' And we had to say 'No', because I didn't have any money; and he said 'Well, I'll pay for you'. And I said 'No, I don't want that, because I still want at least a bit of money in my own pocket'. So I felt guilty about that, because I feel like the kids have missed out because I haven't got the money to take them. It's hard now because they're seeing all their friends going on holiday and they're like 'Mum when can we go on holiday?' And I'm like 'Argh, the twelfth-of-never, the way it's going'.*
>
> Phoebe

Eileen had similar feelings of guilt, but also considered herself lucky to have children who understood the situation.

> *As a family we've never been on holiday. They understand; they're good kids. It's not a case that I don't want to take them; it's just a case that I can't. I don't know many families that don't go on holiday.*
>
> Eileen

Being a self-employed cleaner meant that Emma wasn't paid for time off work. Holidays therefore represented an even more significant cost. She had to rely on help from her family.

> *I can't afford it. So it sounds horrible, but it depends if my Mum can pay for us to go. But then it gets my Mum away as well. But it just depends on what she can afford. I have got relatives; but I don't go to visit them. Because if I don't go to work, I don't get paid. I don't work weekends, so I can take them then. But if I take a week off, I won't get paid for that week.*
>
> Emma

A child recently moving school and the cost of the new school uniform, had made a family holiday out of the question for Phil and Dot.

> *Because* [their son]*'s going into senior school now, we've got expenses there. Uniforms; things like that. Rather than going and spending all the money on holidays, what we're going to have to do is save up for a school uniform.*
>
> Dot

Denise hadn't been able to afford a holiday the previous year and wasn't sure how she was going to manage one in the near future.

> *We didn't have a holiday last year because my little boy had his holy communion. We normally go to Butlins, but there's quite a lot of us and we have to have two chalets. You can get four or five in one chalet, but six? Know what I mean?*
>
> Denise

Occupying the children during the school holidays is a challenge for most families, but it's that much more difficult when money is short. Terri had plans for keeping the children occupied.

> *Well, I have told them. The first two weeks we are doing bedrooms and moving them into my room; and they are going to share. I said to them 'I will paint and decorate it for you'; budgeted for that. I reckon £50 will get paint and stuff for their room. So that's one thing that will keep us occupied for a fortnight. So we will do that. Then other than that, it's my Mum's or we will go to the museum or days out. I am not too worried about it and I have got Sky which is the best thing. They will just watch films; and the other one likes reading.*
>
> Terri

Planning the school summer holidays for the parents included thinking about how to save money and avoid costs. As Grace explained:

> *I take drinks and food with me most of the time; but its hard work having to carry everything. We go on day trips; try and go to the beach. We try to do things that are as cheap as possible and stay away from fairs and things where they just want to take your money. But we're going to see 'The Giants'*[24] *which is going to cost me a fortune. Then maybe on week three we're going to try and do camping in a tent; see how we go there. Last year the school donated a holiday to us which was nice. I mean we did feel like paupers; but it was nice, we'd never been away.*
>
> Grace

Denise dearly wanted to take the children on a foreign holiday one day. In reality however, she wasn't sure that she would be able to take the children away at all. She found it very difficult to put any money aside for anything but the basics.

> *Don't really have any money left by the end of the week or the end of the month. I've just got to budget all the time; make sure I've got money to put away to do something; especially, like, they're on half term next week, you know. You've got to find the money then, to do things with them. Sometimes, I just haven't got it so it is hard, you know. It's just hard, very hard.*
>
> Denise

Luke and Minnie wanted to take their new baby to Luke's parents. However the grandparents didn't live in Britain. Luke and Minnie couldn't afford even a cheap holiday in the UK. The cost of going abroad was completely beyond them.

---

24 Free street entertainment, but with cost of travel into town.

After the baby, we can't afford to go on holiday; and also my wife cannot make money; so the income has certainly dropped. Also the mortgage, we only rely on my own wage, so that's a lot, in the last couple of years.

Luke

Thinking of others

Most of the families, in one way or another, expressed awareness that there were people worse off than themselves. Contributing something to help others can be important for seeing oneself as an active member of society. So, even though they struggled to manage themselves, some of the families nonetheless gave to charity.

Yes, I do give to charity. I give to the Salvation Army. When I was homeless I would have been in serious trouble without them. £19 at Christmas for the gloves and that, and then I give them £10 a month. I know you might say 'It's ridiculous', but to be fair they do help, and my heart breaks for anyone who's on the streets in this weather.

Eileen

Similarly, Karolina gave to homeless people. Luke and Minnie also regularly gave to charity. So too, did Amy.

I sponsor Children's Miracle and Radio City Cash for kids. I give them £5 a month. I used to sponsor Macmillan, but I had to stop. That one was £10, and at the time I was also doing the Cash for Kids and the British Heart Foundation; £5 a month. I've cut it down now.

Amy

Conclusion

Whilst 'the job' is often stressful for those on low pay, security of home and personal and family life can be a compensating and stabilising factor that protects against the strains of working life. Where this is not the case, home insecurity hugely exacerbates those strains. For these families, it was not the case. As we have seen, the families were typically renting their homes and many had stories to tell of negligent landlords, arbitrary evictions, and poor housing conditions. As with the world of work, deregulation played its role in these stories, with landlords finding it relatively easy to evict their tenants without any social accountability, as well as poor enforcement of landlord obligations with respect to repairs and the eradication of damp and mould in the property.

Other problems that were linked to housing included the difficulty of meeting the up-front costs of moving into unfurnished premises, the pernicious effects of the 'bedroom tax' and the loss of community resources in the neighbourhood. The combinations of these and other issues arising from the historic loss of social housing as an option for those living on low incomes was leading to severe detrimental effects for the families.

On top of struggling to achieve home stability come the myriad challenges of family life. Across all the family interviews, one challenge stood out from the rest as a consistent financial pressure: the costs of raising children. One aspect of this was that these costs are not static; rather they change with the children themselves. A sudden growth spurt for instance can within a month or two mean that an entire wardrobe needs to be replaced. Once the teenage years begin, peer pressure and fashion trends come into play. School uniforms, school trips and projects that have to be paid for add to the list. Christmas brings its own depressingly regular annual burden. All parents and carers will be familiar with this list. However, for parents living on the lowest incomes, these costs bring pressures upon the weekly, monthly and annual budgets that can push family finances out of control.

Maintaining a 'healthy family' also presented a major challenge. A healthy diet takes planning if the adults who are working have long hours and are juggling jobs; and is more expensive where money is already tight. We have seen here, cases of parents only themselves eating after their children have eaten a substantial meal, making do with what is left. This resonates with the experience of some of the families Daly and Kelly (2015) interviewed during their Belfast research.[25] Healthy activities for children also bring their own costs. When children get sick the impact upon family life is huge, with working parents and carers having to take time off work with a loss of hours.

Anxiety and depression had come to define daily life for many of the families. Several participants in the study described feelings of embarrassment about having to look to relatives for help. One

25 Daly, M. and Kelly, G. (2015), p. 30.

consequence of living on a low income is social isolation. Going out with friends or even just as a couple, was seen by all the families as being a luxury; something that was simply out of the question, certainly at any time soon. Emma for example, talked about having nothing to look forward to. In these circumstances, it is no great surprise that alongside of (and linked to) insecure employment and rental status, mental health problems were a part of the family story in many cases.

PART III

JUST MANAGING? PERSPECTIVES ON POVERTY

7. Family Views: 'Who's to Blame?'

Throughout the testimonies that have been reported in this work, there were consistent themes of struggle, of constant effort to avoid 'going under' and sometimes of exhaustion. However, there were also moving examples of determination, of overcoming the difficulties faced and of a belief in the future, come what may. There were also notes of questioning and criticism of a society that inflicts such challenges upon people who in the end simply want happy and fulfilled lives, free of worry and stress, for themselves and for their children. Although there were many opinions offered that were political in nature, none of the family members identified themselves as 'political' in the sense of party affiliation or activist orientations. However, many of the comments made along these lines resonated with the *zeitgeist* of opposition and social critique that had emerged around the issues covered in the interviews.

The sense of social injustice conveyed in many of the interviews often focused upon income inequality. The UK has one of the most unequal distributions of wealth by income of all the industrially developed economies. In 2017, those in the bottom income decile of the population had an average annual net income of £9,277. Those in the top income decile had more than nine times that (£83,897). The polarisation of wealth in British society has been dramatic over the last two decades. The distribution, assessed in broad terms, has seen a huge shift towards the highest income holders, a relatively unchanged picture for those in

 https://doi.org/10.11647/OBP.0112.07

the middle strata of the income spectrum and a marked reduction for those at the bottom.[1]

The point was not lost on many of the families, that with each successive budget the government bias towards business and the 'already wealthy', and against the poor was proven once again. So whilst they struggled from week to week against a backdrop of cuts to the services upon which they relied, and new costs resulting from the loss of many of those services, businesses in the UK had enjoyed repeated reductions in Corporation Tax as it fell from 28 percent to 24 percent in April 2013, and then to 21 percent in April 2014; the lowest in the western world. In the March 2016 budget it was reduced once more to seventeen percent. At the same time and relatedly, high profile news stories had emerged of major companies such as Starbucks, Vodafone and Google having paid negligible amounts of tax, despite huge profit levels.

It was no surprise then that many times families expressed the view that the government was hopelessly out of touch with the life experience of those on low incomes. More than this however, a sharp sense of unfairness was clear in what participants had to say about the causes of the difficulties they faced.

This is what they said.

On politicians

They're cutting everything, but not their own wages; disgusting. But they get all their expenses paid for don't they? Why doesn't the normal Joe Blogs get their expenses paid? My partner pays £15.50 a week and he can't get that back in expenses. We're supposed to live on so much. How come they can, say like, when they're earning say £60K, and they're still claiming expenses for the house and the mortgage and when they've got a house somewhere else. You only need one house, surely. You don't need any more. It's pure greed, pure greed.

Grace

It sickens me and saddens me, that they've [politicians] *never known what it's like to come home from school and nothing be in for tea. They've never known what it's like to have holes at the bottom of their shoes. I did. I'm not saying kids*

1 Equality Trust (2017), 'The Scale of Economic Inequality in the UK', https://www.equalitytrust.org.uk/scale-economic-inequality-uk

should live like that because mine certainly do not. What I'm saying is, they've had everything handed to them, including top of the range education; and they take it all away from our young people and it just saddens me. It upsets me and, as I say, I'm trying to remain completely polite.

Eileen

On social class

Well, I think there is a class thing. They think if you are working class then you're not educated or you're thick. You do get that day-to-day. I've worked in a hotel and you get some people coming in and they think you're stupid; but I'm not illiterate. I might sound common to you. Just because I've got a slight accent doesn't mean I go home and sit in a pile of poo. My house is spotless, but you know how people come across. They do think they're better than you. I would never treat anybody any different; whether you're a cleaner or a doctor. I want to treat people all on the same level. I say that to all my children; that you treat everyone the same. If they give you respect, you give respect back. But I do think there is a class issue. I think that people who do have money think they're better. They probably have had better education, that's why I fight for all my children.

Grace

I think it varies depending on the people. I think there are things you're certainly excluded from if you haven't got money or access to people with money. Nobody really knows your exact financial situation, but only what they can see; like the symptoms of it. I suppose, but yeah, people make judgements don't they?

Fiona

They look down their nose at you and they're like 'What do you mean you can't afford that?' And you're like 'I can't afford it'. 'What you're not going away again?' The poor kids'. And it is horrible: 'Budget your money better?' How can we budget? You know what I mean?

Phoebe

Because it is a class thing; people who've got the money seem to be able to pay for whatever they want. They can pay for the best education; the best. Obviously, everyone has got opportunities, and everyone's entitled to an education. But it's the standard of your education, isn't it?

Liz

Sad to say, but where you are born and education, you know [limit one's life] [...] *if you are in a deprived area. They are just taking everything from the working class, aren't they?*

Sue

I think it's all about money; everywhere that you go; everything that you do. If you haven't got money, there's no life. Class as well. It depends where you've been born; what country; what family; your education.

Karolina

I do believe that there is a class system, and I think if you're born into a certain class it is very hard to move away from that. Obviously money and class go hand-in-hand don't they? That's how you determine whether you're working class, middle class or upper class.

Amy

On discrimination

I hear people talk and moan and complain about 'These immigrants' and 'Send them back' and 'We shouldn't have any more'. Then the first thing that springs to mind is that people who consider themselves British who are here—sounds very harsh I know—but they weren't originally here. They weren't indigenous. They came from other countries. Some Vikings from Scandinavia, and some, a lot, from Ireland. We have a lot of Irish immigrants. We have a vibrant Afro-Caribbean community here; and I think Somalis. But you get lots of 'Oh they should go back, we should close our borders'. I like to challenge those attitudes, because a lot of them are very ignorant.

Cath

I keep feeling that way. Look at me, I'm foreign. And I don't ask people for money. I'm trying to sort out my life. I know some people are where they are because of drugs or alcohol; but it is difficult to be Polish and live in the UK. It is, especially now with the Government blowing everything up about the immigrants.

Karolina

I have thought about it. I think it is, after all, still the language barrier. I have been to those English classes and actually have studied for a few years. Now the government has cut the funding on many, enormously. Many places have now closed down, so I cannot go there again.

Jiao

On fairness

I'm always talking about it; decrease the gap between the richer people and the poorer people. It's simple. The way I see it, the more I work, the more I earn, the more I'm going to get taxed. So the Council Tax for one; if we need to lower the debt, why can't we lower the debt from some of the people who are getting paid big amounts of money? We're all the same; we all feel the same; we all bleed the same. What's different is where we have to really, really struggle and people who have got loads of money that don't have to struggle? They kind of flow through life and their priorities are just what colour car they're going to buy, and those types of things; what holiday they're going to go on this year. Why can't it be fairer basically? And then I think, that would get rid of the deprivation and you would probably see a lot less crime.

Brenda

On family backgrounds

I think now, when I look back, I would have liked to have gone to university. But at the time, at that age, my family didn't have any money and I wouldn't have been able to afford it. My Mum and Dad were separated when I was younger and, yeah I think I would have liked to have done more education and gone to university when I was still at home. I don't think I'd be able to now. It would have been a good opportunity. But my Mum was always short of money, because she had me and my brother, and I started working when I was fourteen. We used to work after-school and weekends to help my Mum out with money. So it was more like, we had to get straight to work really to help out. University was never an option really; we had to get into work. For my daughter, I'd like her to have the opportunity of university. Even that's more expensive now, isn't it? But I would like her to have that opportunity. So, fingers crossed she will.

Kay

And also, one of the things that used to come up a lot with my family was 'There's no jobs, no opportunities for Black people in Liverpool'. They said Liverpool's a racist city, so it was a case of 'This is how it is' kind of thing. They said 'People like you, don't try and succeed'; 'Don't try and push yourself because it's pointless'; 'There's only a certain level that you'll be able to get to'. I've always wanted to travel, but there's just no money to do it. I remember when I was doing a course when I was about eighteen. It was winter and the only shoes that I had were open-toed. So, I quit the course because I didn't have the shoes to do it. I'm not saying I was poor; but it was that embarrassment thing. Sometimes I didn't have the bus fare. So, I'd walk.

Brenda

As a child I think I missed her [mother] *not coming to the school play, to watch me being an angel, and things like that. She'd always be like 'Hurry up I've got to go to work'; and I'd think 'Oh you think work's more important than me'. She didn't, but growing up, that's how I felt. And I mean I do two days here* [volunteering] *just to try and better myself; just to try and get into a job which fits round the children. Even a dinner lady, anything, just a few hours each week.*

Grace

On income inequality

I get really emotional about the inequalities. I just think of the greedy fat cats at the top. It does annoy me; but I am more compassionate about the poor people who don't even realise the Government puts so much stress on them. I suppose it is me really as well; we are one of the richest countries in the world, aren't we?

Sue

There was a footballer on the news this morning moaning that he doesn't play football anymore. He is moaning because he doesn't get the wage anymore. What he is moaning for? Driving round in these cars that we can only dream of if we drove. I don't drive, but if we did! And the houses! I could only dream of owning a house like that.

Terri

It is unfair; it should be smaller the [pay] *gap, because some people have got everything. They don't need to think about tomorrow; what they are going to cook; what they're going to buy; whether they've got money for that. People who do work, they need to have that in mind every single day. I keep thinking about the money every day. It's such a difference between the lifestyle of these groups. The lower group and the higher group; it's getting wider.*

Karolina

On the National Minimum Wage

The Living Wage? Employers need to realise that there has been no increase in benefits, or a one percent increase, and it just doesn't cover things. You are talking about years and years of debt and vicious circles building. I would like someone to come along and offer me a job that pays good money. Ideally, I wouldn't want to claim benefits.

Amy

I think things need to be sort of levelled out with regards to money. I think I used the example last time of the footballers. It is a ridiculous amount of money, when there are people begging on the streets, who are trying to get a job because they have got no home and things like that. I am not saying they shouldn't be paid a good wage. It would be nice for us all to have a wage and be able to go to the shops, and not take the calculator sort of thing. Not have to buy the value stuff because you can't afford the non-value; you know what I mean?

Colette

On education and a 'second chance'

Well, to be honest, I think that's just my own fault. I did go to school, don't get me wrong; but I didn't do very well, and I think that's why I've had to go back now. And I think to myself, 'Well I'm 32 now; I've had to go back to college, and do Maths and English again; and it's all new to me, when I should have just got my head down at school'. But I just couldn't then. Well, I tried my best; I just wasn't good enough.

Denise

I think I've probably wasted opportunities really, and again it's down to circumstance; things like the kids and stuff like that come along. I've got a good education; I've got a good brain in my head; I can apply myself to all sorts of things.

Carol

I left school to go into a factory where I was earning £119 a week when I was sixteen. It was a lot of money and I just saw the pounds. It was like twenty-two years ago or something, since I left school. So, even though things had changed—like the feminism-thing movement—but we were still expected to leave school, get married, have kids, bring our families up type of thing. That was always still there at that point. To be honest with you my family always encouraged me to do what I wanted to do and my Mum always worked as well as my Dad. I was thinking about it last night, how some people do always seem to work.

Amy

You can make opportunities for yourself. Once you are educated you can go on then to get a better job, a well-paid job, you know it makes a massive difference. I do think the opportunities, when you come from this area, for women was basically when you got out of school, you had children and that is what you did. You just had babies and then you just went on the dole. There was nothing else.

Ruth

It's support; having that support. It's where you come from; it's who you are; it's the difference between being a parent who can assist your children into doing whatever it is that you want them to do. I funded myself in university, but now I'm in £30,000 worth of debt, and now I'm going 'Was it worth it?' I could have done what I'm doing now without that; but it made me grow up and it made me understand the world a lot more than I did when I went to university. I do think that what I learnt in university should be offered anyway without those charges being put on, because it was just basically opening up the world to me.

Brenda

I think access to appropriate education is a massive one isn't it? Certainly how you're able to interact with those opportunities for education really can make a big difference to children. As you get older things like being able to study again or go back to re-train or keep adding things, make a big difference to the level of work, to where you fit into your career path or whatever. And sometimes it's not that the opportunities aren't there; it's being able to take them up isn't it? Money though, money's the big one; if you can't afford to just get by, you're not going to be able to afford to develop.

Fiona

On opportunities for children

I think what needs to happen is more opportunities for education. They need to be available; that's the key word, the 'opportunities', and being able to have the choice. When I was growing up, it was kind of like 'What do you want to be?' So yeah, just more opportunity for kids to go off and get a good education. Now with university fees it's not helping anyone. The kids who are benefitting are the kids whose Mums and Dads have got loads of money to give them.

Brenda

It has to be a good education, doesn't it? It's having the opportunity to be able to make something of themselves. Money is going to come later on, isn't it? You're going to have to get a good job before the money comes into it. I think it's what you make of it, and as long as your kids are happy and stuff like that, I think everything else is extra isn't it? You just want to make sure your kids are getting brought up properly and they've got all the opportunities that you probably didn't have when you were younger. It's the only thing you can do, isn't it?

Janet

I think it's also important to be an individual as well, and show your children drive and passion and work. Maybe that stems back years from when mums never worked and that's maybe why there's so much unemployment in the area. They haven't seen that side of life. I think it's like a drive with me; I've always been a little bit like that. I was walking donkeys on the beach when I was twelve! I've done dog walking and worked in hotels when I was thirteen. I've always wanted my own money, and my own bit of independence; and I think that's just normal to me. So, I want that for the kids.

Sian

I think education is very important and I don't necessarily mean academic education. I mean you will find young people who aren't academic, they're never going to be academic; but they need more vocational training. I think more 'hands-on', more opportunities, more apprenticeships. Definitely more apprenticeships for young people. Education is very important.

Eileen

I have really pushed them, and motivated them. I mean they're all in some type of either employment or further education. I hope they're all career minded.

Emma

On blame

I think if you talk about fairness, it's got to be about removing the barriers so people can achieve and do what they're capable of, without removing safety nets for people. I suppose it's about making sure that people see things as a society, isn't it? What's the quote about 'Your society's only as strong as the weakest people and how you look after and care for those people'. I don't think there should be kind of anything about punishing people for being in that position, even if it's through choice; even if they are choosing not to work and to live on benefits. It's hardly a desirable lifestyle, so you know, as somebody who works really hard, if I get to be really successful and have to pay tax that supports other people, I don't begrudge paying that. I would rather people who wanted to work, had the opportunity to, than trying to force people who are happy just getting by on £60 a week to do it.

Fiona

I don't blame people who are on the dole and not working, because at the moment it seems as though they're better off. I just think there should be more of a balance between everyone. At the moment there have been times in the last few weeks where I've thought 'Am I better-off not working?', because I feel like I'm getting penalised all the time for having to give extra money back. I just think there should be more encouragement and more help. It just doesn't seem fair does it?

Joy

Everybody's feeling the pinch. There are people who live off benefits and they really need those benefits; and people are getting sanctions. I really feel for them because they have got no income whatsoever once that sanction goes into place. We are struggling as well, everything is going up in price, and the benefits don't go up to meet those needs. So the money has to come from somewhere else.

Amy

On taxes

You need to make people feel more appreciated and give them more back. Do you know what I mean? Working Tax Credits? You have got to work 24 hours, with a family of four children. I can't physically work 24 hours to get Working Tax Credits. It's given to you like a bonus. It isn't a bonus if it's needed.

Ruth

What is stopping [things] *being fairer, I think is the Government by saying that people on benefits are 'scroungers'. I'll tell you, the biggest culprit is taxes. Billions and billions all these big companies owe, and they're discriminating against people who they call 'scroungers' who are claiming benefits. No wonder they're stressed-out going to the job centre. They say the Government's got no money; but what about all the backhanders! They're all part of these companies. They've all got something in these companies that go offshore, and owe billions. I just don't understand. And the press, they just publish what they want us to know. It's ridiculous.*

Sian

What I would change now is for the Government to stop taking money off the welfare bill and make [two well-known telephone companies] *pay their tax bills. Simple solution: £6 billion* [well-known company] *owed in 2010 and they cut £7 billion off the welfare. Stop taking off the poor. Does the Government want to be remembered as 'the Government that introduced foodbanks'?*

Eileen

On the NHS

You know, as a nurse, they are all saying 'Oh it costs this much to look after alcoholics. You know what is happening now, with youth culture? So many millions, it is costing with all the alcohol problems. But why don't they go to the alcohol companies? They don't care do they? You know, make a healthier option and just say no more blank cheques. Yeah, and all the big companies that sell all the bloody products should be made accountable. They should pay the bill for the NHS.

Sue

We tried the other hospitals. The only hospital that had any appointments left at all was the Royal, and when I phoned up there was one appointment left between now [November] *and April. In Whiston, St Cath's, Runcorn, all the hospitals, one appointment and that's it. It's just not good enough. Let's hope there's a cancellation. But again it's funding; that's what it's all down to at the end of the day isn't it? The Government are talking about wanting us to pay for our medical care and things, and I think you're creating a situation where we're going to end up like America: if you haven't got the health cover then what are you left with? Those free hospitals in America, good grief, they're just atrocious; and it's like the worst possible care. You can't treat people like that, you really can't. Just because they can't afford to pay for the medical care. There's something very, very wrong, you know? Poor politicians are debating about whether they should have their champagne budget cut. Dear me; what a dilemma!*

Carol

On social justice

There's so much injustice, right across the nation; it's like where do you start? Where can you possibly tackle that sort of thing? A lot of it is attitude as well, I think, and ignorance. The Government? I don't know what world they're living in at the end of the day. I think they're seriously out of touch with people.

Carol

They're saying there's no money and people are 'scroungers' and this that and the other. They're all millionaires in their own right; and they get big expenses and jobs. How can that be justified; how? But the rich get rich and the poor get poorer.

Sian

… and finally

Things can only get better for the kids, can't they? That's my answer to it. I'd like to see them abolish zero hours; up minimum pay; and [have] *better opportunities for kids leaving school. More apprenticeships. Life isn't living on the dole.*

Tammy

I do feel that the Government is just not in touch with us. I really do feel that. That's the beauty of this [research] *at the end of the day; and that's where that's going isn't it? And I hope they do read it; and I hope it opens some eyes for them.*

Carol

8. Liars, Thieves and Honest Scousers

The emotional spectrum of these interviews was wide. In some, the dominant note was one of deep frustration; in others, it was one of stoicism. Some families found talking about their situations upsetting, whilst for others it appeared to provide some outlet for them to express how they felt. There were moments of despair certainly; but there were also moments of determination that the family would not be dragged under by sheer circumstance. Often the discussion would alternate between these different moods within the same interview. Many of the interviews however, were characterised in places by one very striking emotion: anger.

Anger is not necessarily expressed angrily; and it is not always loud. Anger can be in the force of what is said; in the logic, rather than the outward expression; and in the inference, rather than what is heard in the literal statement. This was the kind of anger apparent here. It occurred most often when the families came to the question of 'Who's to blame?' On this subject, time and again participants protested the manifest unfairness of what was happening to them and their families, in relation to what they saw in society around them.

The unfairness of the austerity measures instituted by the 2010–2015 Coalition Government and intensified by the 2015 Conservative Government, has already been described. We have seen that the effects of what those governments led the electorate to believe were the 'deficit reduction' measures of responsible and fair administrations, were in

 https://doi.org/10.11647/OBP.0112.08

fact grossly unfair and disproportionately detrimental to the least well-off in society. This is demonstrable in monetised terms. However, it is how these measures have played out in the lives of real people and their families that is captured in this study.

The impact of low pay was described in many ways and with respect to many different interview themes. We will revisit a few of these here. Low pay of course meant a constant struggle to make ends meet for all the families. It also meant debt for many, the stress of managing that debt and constant worry about debt-collectors, bailiffs and repossession. With low pay, usually come long hours and multiple jobs, the results of which are all too predictable: constant tiredness and fatigue; irritability at home; insufficient time for children and family life; becoming 'run-down'; health issues, mental and physical; a monotonous routine; and so on.

Insecurity of various kinds adds to the toxic mix of detriments that create downward cycles of social and psychological malaise. Insecure work contracts, insecure tenancies and insecure finances all conspire to make life worrisome and unpredictable for those whose lives are defined by these realities. Renting a house—that may need long-waited-for basic repairs, that is cold and that is unsuitable for a disabled child or lacks the adjustments required for an elderly dependent for example—can bring its own life-limitations and difficulties. The combinations of these and other problems of life are punishing for the health and well-being of adults. They are even more so for children. Children who do not see enough of their parents are emotionally deprived; children who rarely have new clothes bought for them are materially deprived; children who have few days out and never get to have a holiday, have little to look forward to; children who are cold get sick; children who are sick miss school; and so on. This litany could be extended considerably. The point here is that the unfairness that pervades this entire topic is even more cruelly apparent when we consider the lives of the children and young people who were born into, and are growing up in, the economic, social and cultural poverty of 'austerity Britain'.

The political logic used to justify government action that has produced such constant struggle for these families, also calls for careful consideration. We have seen that UK government domestic policy has not been 'fair' as purported. However, the intention, the electorate were informed, was that welfare spending would be reformed with aim of concentrating support upon the 'most vulnerable' in society. Quite how cuts to the Disability Living Allowance, the abolition of a swathe of emergency services and crisis support payments, the introduction of a new and draconian regime of benefits sanctions and cuts of 68 percent of the budget for local services in the most deprived English city (Liverpool) could be seen as protecting support for the 'most vulnerable', is impossible to fathom. The underlying logic itself however, does not bear the slightest scrutiny. Concentrating support upon the most vulnerable, means withdrawing support from those who are merely 'vulnerable'. With support withdrawn, the families who are vulnerable will quickly join the category of the 'most vulnerable'. Refocusing the definitions of need upon which vulnerability is indexed, to keep the numbers small and the service demands within departmental budgets, in turn means that the thresholds of need used to trigger state support are repeatedly raised. The result is a vicious policy cycle of ever decreasing state support in which families that are in need (though not yet the 'most needy') are pushed over the edge and into crisis. Such is the logic of 'welfare reform' in the UK.

The families who took part in the study were vulnerable in the sense that little or no slack existed in their week-to-week finances. The low incomes upon which these families had to rely, meant that no amount of careful planning could protect them from an unexpected demand upon the family budget. A benefit overpayment that must be repaid, a delay in money that is due, a higher than normal heating bill, the costs of an illness of a working adult or a poorly child, a cut in hours and so on are the kinds of unforeseen events that could (and did) push family finances all too easily out of control. Where money is so tight, no reserves exist to buffer households against contingencies that often arise because of that very circumstance. The effect is that families live constantly on the edge of an inexorable downward slide into situations of accumulating debt, inability to pay bills and rent, dependence upon loan sharks and the prospect of eviction.

All the families were surviving: just. Yet each of these families also conveyed a palpable sense of the fragility of their situations, and the closeness of the line between 'just about managing' and financial collapse. None were destitute and all had homes. It is increasingly apparent however, that destitution is no longer a haunting memory from a bygone era, a signifier of 'how much has changed'. In the era of foodbanks and the return of child hunger, it is a real and present threat to many families living on insecure and restricted incomes and with a disappearing safety net beneath them. This throws into new relief the meaning of 'absolute poverty' as distinct from 'relative poverty'. In the language of public policy these terms have precise technical definitions. Currently, whilst 'relative poverty' is defined as household income of 60 percent or below of the median income, 'absolute poverty', as a basic and unchanging minimum is defined by the UK government's Department of Work and Pensions as household income of 60 percent or below of the 2010/11 median.[1] However, in its more popular usage 'absolute poverty', conjuring up the image of the family living in penury and utter desperation, has made its return as a frightening spectre. This was not the reality for these families. However, to different degrees, its possibility represented a blackening cloud under which they were living.

All the families had at least one working parent. That was the basic criterion for their inclusion in the study. All were reliant upon that income, even where some element of state support existed. What was also clear however, were the levels of commitment to working that were repeatedly expressed in many of the interviews. Indeed, it is no exaggeration to say that a strong work ethic characterised the family testimonies on this subject. Owen Jones (2016) in *Chavs: The Demonization of the Working Class*[2] points out that despite virulent tabloid stereotyping of benefit claimants and especially single mothers, as seeking to avoid work, most single parents want to work.[3] For some of the families, this commitment to working was about maintaining a sense of connection with the world. For others, it was about being economically self-reliant, and so materially and psychologically independent. For still others, it was about not having to endure the increasing indignities and irrationalities of the benefits system. For many, it was about providing an example to children. The reasons varied; all however were rooted in

1 McGuinness, F. (2015), *Poverty in the UK: Statistics*. Briefing paper 7906, 6 November. House of Commons Library.
2 Jones, O. (2016).
3 *Ibid.*, p. 217.

a desire not to 'go under' by having to resort to state support that would only come accompanied by a bullying culture and whole new types of stress.

These families, in the attitudes they expressed towards work and the wariness they obviously felt towards the benefits system, were behaving exactly in the ways demanded of them by the crusading agendas of the Coalition Government of 2010–2015 and its Conservative successor. As we have seen some had set up their own small businesses, entirely in line with government exhortations. Far from moving forward with a new and rising prosperity however—and having conformed to the expectations required of them by government employment policy, because of increasingly restricted options and tabloid hectoring, but also by choice—they were now being punished by constant worries arising from the insecurity and unprotected nature of their economic and social situations. To indulge for a moment the proponents of the morally prejudiced and entirely bogus distinction between the 'deserving' and the 'undeserving' poor, these families would clearly count as 'deserving' in the sense that has been peddled over the years by home secretaries, centre-right think tanks and right-wing newspaper editors. Their reward however, was a life of constant struggle, trapped on low pay with no way back, up or out.

It is this last aspect, that of the entrapment of working families on low incomes, that reveals the true effects, and even intentions, of the austerity policy regimes of the governments that came to power following the 2008 banking collapse. The 'bunching' effect whereby the wages of workers become stuck at or close to the national minimum, has been shored-up by the erosion or removal of important state protections, the introduction of new caps and conditionalities for benefits, pay freezes, the introduction of fees for adult education courses and trends towards casualisation, hourly-paid status and self-employment. It is the extension and intensification of low wage *dependency* then that is the real achievement of recent government welfare reform and incomes policy.

As we have seen, in many interviews participants expressed their view that government ministers were 'out of touch' with realities of life for those coping on low incomes. Since 2010 the popular perception of the socially privileged background and status of political elites has hardened into a firm consensus. The gap between the social position of many government ministers and that of the people whose lives they have comprehensively harmed, has never appeared so vast. However, as we have argued here, this is not simply a matter of privilege and social position. The very methodologies by which the impact of government policy has been predicted and tracked were skewed from the beginning. The tendency for example to produce impact assessments for separate policies in isolation from one another, means that the combined and cumulative effect upon communities, families, social groups and individuals is eclipsed. Repeatedly, these families talked about the ways in which their problems piled up from the whole range of pressures upon their budgets and available time. The demands of work, routines for child-care, school costs, bills, and debt repayments along with health problems for some, difficulties with landlords and unpredictable hours created a punishing cycle that was clearly pushing many to the edge of being able to cope. It is the full complexity of these problems of life that government impact methodologies fail to capture. The result has been that legislative processes have not been informed by evidence that is genuinely reflective of the lives of the poorest in society. The 'out-of-touch' character of government in the UK over recent years is not simply the result of social blind-spots. It is wilful.

The 'thing' of course, with which UK governments since 2010 have been in very close touch, has been their own agenda of the realignment of the structures of class in British society. The rolling back of the welfare state has been one major project that was inaugurated by the 1979 Conservative Government led by Margaret Thatcher, and launched into a new historical phase by the 2010 Coalition and 2015 Conservative governments.[4] Now, considering the draconian departmental budget cuts for public services, long-term falls in the provision of social housing and leaps in rates of eviction as well as the spectacle of foodbanks in one of the largest economies in the industrialised world, comparisons with the British society of the 1930s no longer seem far-fetched.

The comparison with which we began was to that of British society of over a century ago. The circumstances of the working poor of course are separated from those of today by time and by many types of social-historical change. As we have seen however, they also resonate with one

4 Mendoza, K. (2015), *Austerity: The Demolition of the Welfare State and the Rise of the Zombie Economy*, New Internationalist Books.

another over the intervening generations between them. One crucial point on which they connect is that of insecurity. Indeed, throughout our discussion the sense of these families being at a 'tipping point' has emerged from the obvious fragility of their circumstances; from an awareness that one more financial demand or one more challenge in life, can push carefully managed arrangements over into unmanageable chaos. The Lambeth families of the 1913 *Round About A Pound A Week* report recognised this constant possibility in their own lives. So too did these Liverpool families.

The notion of a 'tipping point' can have another meaning however. The historical period of the Fabian Women's Committee study was one of strife and political, social and economic conflict. Revolts of 'the Irish', 'the women' and 'the workers'[5] for example were as much part of that historical era as were the indigence and squalor of the working-class districts. It is noteworthy now, that amongst these families, when the matter of 'blame' arose, it wasn't aimed at the familiar targets offered daily by tabloid columnists for the venting of social ire: immigrants; refugees; Muslims; benefits claimants; and so on. Rather it was celebrity culture, the establishment, cabinet ministers and the wealthy generally.

The merchants of austerity should take note. It is not just family stability that can be 'tipped'. So too can the willingness of those who are 'just managing' to put up with it all.

5 Dangerfield, G. (1997), *The Strange Death of Liberal England*, Serif.

Appendix I: How the Research Was Conducted

The intention behind the *Getting By?* project was to capture what life is like for typical families in low paid employment, and the extent to which they can maintain an acceptable living standard. In defining 'acceptable living standard' the work of the Centre for Research in Social Policy and the Family Budget Unit of the University of York was used. This established a Minimum Income Standard (MIS) and was based on research with the wider public, specifying items that need to be included in a minimum household budget. This is regularly updated and can be accessed as an online calculator. The MIS forms the basis for setting the Living Wage (outside London).

Participation in the project was open to Liverpool families that had at least one child under eighteen years of age, and with at least one member of the household in paid employment, whether this was part- or full-time work. Another selection criterion was that the family income after tax and National Insurance, but taking account of tax and welfare benefit payments and paid employment, had to fall below the MIS in the UK. The families could be either lone parents or couples, and could include extended families living within the same household and sharing their finances. A decision was taken not to seek out families whose situation was extreme; for instance, families who were about to become homeless or where there were issues with alcohol or substance misuse.

The project was widely publicised through an interview on BBC Radio Merseyside at peak listening time; and through local Community

 https://doi.org/10.11647/OBP.0112.09

and Voluntary Sector organisations, including Citizens' Advice Bureaus, registered social landlords and credit unions. Publicity was circulated via electronic newsletters and broadcasts such as those of Liverpool Charity and Voluntary Services, as well as widespread circulation of a flyer for interested groups or organisations. An information sheet was also produced for families who expressed an interest in the project.

From late November 2013, the process of recruiting the thirty families began. The families were mainly recruited via contact with community organisations from across the City. An effort was made to include ethnic minority families to reflect Liverpool's demographic profile, but also because they are disproportionately highly represented amongst groups in low-paid employment. Families were recruited from Chinese, Black British, Polish and Somali backgrounds.

At the same time six community researchers were recruited and trained, one of these being a Cantonese speaker. In addition, a participant information sheet was produced detailing the methodology, including ensuring informed consent and confidentiality, and explaining how the information gathered would be analysed. One of the project's two academic advisors then reviewed the research for ethical aspects. This ensured that appropriate ethical standards were met.

The families each took part in five separate recorded in-depth interviews over a year. The initial interview for each family established informed consent and gathered basic demographic and income data. The spending diary was also explained. The interviewers also asked for general information about how the family was managing financially. The first round of interviews took place at the end of 2013 and the start of 2014.

In the spring, summer and autumn of 2014 (at approximately three month intervals), the families took part in further interviews. These were informed by the responses to the first and subsequent interviews, which were subject to thematic analysis. They were also informed by regular debriefing of the community interviewers. Recurring interview themes were identified and then subject to further inquiry. The interviewers followed up any specific issues affecting their families, for example the challenges facing a family with a disabled member.

In the months when the families were not being interviewed the community researchers contacted them by phone. The point of this was to find out whether the family were having any difficulties keeping their spending diary, and to see if there had been any significant change in their circumstances that would need to be taken account of in the next interview.

The final interviews at the end of 2014 reviewed the families' experience of the previous twelve months in managing their finances and their use of the spending dairy. It also focused upon their thoughts about the future and further changes to tax credits and welfare payments.

Participation in the project was incentivised, with the payment of £30 for the first interview and then £5 a week being saved over the duration of the family's involvement. At the end of the project the families received the remaining amount.

Each family's income and expenditure was recorded by them in a printed spending diary. The data from the spending diaries was collated and analysed. Where families had not completed 52 weeks, their aggregated weekly spend was weighted to provide an annual figure for various items of income and expenditure.

The information from the spending diaries for each family was broken down into the following elements: rent; utilities (water, gas and electricity); fuel; weekly shopping; food; transport; clothing and shoes; unexpected costs; paying back debt. One family amended their spending diaries to identify 'food and fuel' costs separately.

Over the course of the year six families dropped out of the project. The first families to leave the project were those with the largest number of children. One person decided not to continue when they got married, and their new partner was in a well-paid job. Another person didn't want to continue when they lost their job. Another got a new job and decided not to continue. The last person dropped out due to family circumstances. None of these families completed spending diaries.

For the duration of the project a website provided an open forum for discussion about issues to do with poverty and austerity as it affects Liverpool families. It also provided links for advice and help, and signposts to relevant services.

Appendix II: Family Circumstances and Spending

Pictograms are given for the annual financial outgoings of those families who completed their spending diaries over the whole year of the study. One family amended their diaries slightly and included their own categories of 'food alone' and 'fuel alone'. Where spending diaries were not fully completed over the year, the families' circumstances are provided after the charts shown below.

All names have been changed to provide anonymity.

 https://doi.org/10.11647/OBP.0112.10

Mark and Ruth

Children: four. Work (Ruth): office work (part-time). Work (Mark): unemployed. Home: social housing.

	Weekly spending £s	Annual spending £s
Income	594.60	30,919.45
Spend	605.37	31,479.19
Balance	- 10.77	-559.74

Breakdown of spending

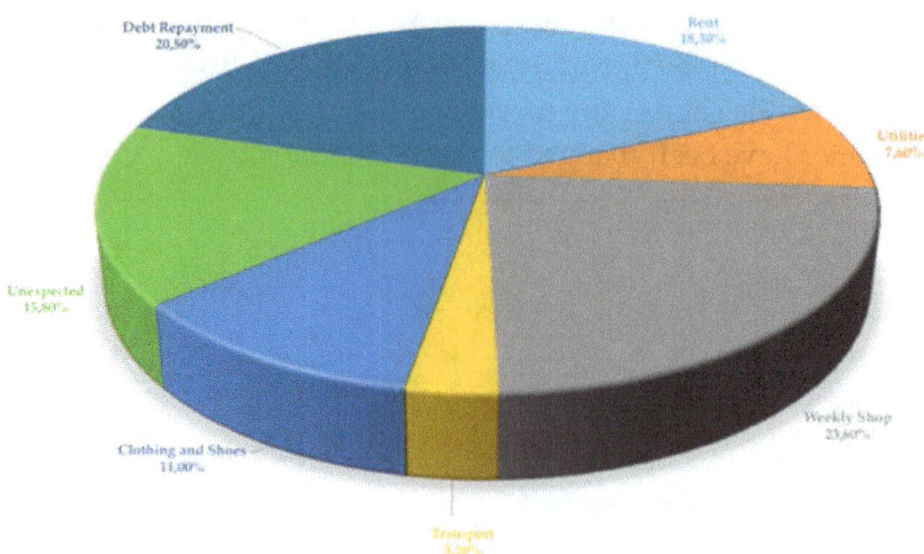

Colette

Children: two. Work: teaching assistant (temporary). Home: privately rented.

	Weekly spending £s	Annual spending £s
Income	446.62	23,224.10
Spend	455.07	23,663.89
Balance	-8.46	-439.78

Breakdown of spending

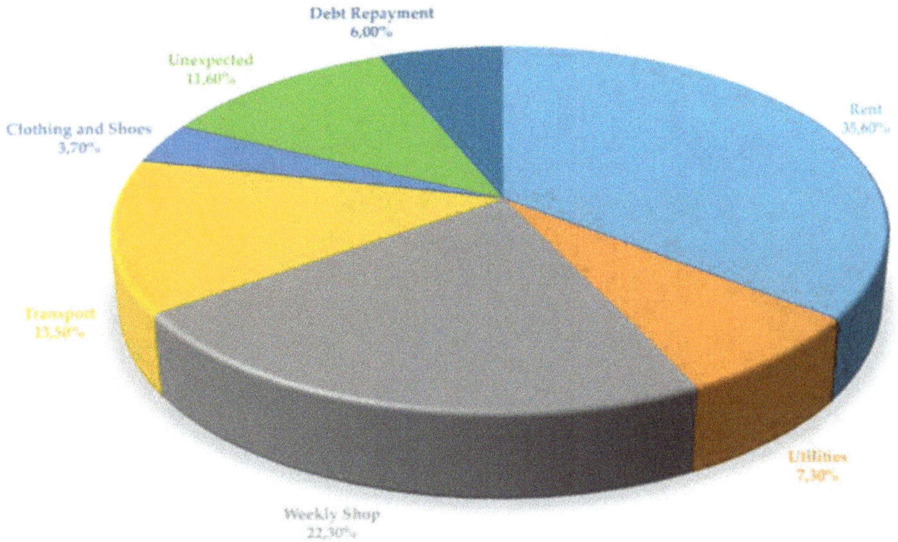

Zoe

Children: two (one at home). Work: student nurse (plus agency work). Home: privately rented.

	Weekly spending £s	Annual spending £s
Income	375.92	19,547.65
Spend	367.35	19,101.95
Balance	8.57	445.70

Breakdown of spending

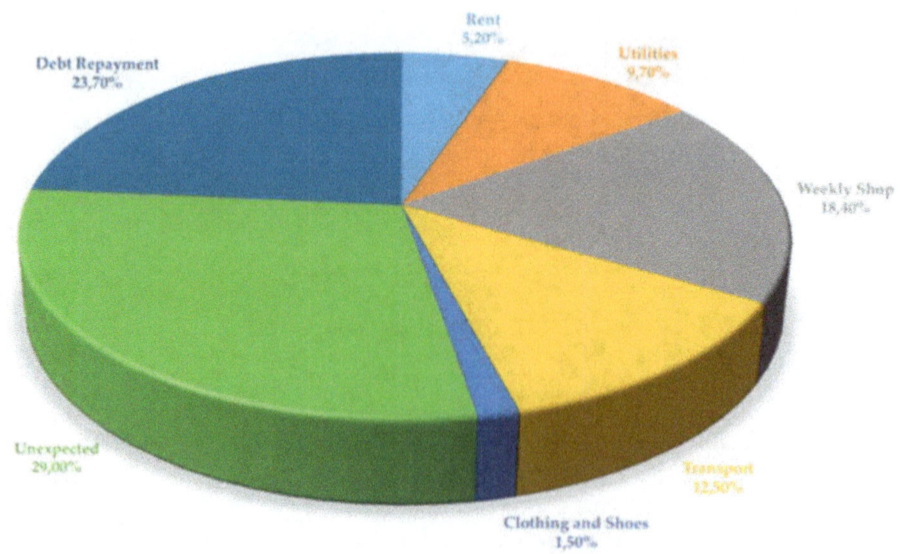

Tammy and Malcolm

Children: two. Work (Tammy): unemployed. Work (Malcolm): service sector (zero-hour contract). Home: privately rented.

	Weekly spending £s	Annual spending £s
Income	410.19	21,330.00
Spend	505.59	26,290.67
Balance	-95.40	-4,960.67

Breakdown of spending

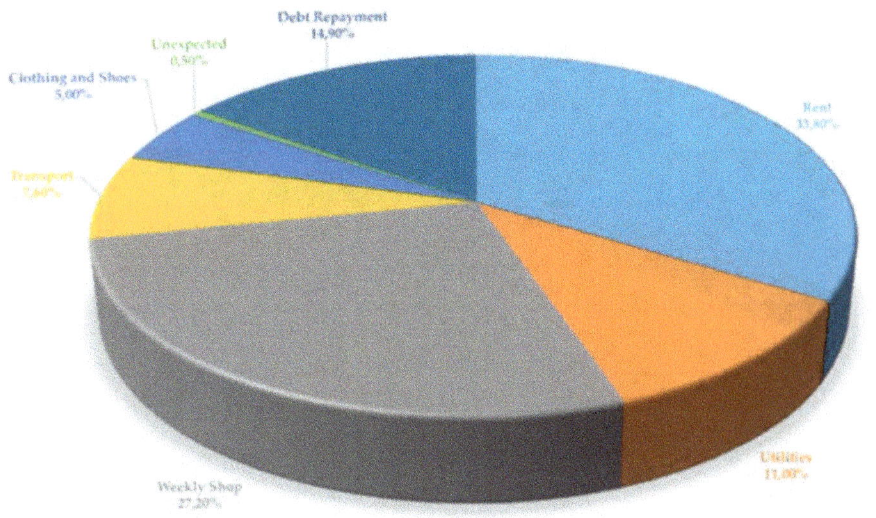

Eileen

Children: three (two at home). Work: cleaning (part-time; two jobs). Home: privately rented.

	Weekly spending £s	Annual spending £s
Income	542.98	28,234.73
Spend	490.71	25,516.78
Balance	52.27	2,7171.95

Breakdown of spending

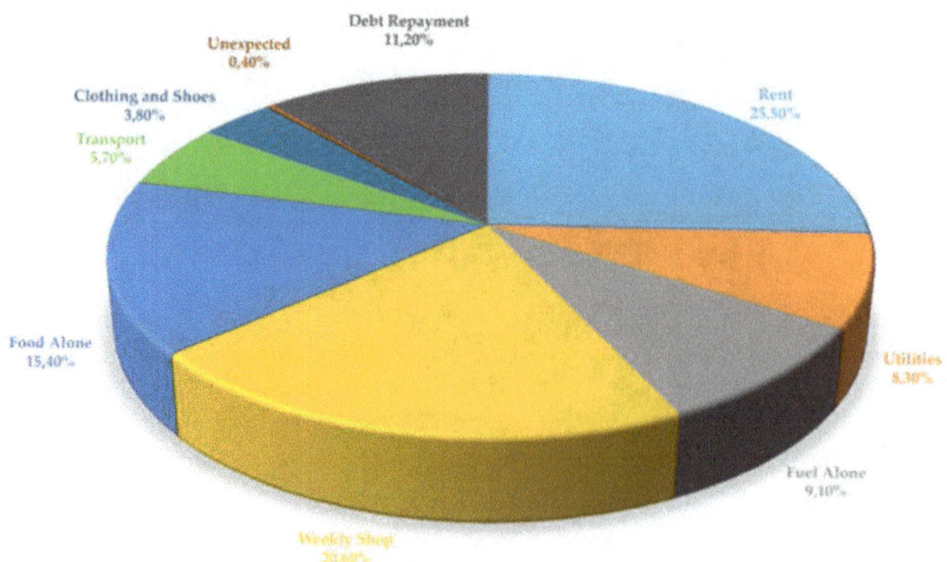

Emma

Children: four. Work: cleaning (self-employed). Home: owned with mortgage.

	Weekly spending £s	Annual spending £s
Income	343.72	17,873.39
Spend	403.32	20,972.45
Balance	-59.60	-3,099.05

Breakdown of spending

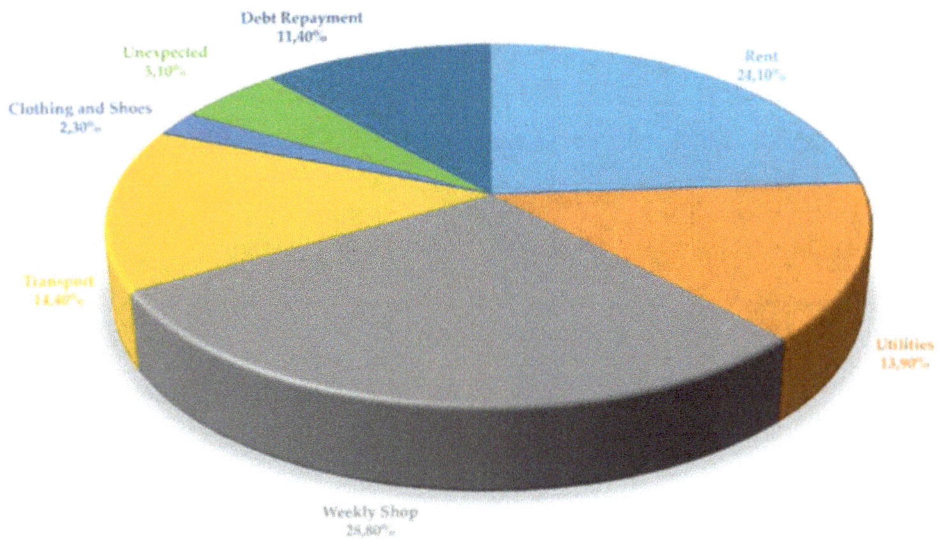

Amy

Children: four. Work: voluntary sector (part-time; two jobs). Home: privately rented.

	Weekly spending £s	Annual spending £s
Income	533.54	27,744.00
Spend	490.00	25,528.53
Balance	42.61	2,215.47

Breakdown of spending

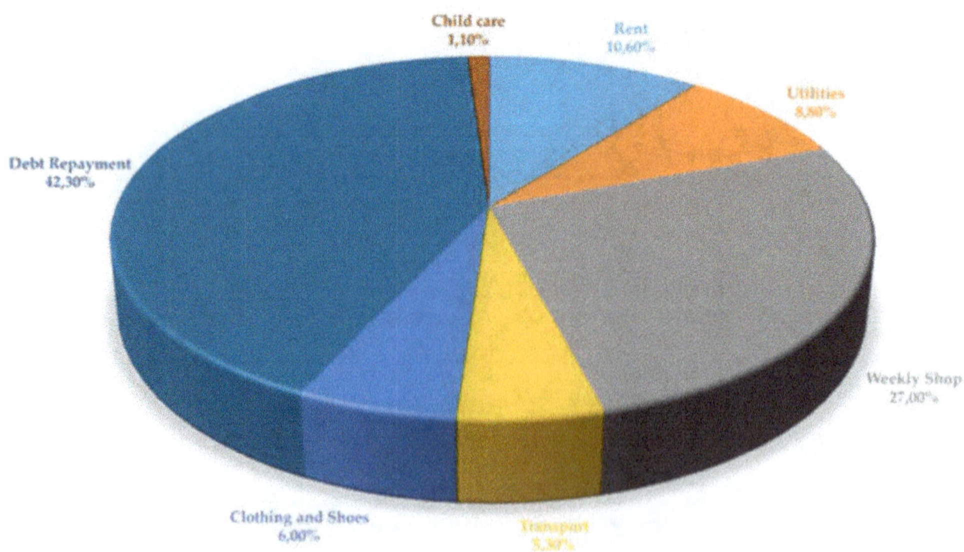

Karolina and Micha

Children: one. Work (Karolina): retail sector (part-time). Work (Micha): factory work (full-time). Home: social housing.

	Weekly spending £s	Annual spending £s
Income	458.31	23,831.90
Spend	414.33	21,545.40
Balance	43.97	2,286.50

Breakdown of spending

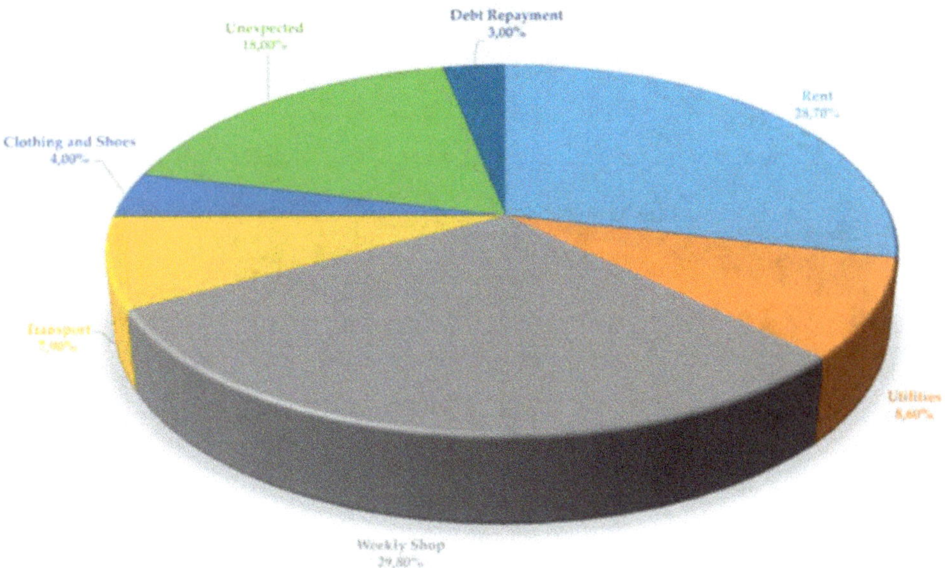

Phoebe and Gavin

Children: four. Work (Phoebe): unemployed. Work (Gavin): manufacturing sector (full-time). Home: social housing.

	Weekly spending £s	Annual spending £s
Income	796.10	36,716.95
Spend	810.40	42,141.05
Balance	-104.31	-5,424.10

Breakdown of spending

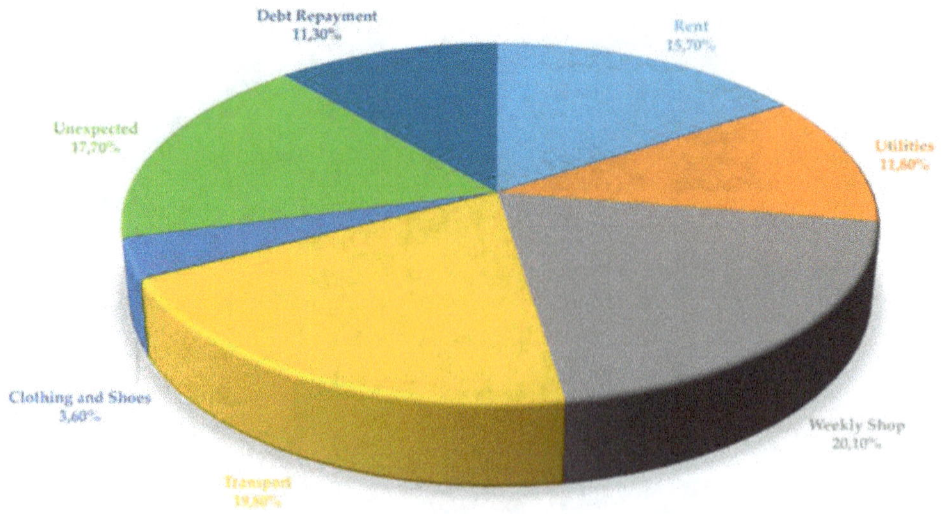

Joy

Children: one. Work: receptionist (part-time). Home: privately rented.

	Weekly spending £s	Annual spending £s
Income	370.12	19,246.19
Spend	326.74	16,990.38
Balance	43.38	2,255.81

Breakdown of spending

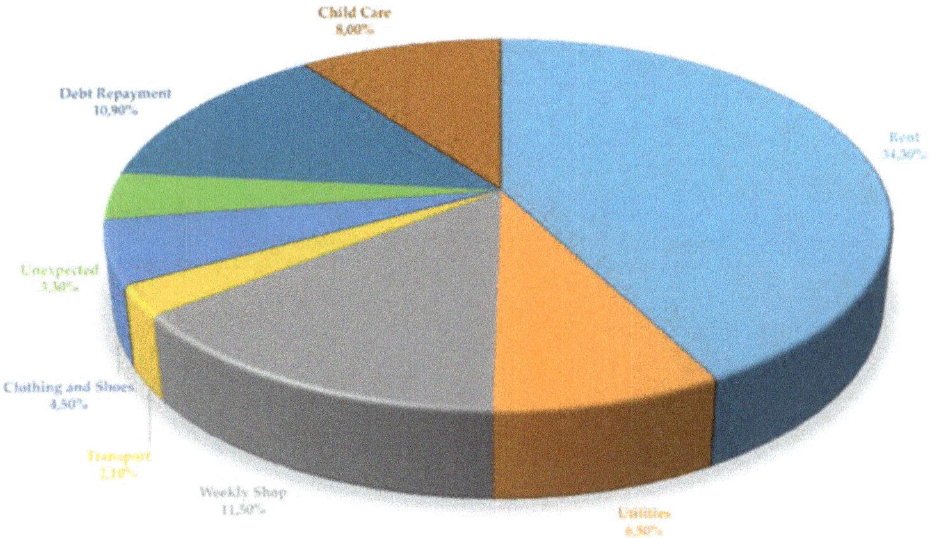

Janet

Children: two. Work: teaching assistant (part-time). Home: privately rented.

	Weekly spending £s	Annual spending £s
Income	456.44	23,734.63
Spend	594.47	30,912.51
Balance	-138.04	-7,177.88

Breakdown of spending

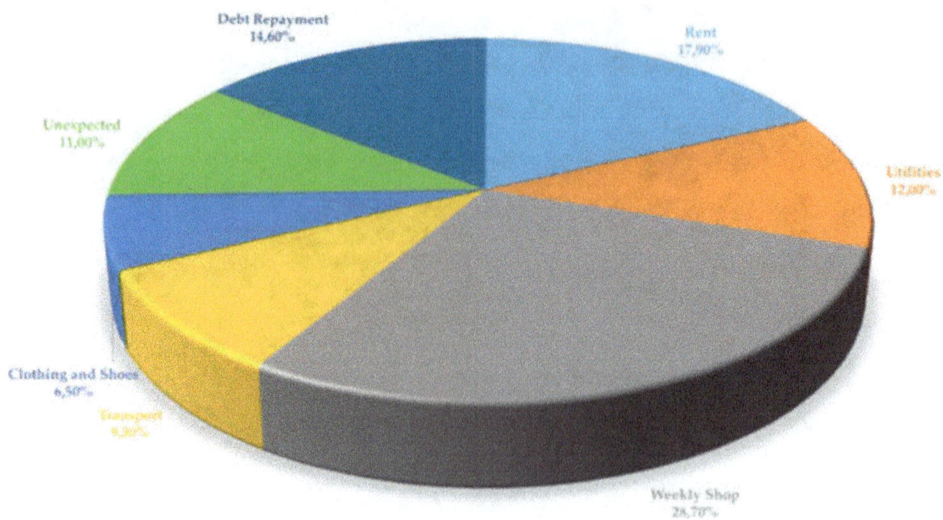

Fiona

Children: two. Work: shop work (self-employed). Home: social housing.

	Weekly spending £s	Annual spending £s
Income	287.92	14,972.00
Spend	230.82	12,002.50
Balance	57.11	2,969.50

Breakdown of spending

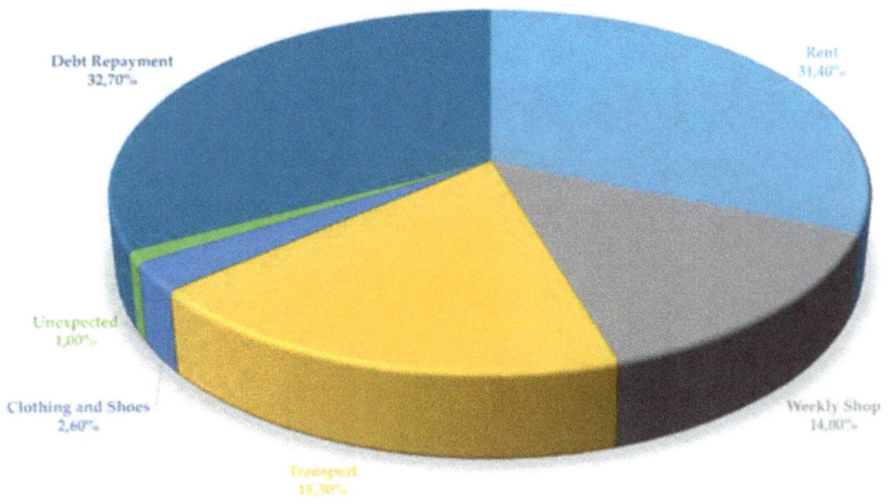

Will and Sam

Children: two. Work (Will): leisure sector (full-time). Work (Sam): unemployed. Home: privately rented.

	Weekly spending £s	Annual spending £s
Income	288.67	15,011.07
Spend	348.20	18,106.28
Balance	-59.52	-3,095.21

Breakdown of spending

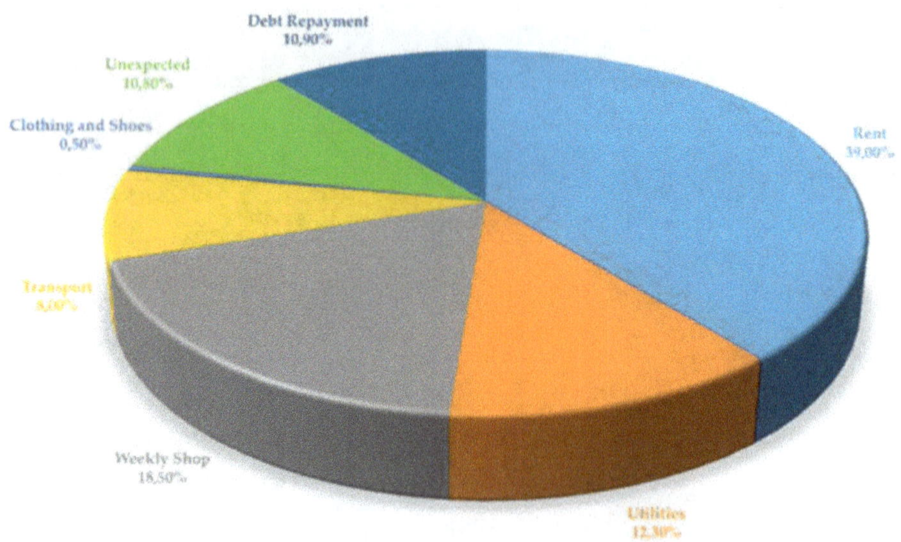

Brenda and Colin

Children: two (a third due). Work (Brenda): leisure sector (part-time). Work (Colin): unemployed. Home: social housing.

	Weekly spending £s	Annual spending £s
Income	361.43	18,794.61
Spend	460.34	23,937,76
Balance	-98.91	-5,143.16

Breakdown of spending

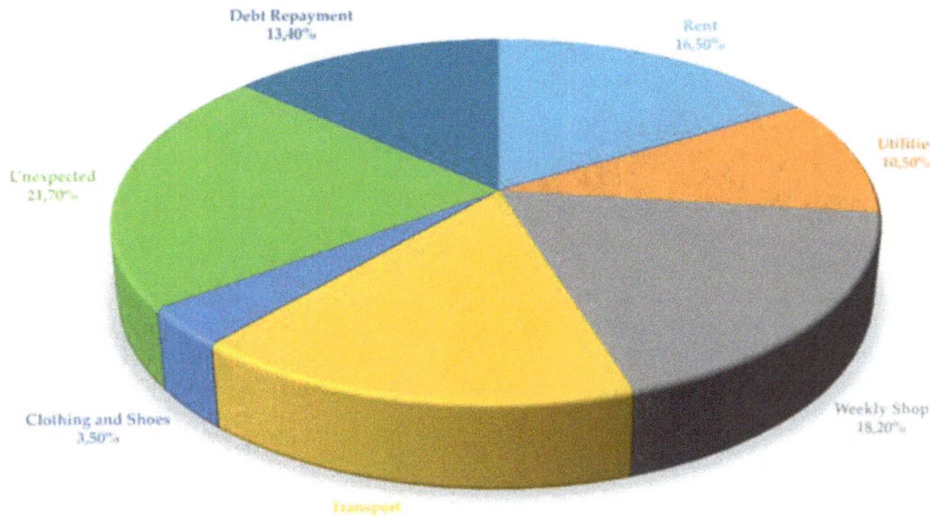

Liam and Grace

Children: four. Work (Liam): chef (hourly-paid). Work (Grace): unemployed. Home: social housing.

	Weekly spending £s	Annual spending £s
Income	452.86	23,548.74
Spend	484.50	25,194.24
Balance	- 31.64	- 1,645.50

Breakdown of spending

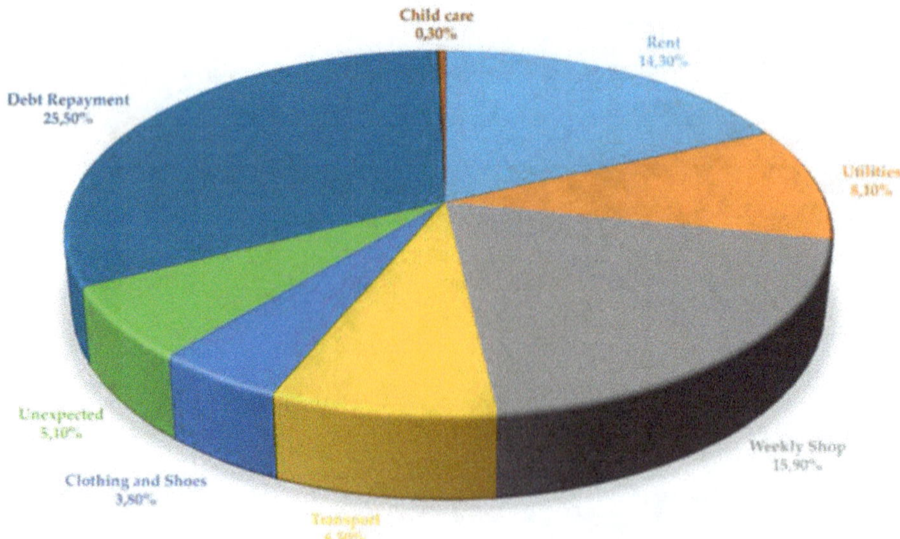

Sian and Steve

Children: three. Work (Sian): unemployed. Work (Steve): driver (self-employed). Home: privately rented.

	Weekly spending £s	Annual spending £s
Income	473.22	24,607.41
Spend	483.94	25,165.13
Balance	-10.73	-557.71

Breakdown of spending

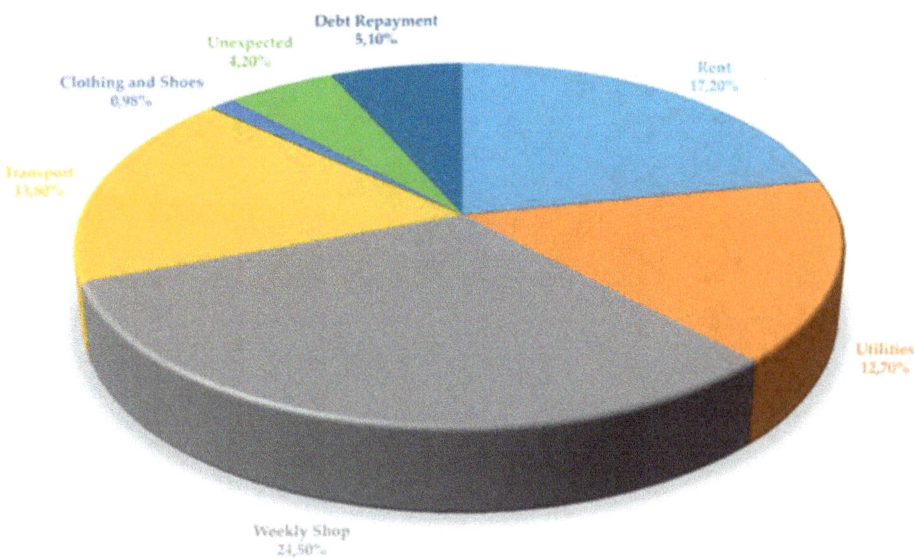

Gaynor

Children: one. Work: cleaner and retail sector (part-time; three jobs). Home: privately rented.

	Weekly spending £s	Annual spending £s
Income	403.46	20,979.92
Spend	395.07	20,543.89
Balance	8.39	436.03

Breakdown of spending

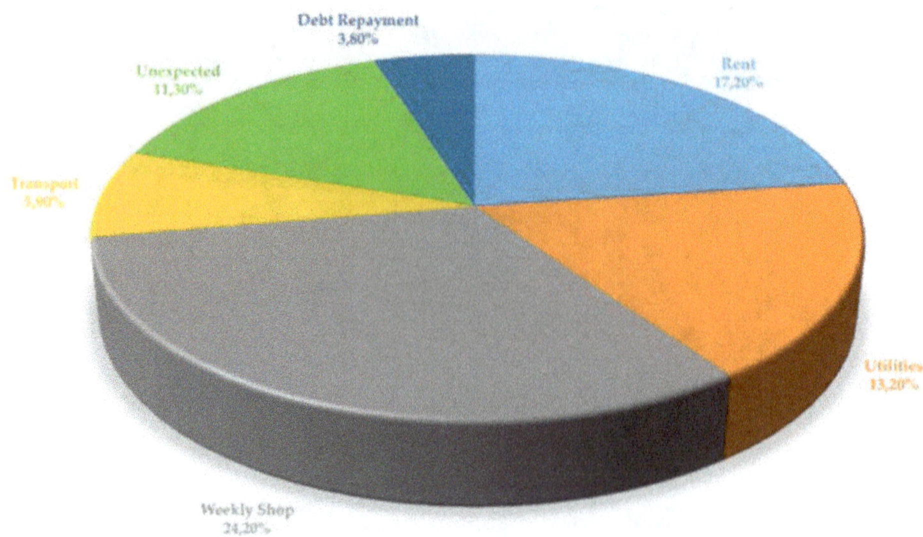

Liz

Children: one. Work: office work (part-time). Home: privately rented.

	Weekly spending £s	Annual spending £s
Income	405.70	21,096.60
Spend	432.79	22,504.85
Balance	-27.08	-1,408.35

Breakdown of spending

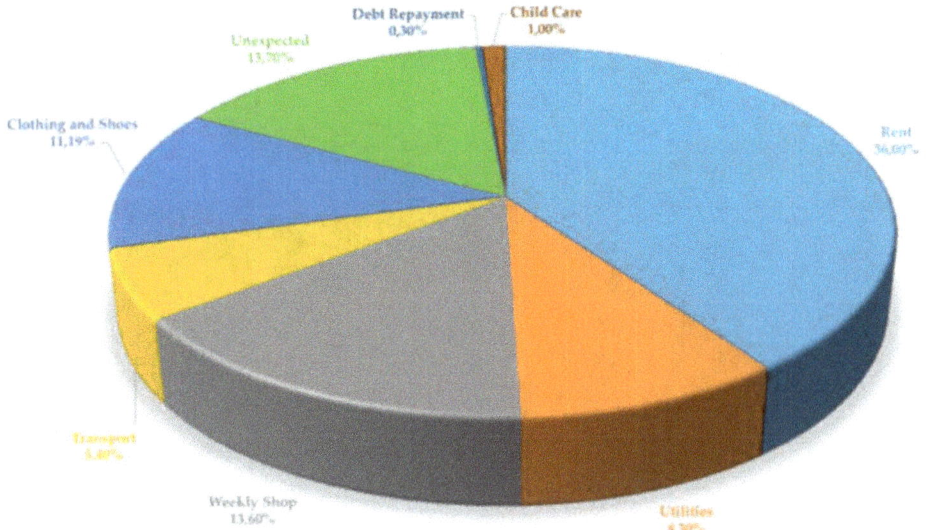

Luke and Minnie

Children: two. Work (Luke): social-care sector (full-time). Work (Minnie): retail sector (part-time). Home: owned with mortgage.

	Weekly spending £s	Annual spending £s
Income	487.25	25,337.01
Spend	461.64	24,005.46
Balance	25.61	1,331.55

Breakdown of spending

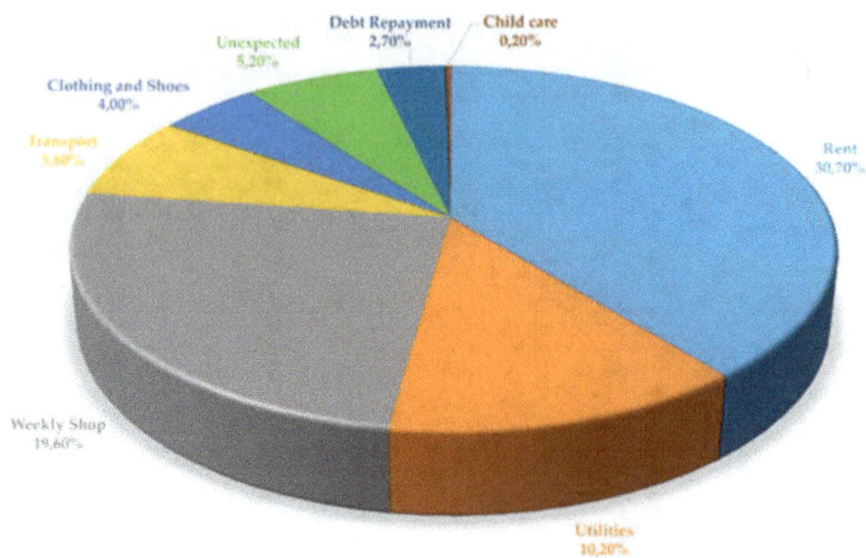

Chang and Jiao

Children: two. Work (Chang): restaurant work (part-time). Work (Jiao): retail sector (part-time). Home: social housing.

	Weekly spending £s	Annual spending £s
Income	358.31	18,632.18
Spend	363.65	18,909.98
Balance	- 5.34	-277.80

Breakdown of spending

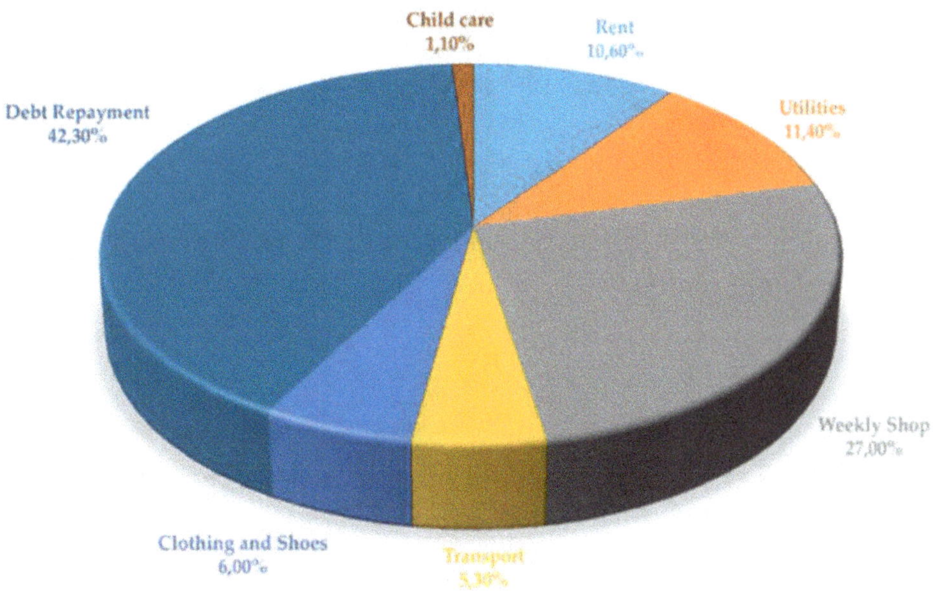

Ali and Rabia

Children: five. Work (Ali): catering sector (full-time). Work (Rabia): unemployed. Home: privately rented.

Jenny

Children: one. Work: catering (part-time). Home: privately rented.

Amber

Children: three. Work: voluntary sector. Home: privately rented.

Phil and Dot

Children: one. Work (Phil): cleaning (full-time). Work (Dot): care worker and cleaner (part-time: two jobs). Home: social housing.

Karen and Steve

Children: four. Work (Karen): unemployed. Work (Steve): civil service. Home: privately rented.

Carol and Ric

Children: two. Work (Carol): unemployed. Work (Ric): Social care sector (hourly paid). Home: social housing.

Terri and Don

Children: two. Work (Terri): unemployed. Work (Don): various (part-time). Home: privately rented.

Denise

Children: three. Work: retail and bar-tending (part-time). Home: social housing.

Nick and Cath

Children: three. Work (Nick): factory work (full-time). Work (Cath): unemployed. Home: social housing.

Carol

Children: five. Work: cleaner (part-time). Home: privately rented.

References

Aldridge, H., Kenway, P. and Born, T. (2015), *'What Happened to Poverty Under the Coalition'*. New Policy Institute.

Armour, R. (2014) 'Charity Shops Buck Trend', http://thirdforcenews.org.uk, 24 March 2014.

Beatty, C. and Fothergill, S. (2016), *The Uneven Impact of Welfare Reform. The Financial Losses to Places and People*, Centre for Regional and Social Economic Research and Sheffield Hallam University, https://www4.shu.ac.uk/research/cresr/sites/shu.ac.uk/files/welfare-reform-2016_1.pdf

Belfield, C. Chandler, D. and Joyce, R. (2015), 'Housing: Trends in Prices, Costs and Tenure', Nuffield Foundation and The Institute for Fiscal Studies, February.

Belfield, C., Cribb, J., Hood, A. and Joyce R. (2014), *Living Standards, Poverty and Inequality in the UK*. Institute of Fiscal Studies/Joseph Rowntree Foundation/Economic and Social Research Council, https://www.ifs.org.uk/publications/7274

Belfield, C., Cribb, J., Hood, A. and Joyce R. (2016), *Living Standards, Poverty and Inequality in the UK*. Institute of Fiscal Studies/Joseph Rowntree Foundation/Economic and Social Research Council, https://www.ifs.org.uk/publications/8371

Blaug, R. Kenyon, A. and Lekhi, R. (2007), *Stress at Work: A Report Prepared for The Work Foundation's Principal Partners*. The Work Foundation, http://westminsterresearch.wmin.ac.uk/11456/

Brinkley, I. (2014), *Zero-hour Contracts: Response to the BIS Consultation*, The Work Foundation. March, http://mbsportal.bl.uk/taster/subjareas/hrmemplyrelat/twf/164300zerohour14.pdf

Coles, S. (2013) 'The Horrifying New Trend in Pay-day Loans'. *AOL Money*, 24 December 2013.

Corlett, A. and Clarke, S. (2017), *Living Standards 2017. The Past, Present and Possibly Future of UK Incomes*. Resolution Foundation Report, http://www.resolutionfoundation.org/publications/living-standards-2017-the-past-present-and-possible-future-of-uk-incomes/

Corlett, A. and Gardiner, L. (2015), *Low Pay Britain 2015*, Resolution Foundation, http://www.resolutionfoundation.org/publications/low-pay-britain-2015/

D'Arcy, C. and Kelly, G. (2015), *Analysing the National Living Wage Impact and Implications for Britain's Low Pay Challenge*. Resolution Foundation, http://www.resolutionfoundation.org/app/uploads/2015/07/RF-National-Living-Wage-briefing.pdf

Daly, M. and Kelly, G. (2015), *Families and Poverty: Every Day Life on a Low Income*. Policy Press.

Dangerfield, G. (1997), *The Strange Death of Liberal England*. Serif.

Davies, A., Hirsch, D. and Padely, M. (2014), *A Minimum Income Standard for the UK in 2014*. Joseph Rowntree Foundation, https://www.jrf.org.uk/report/minimum-income-standard-uk-2014

Davies, E. (2015), 'Cost of School Uniform 2015', Department for Education. June, https://www.gov.uk/government/publications/cost-of-school-uniform-2015

De Agostini, P. Hills, J. and Sutherland, H. (2014), 'Poor Lose, and Rich Gain from Direct Tax and Benefit Changes Since May 2010—Without Cutting the Deficit', LSE / CASE, November.

Department for Communities and Local Government (2014), *English Housing survey-Households 2013–14*, https://www.gov.uk/government/statistics/english-housing-survey-2013-to-2014-headline-report

Department for Energy and Climate Change (2015), *Annual Fuel Poverty Statistics Report 2015*, https://www.gov.uk/government/statistics/annual-fuel-poverty-statistics-report-2016

Dobcheva, Z. (2015), *Credit Unions in the UK—Balancing Social Benefit with Economic Viability*. Centre on Household Assets and Savings Management. Briefing Paper BP9/2015. August, http://www.thenews.coop/100618/news/banking-and-insurance/end-year-review-2015-finance-credit-unions/

Dorling, D. (2015), *All That is Solid. How the Great Housing Disaster Defines Our Times, and What We Can Do About It*. Penguin.

Dorling, D. (2015), *Injustice. Why Social Inequality Still Persists*. Policy Press.

Equality Trust (2017), 'The Scale of Economic Inequality in the UK', https://www.equalitytrust.org.uk/scale-economic-inequality-uk

Foster, D. (2015), 'Eviction is the Last Refuge for Poor Tenants', *The Guardian*, 18 February 2016.

Foster, D. (2016), 'More Families Are Renting and Fewer People Ever Expect to Own a Home', 25 February, https://www.theguardian.com/housing-network/2016/feb/25/families-renting-2016-english-housing-survey

Gallagher, P. (2105) 'Number of People Evicted from Rented Homes has Soared Since Housing Benefit Cuts Began',*The Independent*. 13 August 2015, http://www.independent.co.uk/news/uk/home-news/number-of-people-evicted-from-rented-homes-has-soared-since-housing-benefit-cuts-began-10454150.html

Garthwaite, K. (2016), *Hunger Pains: Life Inside Foodbank Britain*. Policy Press.

Ghelani, D. and Tonutti, G. (2017), *The Impact of the Two-child Limit to Tax Credits*. Policy in Practice, April.

Guertler, P. and Royston, S. (2013), 'Fact-file: Families and Fuel Poverty'. Association for the Conservation of Energy, http://www.ukace.org/wp-content/uploads/2013/02/ACE-and-EBR-fact-file-2012-02-Families-and-fuel-poverty.pdf

Hall, S. and Perry, C. (2013), *Family Matters: Understanding Families in an Age of Austerity*. Family and Childcare Trust.

Hannon, C. (2013), *Living Precariously: Families in an Age of Austerity*. Family and Childcare Trust, May.

HMS Treasury (2014), *Impact on Households: Distributional Analysis to Accompany Budget 2014*, http://socialwelfare.bl.uk/subject-areas/government-issues/social-policy/[Treasury]/impact14.aspx

Howard, R. (2015), *Warmer Homes: Improving Fuel Poverty and Energy Efficiency Policy in the UK*. Poverty Exchange, https://policyexchange.org.uk/publication/warmer-homes-improving-fuel-poverty-and-energy-efficiency-policy-in-the-uk/

HRZONE, Acas, CIPD (2015), 'Workplace Trends of 2015. What They Mean for You', http://www.acas.org.uk/media/pdf/t/e/Workplace-trends-of-20151.pdf

Jaleel, G. (2014), 'Liverpool is the Hardest Hit Major UK City in Government's Latest Round of Funding Cuts', *Liverpool Echo*, 19 January, http://www.liverpoolecho.co.uk/news/liverpool-news/liverpool-one-worst-hit-country-8313557

Jones, N., Conklin, A., Suhrcke, M. and Monsivai, P. (2014), 'The Growing Price Gap between More and Less Healthy Foods: Analysis of a Novel Longitudinal UK Dataset', PLoS ONE 9(10): e109343, https://doi.org/10.1371/journal.pone.0109343

Jones, O. (2016), *Chavs. The Demonization of the Working Class*. Verso.

Knight, K. 'Forget the Local Museum! How Far-flung School Trips Costing up to £3,000 are Leaving Parents Broke—and Fuming'. *Mail Online*, 25 June 2015.

Lansley, S. and Mack, J. (2013), 'A More Unequal Country?', *Poverty and Social Exclusion Newsletter*, 16 April.

Lansley, S. and Mack, J. (2015), *Breadline Britain. The Rise of Mass Poverty*. Oneworld.

Liverpool City Council (2012), *The Liverpool Economic Briefing*, http://liverpool.gov.uk/media/9996/liverpool-economic-briefing-february-2012.pdf

Liverpool City Council (2017), *Welfare Reform Cumulative Impact Analysis 2016. Interim Report February 2017*, https://www.lcvs.org.uk/events/report-launch-liverpool-welfare-reform-cumulative-impact-assessment/

Loopstra, R., Reeves, A., Taylor-Robinson, D., Barr, B., McKee, M. and Stuckler, D. (2015), 'Austerity, Sanctions, and the Rise of Foodbanks in the UK', *British Medical Journal*, 350, https://doi.org/10.1136/bmj.h1775

Low Pay Commission (2014), *The Future Path of the National Minimum Wage*, https://www.gov.uk/government/publications/the-future-path-of-the-national-minimum-wage-2014.

McGuinness, F. (2015), *Poverty in the UK: Statistics*. Briefing paper 7906, 6 November. House of Commons Library.

McKenzie, L. (2015), *Getting By: Estates Class and Culture in Austerity Britain*. Policy Press.

Mendoza, K. (2015), *Austerity: The Demolition of the Welfare State and the Rise of the Zombie Economy*, New Internationalist Books.

Mental Health Network (2014), 'Key Facts and Trends in Mental Health: 2014 Update', NHS Confederation, Fact Sheet, January.

Monaghan, A. and Goodley, S. (2014) 'Cost of Childcare Cancels Out Pay for 1 in 10 Working Families'. *The Guardian*, 29 December 2014, https://www.theguardian.com/money/2014/dec/29/childcare-cost-pay-families-aviva

Motwanie, N. (2015), 'No Cold Homes', Turn2Us, https://www.turn2us.org.uk, https://www.turn2us.org.uk/About-Us/Our-Campaigns/No-Cold-Homes/About-the-Campaign

Motwanie, N. (2015), '50% of Working Households Struggle to Heat Homes', Turn2Us, https://www.turn2us.org.uk/About-Us/News/50-of-low-income-working-households-struggling-to

Nettle, D. (2015), *Tyneside Neighbourhoods: Deprivation, Social Life and Social Behaviour in One British City*. Open Book Publishers, http://www.openbookpublishers.com/product/398, https://doi.org/10.11647/OBP.0084

NHS Choices (2016), 'NHS in England—Help with Health Costs', http://www.nhs.uk

O'Brien, M. (2012), *'Fairness and the City'. Public-sector Cuts, Welfare Reform and Risks to the Population of Liverpool and its Wider Region: An Independent Submission to the Liverpool Fairness Commission*. Centre for Lifelong Learning, https://www.liv.ac.uk/media/livacuk/cll/reports/fairness_and_the_city.pdf

O'Hara, M. (2014), *Austerity Bites: A Journey into the Sharp End of Cuts in the UK*. Policy Press.

O'Hara, M. (2015), 'Cut Off: How Austerity Relates to Our Mental Health'. *New Statesman*, 6 October.

Office for National Statistics (2015), *Statistical Bulletin: Consumer Price Inflation*. December 2015, https://www.ons.gov.uk/economy/inflationandpriceindices/bulletins/consumerpriceinflation/2015-10-13

Office for National Statistics (2014), *Households and Household Composition in England and Wales: 2001–11*, https://www.ons.gov.uk/peoplepopulationandcommunity/birthsdeathsandmarriages/families/articles/householdsandhouseholdcompositioninenglandandwales/2014-05-29

Osborne, H. (2015), 'New Consumer Debt Reaches Seven Year High in UK', *The Guardian*, 3 January 2015.

Paton, N. (2015), 'Presenteeism Costs Twice as Much as Sickness Absence', *Personnel Today*, 27 November, http://www.personneltoday.com/hr/presenteeism-costs-twice-much-sickness-absence/

Patrick, R. (2017), *Whose Benefit? Everyday Realities of Welfare Reform*. Policy Press.

Pember Reeves, M. (1984 [1913]), *Round About a Pound a Week*. Virago.

Power, A., Willmot, H. and Davidson, R. (2011), *Family Futures. Childhood and Poverty in Urban Neighbourhoods*. Policy Press.

Pricewaterhouse Coopers (2015), *UK Economic Outlook*, 'UK Housing Market Outlook: The Continuing Rise of Generation Rent', July.

Reed, H. and Portes, J. (2014), *Cumulative Impact Assessment. A Research Report by Landman Economics and the National Institute of Economic and Social Research (NIESR) for the Equality and Human Rights Commission*. Equality and Human Rights Commission. Research report 94, https://www.equalityhumanrights.com/sites/default/files/research-report-94-cumulative-impact-assessment.pdf

Relate (2013), *How is Austerity Affecting Our Relationships? Relationships: Our Support Systems in Good Times and Bad*, https://www.relate.org.uk/policy-campaigns/publications/how-austerity-affecting-our-relationships-relationships-our-support-systems-good-times-and-bad

Rutter, J. (2015), 'Childcare Costs Survey 2015'. Family and Childcare Trust, https://www.familyandchildcaretrust.org/childcare-survey-2015

Save the Children (2012), *Ending Child Poverty: Ensuring Universal Credit Supports Working Mums. How Will Universal Credit Affect Poor Families?* http://www.savethechildren.org.uk/resources/online-library/ending-child-poverty-ensuring-universal-credit-supports-working-mums

Shelter (2016), http://england.shelter.org.uk

Shildrick, T., MacDonald, R., Webster, C. and Garthwaite, K. (2011), *Poverty and Insecurity. Life in Low-pay, No-pay Britain*. Policy Press.

Stephen Clarke, S. and Conor, D. (2016), *Low Pay Britain 2016*. Resolution Foundation, http://www.resolutionfoundation.org/publications/low-pay-britain-2016/

The Children's Commission on Poverty (2014), *At What Cost? Exposing the Impact of Poverty on School Life*, October.

The Mersey Partnership (2012), *Economic Review 2012*, http://www.knowsley.gov.uk/pdf/LC10_MerseyPartnershipEconomicReview2012.pdf

Toynbee, P. (2003), *Hard Work. Life in Low Pay Britain*. Bloomsbury.

Trussell Foundation (2015), 'Foodbank Use Tops One Million for First Time Says Trussell Trust'. Press Release, 22 April 2015, https://www.trusselltrust.org/2015/04/22/foodbank-use-tops-one-million-for-first-time-says-trussell-trust/

Trussell Trust (2015), 'The Trussell Trust's Response to Feeding Britain's Route Map to Ending Hunger'. Press release, 10 December 2015. Response to Forsey, A. and Mason, L. (2015), *Feeding Britain in 2015–16: A Route Map to Ending Hunger as We Know It in the United Kingdom*. Report for the All-Party Parliamentary Group on Hunger, https://www.trusselltrust.org/wp-content/uploads/sites/2/2016/01/Response-to-Feeding-Britains-route-map-to-ending-hunger.pdf

Trussell Trust (2016), 'Foodbank Use Remains at Record High, as New Data Mapping Tool Gives Fresh Insights into UK Hunger'. Press release, 12 April 2016, p. 1, https://www.trusselltrust.org/wp-content/uploads/sites/2/2015/06/Foodbank-use-remains-at-record-high.pdf

TUC (2010), 'In Sickness and in Health? Good Work—and How to Achieve It', https://www.tuc.org.uk/sites/default/files/extras/goodwork.pdf

TUC (2015), '1.7 Million People Missing Out on Their Paid Holidays'. Press release, 30 July 2015, https://www.tuc.org.uk/workplace-issues/employment-rights/working-time-holidays/17-million-people-missing-out-their-paid

TUC (2015), '15 Percent Increase in People Working More Than 48 Hours a Week Risks a Return to "Burnout Britain"'. Press release, 9 September, https://www.tuc.org.uk/international-issues/europe/workplace-issues/work-life-balance/15-cent-increase-people-working-more

TUC (2015), 'A Hard Day's Night: The Effect of Night Shift Work on Work/Life Balance', https://www.tuc.org.uk/sites/default/files/AHardDaysNight.pdf

TUC (2015), 'Action Needed on Workplace Bullying'. Press release, 21 August, https://www.tuc.org.uk/workplace-issues/health-and-safety/bullying/action-needed-workplace-bullying

TUC (2015), 'Number of Commuters Spending More than Two Hours Travelling to and from Work up by 72 Percent in last Decade'. Press release, November, https://www.tuc.org.uk/workplace-issues/work-life-balance/number-commuters-spending-more-two-hours-travelling-and-work-72

TUC (2015), 'Someone Experiences Work-related Stress Every Two Minutes'. Press release, 16 October, https://www.tuc.org.uk/workplace-issues/someone-experiences-work-related-stress-every-two-minutes-says-tuc

TUC (2015), 'Work and well-being: A trade union resource', https://www.tuc.org.uk/workplace-issues/work-and-well-being-trade-union-resource

Wilkinson, R. and Pickett, K. (2009), *The Spirit Level: Why More Equal Societies Almost Always Do Better*. Allen Lane.

Index

www.ingramcontent.com/pod-product-compliance
Lightning Source LLC
LaVergne TN
LVHW082205200926
848484LV00008B/2216
* 9 7 8 1 0 1 3 2 8 8 2 3 4 *